A History of Barbados

A History of Barbados

From Amerindian settlement to nation-state

HILARY McD. BECKLES

CAMBRIDGE
UNIVERSITY PRESS

For my son, Rodney Beckles,
and his generation of Barbadian youth

PUBLISHED BY THE PRESS SYNDICATE OF THE UNIVERSITY OF CAMBRIDGE
The Pitt Building, Trumpington Street, Cambridge, United Kingdom

CAMBRIDGE UNIVERSITY PRESS
The Edinburgh Building, Cambridge CB2 2RU, UK   http://www.cup.cam.ac.uk
40 West 20th Street, New York, NY 10011–4211, USA   http://www.cup.org
10 Stamford Road, Oakleigh, Melbourne 3166, Australia

Reprinted 1999

Printed in the United Kingdom at the University Press, Cambridge

British Library Cataloguing in Publication data
Beckles, Hilary McD.
A history of Barbados: from Amerindian
settlement to nation-state.
1. Barbados, history
I. Title
972.98′1

Library of Congress Cataloguing in Publication data
Beckles, Hilary, 1955–
A history of Barbados: from Amerindian settlement to nation-state /
Hilary McD. Beckles.
p.   cm.
Bibliography: p.
Includes index.
ISBN 0-521-35374-2. – ISBN 0-521-35879-5 (pbk.)
1. Barbados–History.   I. Title.
F2041.B435   1989   89–542
972.98′1–dc19   CIP

ISBN 0 521 35374 2 hard covers
ISBN 0 521 35879 5 paperback

Contents

CONTENTS

CONTENTS

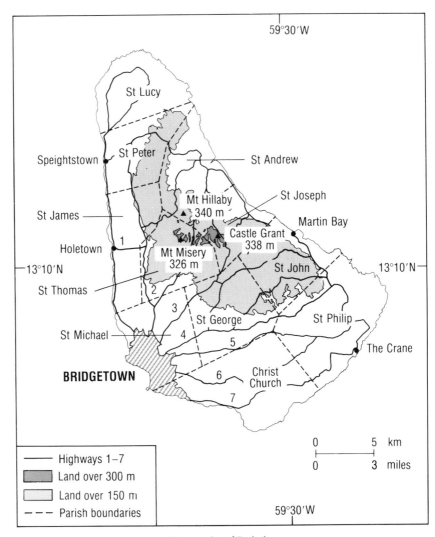

Topography of Barbados

List of Tables

An Amerindian mask excavated in Barbados.

Preface

Perhaps the greatest responsibility one can ever undertake is the commitment to write a general history of one's own country. My decision to do so was not taken lightly. Over the years, many friends and colleagues have suggested that I attempt such a study. When the decision was finally taken in the summer of 1984, shortly before I joined the history staff of the Cave Hill Campus (Barbados), University of the West Indies, the project seemed at once exciting, challenging, and daunting. This ambivalence stayed with me throughout, and has perhaps influenced to a considerable degree its tone and tempo.

The extensive primary research which informs this work is certainly not all my own. In fact, I could not have written it at this time without the detailed and professional research of a number of trustworthy historians and other social scientists. I drew upon the scholarly findings of the Barbados 'school' of historical researchers, especially Professor Woodville Marshall, Dr George Belle, Bentley Gibbs, Ronnie Hughes and Anthony Phillips, Trevor Marshall, Dr Karl Watson, Dr Cecilia Karch, Richard Carter, Velma Newton, Peter Campbell, Robert Morris, Dr John Gilmore, and the late Honourable H. A. Vaughan. The many narratives of local amateur historians, such as Warren Alleyne, Richard Stoute and Sir F. A. Hoyos were also useful. Academic historians outside the region whose works have been particularly important are Professors Claude Levy, Bonham Richardson, Richard Dunn, Jerome Handler, Wilber Will and Gary Puckrein. Any shortcomings found within this work, however, are entirely my own.

During the period of writing, I benefited from the friendship of many persons and the skills of the staff at a number of institutions. Psychological support came from my students during the 1987–88 academic year, Barry Gaspar, Diane and Brian Griffith, Velma Newton and Amanda Hauxwell. Woodville Marshall read the entire manuscript and offered the most valuable suggestions. The University of the West Indies, Cave Hill Campus, offered some financial assistance, as well as the general intellectual context for preparing the work. Sandra Taylor typed successive drafts of the manuscript under the pressure of unreasonable deadlines – and without protest. My family was asked to absorb the persistent stress which followed me home from archives and libraries, and they provided the critical support necessary for the completion of this task. I thank my wife Mary and our son Rodney, for understanding.

The library staff at Senate House and the Institute of Commonwealth Studies, the University of London, were very helpful. At the London Public Records Office, the British Library, the New York Public Library, the United States Library of Congress, and the Barbados Museum, I found the staff to be professional and cooperative, even with some unreasonable demands. The librarians at the University of the West Indies, of course, were always there when needed. To all these people and institutions I here acknowledge my deepest appreciation. Finally, many thanks to my students who, over the years, unknowingly provided the intellectual stimulus required to proceed when my spirit seemed unwilling and unable.

Hilary McD. Beckles
Cave Hill, Barbados

Acknowledgements

The author and publishers wish to thank the following for permission to use photographs:
Barbados Museum and Historical Society, pages x, xvi, 53, 117, 127, 172 (Grantley Adams)
Allsport UK Ltd, page 187 (Sir Garfield Sobers)
Royal Commonwealth Society, London, pages 122, 130, 139, 144 (main photo), 146

Author's acknowledgements

Special thanks to the Royal Commonwealth Society, London, the Barbados Museum, the Institute of Commonwealth Studies, University of London, Mrs Sonya Lawrence, the Barbados Workers Union, and the Barbados Advocate-News for providing the materials that illustrate this book. Thanks to Professors Bonham Richardson, Barry Gaspar, Richard Sheridan, and Dr Karl Watson, who allowed me to talk 'Bajan history' with them at length. The works of Professors Jerome Handler, Gary Puckrein, Claude Levy and Richard Dunn were constant sources of guidance. It was reassuring to have Professor Woodville Marshall on the spot to discuss a number of issues. Thanks also to Professor Edward Kamau Brathwaite for insisting that I had a duty to write this book. Alisandra Cummins and Leslie Barrow at the Barbados Museum, and the Library Staff of the Barbados Advocate-News, did all they could to assist. Tony Seddon and Bob Hands, my editors at Cambridge University Press, treated me as they do their important writers; this was very kind of them. To all, and certainly to those not mentioned, I appreciate your kindness and assistance.

Introduction

A most striking historical feature of this tiny, tropical, Eastern Caribbean island state is the extent to which its development has drawn upon human and material resources on a global scale. Barbados, only 34 kilometres (21 miles) long, 23 kilometres (14 miles) wide and 430 square kilometres (166 square miles) in area, for some 300 years now has found itself involved in the most significant trends that have shaped the modern New World. With this small, coral-capped, open landmass to manipulate, its inhabitants have demonstrated in the process that the magnitude of a country's role in international developments can indeed be in inverse relation to its physical size.

For centuries prior to Europe's sixteenth-century encounter with the island, its indigenous inhabitants had linked its history to that of the American continent by a complex pattern of migration. These first Barbadians cultivated the flat coastal plains, and hunted in the forested interior plateaux which rise gently to no more than 250 metres (800 feet). The hilly Scotland District in the north-east corner of the island, which rises to just over 300 metres (1,000 feet), also provided environmental support for these Amerindians. It seemed logical, therefore, that this work should begin with a brief description of the material and social culture of these first Barbadians.

The colonisation of the island by an English merchant company in 1627 signalled the onset of its integration into the dynamic European commercial world. Within this capitalist orbit it was developed as a slave-based, export-oriented agricultural colony. By 1660 it was commonly described as the 'richest spot' in the English New World Empire on account of the super-profits generated by the sugar industry. Since that time it has maintained its status as an important regional economic and political force, as well as a valuable Caribbean adjunct to the western world order. These historical achievements of European commercialism were built upon the profitability of sugar production and black slave labour – the inter-relation of which shaped the general structure and destiny of most Caribbean societies.

The importation of some 135,000 Africans during the seventeenth century to work as slaves on the earliest English plantations meant that from this time the island's history could not be separated from that of Africa. In addition, these Africans and their creole progeny, who have constituted the demographic majority since the mid-seventeenth century, left behind a dynamic cultural tradition clearly expressed in language, social ethics, religion, dance, song and political radicalism. This culture not only continues to shape the island's contemporary outlook and direction, but reminds all that, aside from it being geographically the closest Caribbean territory to West Africa, there is much of West Africa within it.

However, imposing as they are, these external features of the island's development should not be assigned any supremacy over internal social relations and institutions in assessing the forces which have determined and shaped the country's history. The structurally determining institution of black slavery, for example, was imposed by forces endemic to the wider American colonisation programme of Europe. The commercial domination of the contemporary economy by people of European ancestry, in addition, should not be divorced from the fact that European colonisation of the island, the region and indeed the Americas, established that reality over 300 years ago. Also, that people of African ancestry were to champion the twentieth-century civil rights movement and demand for popular democracy in the country cannot be distinguished from the persistent struggle of their enslaved ancestors for legal freedom and economic security.

Throughout the text it is argued that the persistent struggle for social equality, civil rights and material betterment by blacks, coloureds and some whites, constitutes the central current which flows through the island's history since 1627. This process, generally expressed by historians in the philosophical concept of man's struggle for liberty, equality and justice, is therefore fundamental to the theoretical structure of the work. The evidence, in general, would support no alternative approach as fully. In this sense, therefore, it is a general history which seeks to outline the primary survival concerns of all social groups, and to account for the cohesive as well as the antagonistic nature of their experiences.

There is, however, another important historiographical concern which is addressed in this work; that of the marginalisation of black people in previous histories of the island. Since 1657, when the first such history of the island was published, at least half a dozen others have appeared. Some of these histories have contributed significantly to our knowledge and understanding, though all have been criticised at one stage or another for ignoring and suppressing the island's rich and characteristic African-derived traditions. Conscious of this problem, my search for a rigorous and unbiased approach to the collective historical experience of all the island's inhabitants was guided by standards of historical scholarship expected of a professional historian. At the same time, the structure and intellectual level of the analysis, and the language used, reflect my long-held concern that students, teachers and the general public should be provided with a well-researched but clearly written general history. Footnotes and references are kept to a minimum, though the bibliography may assist the specialist reader in need of additional information.

An Amerindian zemi, which is worn around the neck, excavated in Barbados.

CHAPTER ONE

The first Barbadians,
c.650–c.1540

Barbados, unlike some of the other islands in the Caribbean, was not inhabited during the Archaic Age. Stone Age man, who did not practise agriculture but relied upon fishing and food gathering for survival, never did settle on the island. Rather, it was first inhabited by an Amerindian migrant group now called the Saladoid-Barrancoid about AD 350–650. These people have been so named after the places in the Orinoco Basin in South America where the artefacts of their ancestors have been found.

Little was written about these earliest Barbadians by the Europeans who encountered them in the sixteenth century. The Spanish who visited the island during the first quarter of the century merely stated that it had had many Amerindian settlements, while Pedro a Campus, a Portuguese explorer, on landing there in 1536, reported that it was uninhabited. The English mariners who explored the island in 1625 confirmed the finding of Pedro a Campus. However, the settlement party from England that landed in 1627 stated that though the island had no Amerindian community, they found substantial material evidence of their recent habitation.[1]

In recent years, however, knowledge of the island's Amerindian heritage has been greatly expanded by the findings of a number of professional archaeological investigations. Some historians remain sceptical about such research and suggest that caution should be exercised in using it as the basis of firm historical judgements. They also complain that these researches, such as those presented by Peter Drewett and Arie Boomert, deal more with material cultures than with considerations of ethnic peculiarity.[2] As a result, the names of inhabitants found within this literature relate more to periods of material development than to ethnicity. This poses a number of problems for the historian, one of which is that he has been generally unable to link satisfactorily distinct historic periods and material expressions to exclusive ethnic groups.

One increasingly acceptable conclusion from this research, however, is that it should no longer be stated that the first settlers were a culturally distinct group of so-called peaceful Arawaks who were displaced in the fourteenth century by another distinct group of so-called warlike Caribs. Instead, archaeologists have shown satisfactorily that the successive waves of Amerindian migrants to the island from the South American mainland were from the same basic ethnological background.

The Saladoid-Barrancoid people probably spoke a language akin to what became known as Arawakan. More certain, however, is that they were skilled farmers and fishermen, as well as being accomplished in the ceramic crafts. That they traded their wares among other Amerindian communities throughout the Caribbean area has also now been established. Some ceramic artefacts found on the island, as well as neighbouring islands, show a marked degree of similarity. This might be the result of extensive trading and migration, common cultural elements, or a combination of these and related factors. These artefacts have also been used to show that Barbados was of marginal importance to these Amerindians, and was isolated from the main streams of their migration from the Guianas into the Eastern Caribbean.

Greater quantities of artefacts exist pertaining to the second wave of Amerindian migrants which took place about the year AD 800. In the Guianas where these people had settled in large communities before migrating into the Lesser Antilles, they referred to themselves as the Lokono. The Spanish *conquistadores* of the early sixteenth century, who claimed an intimate knowledge of these people in the Greater Antilles, referred to them as Arawaks, though the name was never a self-ascription. In Barbados they lived in small, scattered village communities, organised under chiefs. These villages were strung along the coastline where fishing grounds were good (Figure 1). There was one cluster of some twenty settlements situated at the north-eastern tip of the island. These settlements, particularly those at River Bay, Stroud Point, Jones Bay, Laycock Bay and Chandler Bay, were located along the edge of the northern plateau beside fresh-water streams; those at Sandy Hill and Horseshoe Bay were situated upstream, on farming lands. A principal factor in the explanation of the concentration of settlements in this area is its unique topography, which was manipulated for strategic defence. Perched on the edges of jagged cliffs which descend steeply some 20 metres (60–70 feet) to a shoreline battered constantly by huge Atlantic ocean breakers, these villages were protected naturally by a coast which was extremely difficult, if not impossible, for Amerindian seafarers to navigate. Attacks were likely to be from the landward side, and the openness of the terrain would reduce significantly the surprise element. A small number of settlements were also located several miles inland. Those identified so far were at Greenland, St Luke's Gully, Mapp's Cave, and Three Houses. The people living in these villages were farmers with specialised knowledge in the cultivation of cassava and potato roots as well as maize grain. Domestic industrial activity included production of cotton textile goods and ceramics.

The selection of village locations was influenced by military defence considerations, easy access to reliable fresh water, and the availability of flat fertile ground for cassava cultivation. They were great consumers of shellfish, mainly conch and whelks, but also ate oysters and scallops and a variety of fish. Their taste in foods can be detected from the shells and bones found in their many excavated middens along the southern and eastern coasts of the island. Hoes for the cultivation of cassava, and axes, were made from conch shells. Their edges were sharpened by rubbing them on sandstone, and handles were made of wood. Some of these implements (without their handles) have been found at excavated sites throughout the island.

The available archaeological evidence shows that the third distinct wave of migrant settlers in Barbados took place during the mid-thirteenth century. These Amerindians, from the same ancestral stock as the previous migrants, confusingly named Caribs by the Spanish, also used the Guianas as the springboard for their island migration. These migrants were a more materially developed and politically organised people than their pre-decessors – whom they subdued and dominated. They were also advanced grain and root cultivators, and used cassava and maize as their staple diet. In addition, they were expert fishermen and had an advanced knowledge of cotton textiles and pottery. Spanish colonists who engaged in military hostilities with these Amerindians in the Eastern Caribbean claimed that they were identifiable at sea by their long dugout canoes (some of which were as much as fifteen metres, or fifty feet, long), in which they traversed the Caribbean Sea as traders, and in defence of their newly acquired territories.

Several excavations of Amerindian settlements have been carried out in Barbados. Evidence from those at Maxwell, Greenland and, more recently, Chancery Lane, suggests that it was common for successive migrant groups to establish settlements as temporary camps for fishing and crab-hunting expeditions, and that the more longstanding villages clung to the few coastal springs and natural ponds. The evidence also shows that in spite of

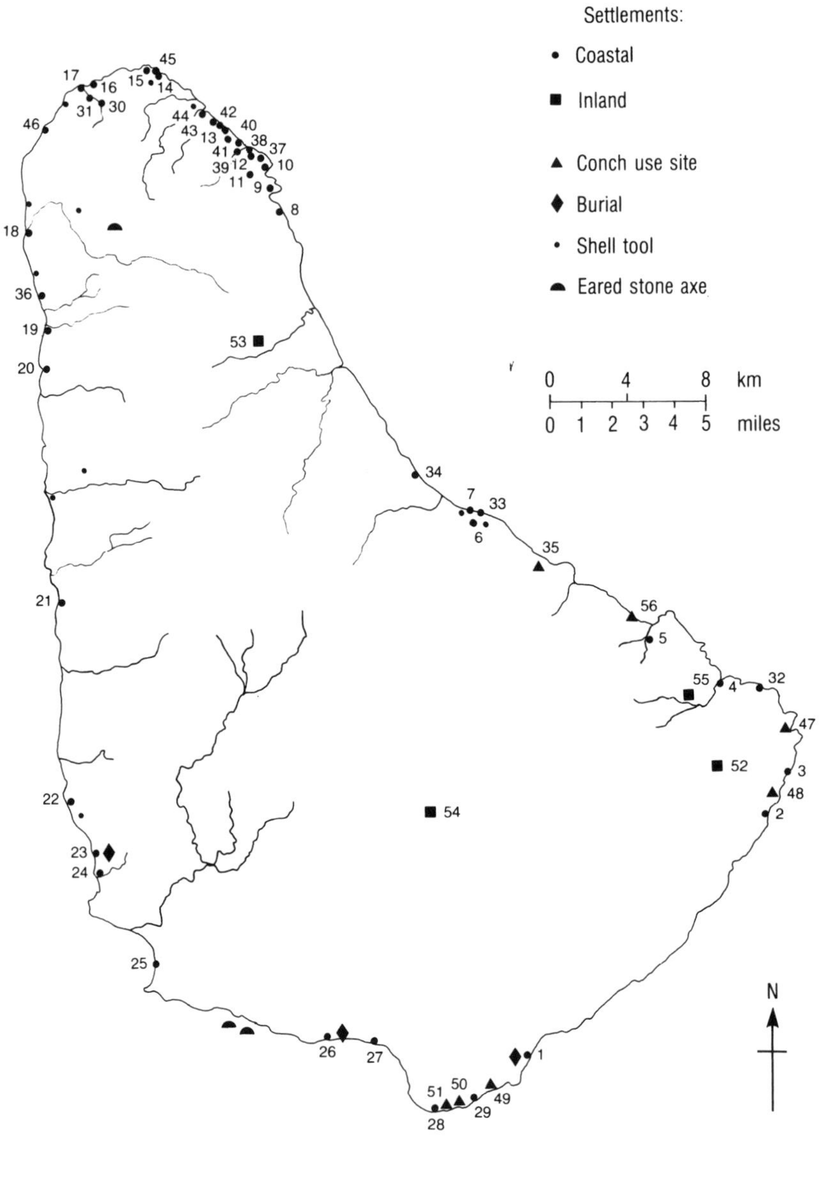
Settlements:
Coastal
Inland
Conch use site
Burial
Shell tool
Eared stone axe
0 4 8 km
0 1 2 3 4 5 miles
N
1
2
3
4
5
6
7
8
9
10
11
12
13
14
15
16
17
18
19
20
21
22
23
24
25
26
27
28
29
30
31
32
33
34
35
36
37
38
39
40
41
42
43
44
45
46
47
48
49
50
51
52
53
54
55
56

Fig. 1 Prehistoric Barbados

Prehistoric sites on Barbados

1 Chancery Lane, Christ Church
2 Sam Lords, St Philip
3 Palmetto Bay, St Philip
4 Culpepper, St Philip
5 Conset Bay, St John
6 Andromeda Gardens, St Joseph
7 Hillcrest (site A), St Joseph
8 Pico Teneriffe, St Peter
9 Cove Bay, St Lucy
10 The Landlock, St Lucy
11 Pie Corner, St Lucy
12 Indian Mound, St Lucy
13 Goat House Bay, St Lucy
14 Sandy Hill, St Lucy
15 Horseshoe Bay, St Lucy
16 Cluffs (site A), St Lucy
17 Stroud Point, St Lucy
18 Maycocks Bay, St Lucy
19 Heywoods, St Peter
20 Speightstown, St Peter
21 Hole Town, St James
22 Fresh Water Bay, St Michael
23 Brandons, St Michael
24 Indian River, St Michael
25 Beckles Spring, St Michael
26 Maxwell, Christ Church
27 Oistins, Christ Church
28 South Point, Christ Church
29 Silver Sands, Christ Church
30 Cluffs (site B), St Lucy
31 Cluffs (site C), St Lucy
32 East Point, St Philip
33 Hillcrest (site B), St Joseph
34 Cattle Wash, St Joseph
35 Martins Bay, St John
36 Littlegood Harbour, St Peter
37 Cuckold, St Lucy
38 Laycock Bay, St Lucy
39 Chandler Bay (site A), St Lucy
40 Chandler Bay (site B), St Lucy
41 Kings Bay, St Lucy
42 Jones Bay (site A), St Lucy
43 Jones Bay (site B), St Lucy
44 River Bay, St Lucy
45 Sandy Hill, St Lucy
46 Lower Crab Hill, St Lucy
47 Kiteridge Bay, St Philip
48 Cave Bay, St Philip
49 Round Rock, Christ Church
50 Green Garden, Christ Church
51 The Chair, Christ Church
52 Mapps Cave, St Philip
53 Greenland, St Andrew
54 St Luke's Gully, St George
55 Three Houses, St Philip
56 Conset Beach, St John

Source: P.L. Drewett *et al.* 'Archaeological survey of Barbados', *JBMHS* 38:1 (1987), pp. 58, 69

the lack of hard stone and abundant fresh water the island developed many large-scale communities that depended upon fishing and large-scale farming.

Permanent Amerindian settlement ended during the early sixteenth century. These inhabitants did not depart from Barbados of their own accord; many were the victims of Spanish slave-raiding missions. It was during this time that Spanish *conquistadores* organised regular expeditions into the Lesser Antilles for the capture of Amerindians to work the sugar estates and mines in Hispaniola and elsewhere. Such raids could have significantly depleted the island's population by the mid-sixteenth century. Some of those who escaped these slave missions fled to the mountainous neighbouring Windward Islands where they consolidated their defence against the Spanish. Such developments explain why a Spanish writer noted in 1541 that the island had no indigenous people.

During the second half of the sixteenth century, Amerindians in the Lesser Antilles, referred to by Europeans as Caribs, managed to organise a military force in the Windwards – St Lucia, St Vincent, Grenada and Dominica – which held up the pace and undermined the effectiveness of European colonisation. Because Barbados lacked a mountainous topography, it was not considered attractive for these purposes of self-defence. As a result, though the island remained part of the Amerindian survival environment, it was not ideally suited for their long-term community development.

Barbados, then, was settled prior to English colonisation by a succession of Amerindian migrants from South America, the last of whom were forced to defend their spheres of influence against Europeans in the sixteenth and seventeenth centuries. This military consideration reinforced the status of Barbados as a 'backwater' within the Eastern Caribbean Amerindian world. Certainly, the defence factor is important in understanding the island's subsequent history, since English colonists did not encounter inhabitants resisting their presence with weapons, and were able easily to get down to the immediate task of planting crops and establishing trade systems. St Kitts, the first English settlement (1624) in the West Indies, for example, was hampered for decades by persistent Amerindian military opposition, and was quickly surpassed by Barbados in both population growth and commercial value. The absence of Amerindian settlements in the island in 1627 is undoubtedly an important factor in explaining why its English colonists easily surged ahead as the most prosperous in the West Indies during the seventeenth century.

CHAPTER TWO

English colonisation,
1625–1644

Although Columbus made no claim to have visited Barbados on any of his four voyages to the Caribbean, both Spanish and Portuguese *conquistadores* reported landing there during the early sixteenth century. The party of English mariners who arrived there on 14th May 1625, under the command of Captain John Powell, and claimed the island on behalf of King James I, were the first Europeans to set in train a programme for its colonisation. It was not until 1627, however, that colonists arrived from England with the intention of establishing a settlement.

The colonising expedition landed on the leeward coast, at the present site of Holetown village, on 17th February. It was headed by Henry Powell, younger brother of John, and organised and financed by two London merchant brothers, Sir Peter and Sir William Courteen. The settlement project was the result of two years of negotiations between John Powell, mariner of the Courteen family, and the knights. From his 1625 visit to the island, on a return voyage to Brazil, John Powell had considered its location and topography ideally suitable for an agricultural settlement. It possessed rich and open land and, perhaps most importantly, was believed to be uninhabited by politically organised Amerindians.

The constitutionality of the original settlement has remained unclear in places, owing to inconsistent and opposing documentary evidence. A traditional interpretation suggests that Sir William Courteen, after obtaining a patent from King Charles I, equipped four ships with eighty colonists under John Powell's management to undertake the settlement. Also, that by July 1628, Courteen's finance syndicate had made an investment of £10,000 in preparing the colony for large-scale agriculture. More recently, it has been argued that Courteen had no settlement right to Barbados, since he received no royal patent, and that Powell's landing party were possibly no more than squatters.

During 1627, however, Courteen's syndicate held possession of the island. As leader of the colonising agency, he was the island's first effective proprietor, and was therefore responsible for the nature of colonial structures. Under his scheme, colonists were given some assistance with capital, but not with labour. They were not given freehold ownership of land but were to produce crops and hand them over to the syndicate's resident agent. In return, they were paid an annual wage of £100 by the syndicate, out of which they maintained themselves and their labourers. Barbados, then, was initially a company-sponsored colony, and pioneer colonists were employees rather than freehold farmers.

By April 1627, Courteen's colonists had established a resident Governorship under John Powell Jr. This regime was short-lived. On 22nd July, Charles I granted letters patent for the settlement of Barbados and other 'Caribbee islands' to James Hay, the first Earl of Carlisle. Under this royal concession, the earl assumed the status of Lord Proprietor with full responsibilities for the defence and administration of the colony. As royal proprietor, Carlisle was empowered to enjoy full jurisdiction over all inhabitants. He was also given full powers to establish civil institutions and offices such as legal systems, religious bodies and political organisations. More importantly, he was empowered to dispose of the colony's land, exact duties on its trade, and create honorary titles for its inhabitants.

The issue of Carlisle's patent led to the development of legal and administration conflict and political turmoil in the colony. Adding to the crisis was the erroneous subsequent issue of a royal patent to the Earl of Pembroke, which included Barbados and several other islands. The legal ownership of the island, therefore, was enveloped in confusion, though there was some clarification on 1st April 1628, when Carlisle obtained a second patent which was intended to revoke that of Pembroke. During the interim, the various representatives of the two earls engaged in a wrestle for political power on the island, but the Powell faction managed to stay in charge of government by means of firm defiance of both contenders.

Upon receipt of his second patent, Carlisle issued land grants to a London Merchant group that had assisted in financing his proprietorship. As this merchant syndicate was also given permission legally to administer these lands, they quickly dispatched Charles Wolverston, a knowledgeable man on West Indian affairs, to the colony as their agent. He landed in Barbados in June 1628, and by August had brought the entire island, including Powell Jr and Courteen's men, under his authority. On 4th September he was selected Governor of Barbados.

Wolverston consolidated his rule by means of the appointment of twelve Justices of Peace, and by carefully excluding Courteen's men from civil offices. By the end of 1628, he had established in government the proprietary authority of Carlisle at the exclusion of other interests. But the political struggle did not end there, as the battle for ownership ensued. Wolverston was accused by colonists with capital of imposing the unpopular Courteen's land policy which kept them as tenants-at-will with rights to use land only upon the payment of a proprietary rent. They wanted freehold ownership with the full rights of private property. With this objective in view, members of the alienated Powell faction succeeded in leading a successful but short-lived uprising against the Carlisle Proprietorship. Governor Wolverston was deposed and deported. Carlisle soon regained command of the colony with the assistance of Royal authority, and dispatched Sir William Tufton as his new Governor.

Tufton arrived at Barbados in September 1629 with proprietary instructions to establish a firm loyalist administration. In spite of stout resistance from many leading colonists, he succeeded in taking command of government. One of the measures he took in laying the foundation for political administration was the division of the island into six parishes. He refused to appoint an advisory Council from among prominent inhabitants. This policy made his rule unpopular, and petitions were dispatched to Carlisle complaining of his autocratic style. He was described as favouring the poor and being insensitive to the interests of the island's elite. His attempts to ameliorate the working conditions of white indentured servants added to his unpopularity among planters. With such criticisms of his Governor, Carlisle had little choice but to recall him. Henry Hawley was dispatched to Barbados on 15th March 1629, as his replacement.

Hawley arrived on 30th June, and Tufton, disgruntled by his dismissal, organised a feeble attempt to depose Hawley. He lost, and was executed for sedition. Following this event, Hawley imposed his authority upon the colony, and can be accredited as the person who, though ruthless, brought order and stability to frontier Barbados. He established an advisory Council of twelve prominent men, and ruled the island autocratically throughout most of the 1630s.

Carlisle was also faced with the task of diffusing the widespread discontent among planters that was created by Courteen's land policy. In addition, demand for a political system which offered colonists some measure of control over their economic affairs was increasing. Carlisle responded to the former demand, and instructed Hawley to nullify Courteen's land tenure system and to issue land to credible colonists in return for a quit rent of forty pounds in weight of tobacco annually. Furthermore, each planter was to provide his own capital and labour, and

9

pursue his own agricultural policy. Carlisle's system of land tenure made it difficult for men without access to large sums of capital to become substantial landholders. By the early 1630s, then, political and economic conditions were established for the development of a society dominated by a small landed elite.

POLITICAL ORGANISATION

The royal patent issued to the Earl of Carlisle did not specify the nature of political institutions through which he should exercise his authority. The patent merely stated that all laws which he may impose should be 'with the consent and approbation of the freeholders'. This provision was to ensure that colonists enjoyed some degree of influence over decisions which would affect their social and economic interests. Only under emergency situations was the Proprietor entitled legally to enforce laws without some measure of local consultation. This provision had the practical effect of nullifying the previous stipulation, since definitions of 'emergency situations' resided with the Proprietor. In addition, he could delegate governmental authority to governors who would have full executive power in the colony.

The executive powers of a Governor were extensive, and similar to those which the Crown had given the Proprietor. The Proprietor, during the early years, merely required his Governors to refer all important decisions for his confirmation, and to implement the details of his policies. From the earliest times, Governors appointed an advisory Council to inform them on colonial interests and opinions. Councillors were in effect 'yes men', whose loyalty to the Governor had to be unswerving. All legislative, executive and judicial authority resided in this body. It passed laws, issued proclamations, tried criminals and gave sentences. A spirit of arbitrariness pervaded all the doings of the Council, and popular liberties were practically non-existent.[1]

Only prominent members of the white community were considered by Governors fit for political office. Indentured servants, wage labourers, blacks and Indians were excluded from administrative and electoral participation. As in England, Barbados' political culture was neither democratic nor egalitarian, and those without property, education and status were not considered eligible for political rights. Governor Henry Hawley, in particular, was notorious for his exercise of power against persons whose only failure, according to one contemporary, was 'their ignorance of laws and the signs of the times'. He abused his right to allocate and retrieve land in order to suppress his opponents. Neither did he at this stage encourage the demand for representative institutions which involved the lower sections of the white community.

The movement towards greater civil rights and political representation within the white community began in early 1636, when Barbados was put in trust by James Hay, the First Earl of Carlisle. Nearing his death, the Proprietor hoped to repay his debts, and the colony was placed in the hands of Sir James Hay and Archibald Hay, his two cousins. All proprietary money was collected and used to disemburse his creditors. In September that year, Peter Hay arrived in Barbados as the agent for the Trustees. Governor Henry Hawley departed for England shortly afterwards, and left his brother, William Hawley, in charge as Acting-Governor. Robert Rich, the second Earl of Warwick, proposed to purchase Barbados from Carlisle. The Trustees refused Warwick's offer, even though the Second Earl of Carlisle was willing to negotiate.

Warwick was a tactful campaigner. He appointed James Futter, a political opponent of Governor Hawley, as his Barbados agent. Through Futter, he proposed that upon his ownership of the colony, he would democratise government by allowing a greater degree of representation. A sizeable number of planters supported him, and in early 1639 Peter Hay informed the Trustees that the Council was still loyal to the Proprietor, but the majority of propertied inhabitants were behind Warwick. Warwick was categorically refused the purchase of Barbados, and the Trustees then embarked upon a policy to break Hawley's regime in his absence.

The decision to remove Hawley was based upon the perception that Warwick's success in gaining popular support among colonists reflected their disenchantment with his administration. The Trustees knew that this would not have been an easy task, especially since Peter Hay, their agent, had been thrown off the Council by Acting-Governor William Hawley. Sergeant-Major Henry Huncks, none the less, was appointed Governor by the Trustees in place of Henry Hawley. He was instructed to expect some measure of resistance from the deposed Hawley, who arrived back in Barbados in May 1639. As expected, Hawley began to mobilise his forces against the Proprietor and the new Governor.

One of the most important statements Hawley issued, in order to swing freeholders to his cause, called for the election of burgesses for a General Assembly in order to give planters political authority on the island. He proposed that two representatives from each parish be selected. Each planter who held ten or more acres of land would take part in the process. By this policy, Hawley proposed to enfranchise about 1,500 Barbadian colonists. With an armed party of planters, Hawley succeeded in removing Huncks from office, and proceeded to make administrative provisions for the establishment of the Assembly in the same year. The Assembly met from time to time and debated political issues, but these gatherings at this time had no constitutional significance. Hawley continued to rule autocratically and the Assembly under him functioned as little more than an advisory body. When Carlisle was informed of these developments he dispatched a five-man commission to Barbados to terminate Hawley's rule. He was arrested, sent back to England a prisoner, and had his property confiscated. Huncks was re-instated, but served for only one year. In 1641, he was replaced by Philip Bell. It was under Bell's administration that the Assembly took its modern form, with the right to initiate legislation.

The 'parliament' established by Hawley in 1639, soon considered an indispensable political institution by planters, consisted of eleven councillors and twenty-two 'chosen burgesses'. Under Bell's regime, the number of parishes was fixed at eleven, and two delegates represented each parish to make up the full composition of the House. Though the number of councillors changed over time, the composition of the Assembly remained unaltered throughout the slavery period. Bell's administration was also influenced by the civil war in England, which had the effect of forging closer relations between the Council and Assembly. Most colonists had attempted to maintain a neutral position on the civil war, and Bell succeeded in establishing a large measure of functional unity of the two branches of the legislature in order to reflect that neutrality. The result was that extensive powers of self-government were achieved by the planter elite. The Assembly met frequently and considered most matters of policy, to the extent that it has been suggested that it bore a major part of the island's government. Many planters served in both Council and Assembly, which assisted in reducing the level of tension that had hitherto featured in their relations. James Drax, for example, was Councillor and Assemblyman under Bell's government.[2]

THE PLANTER ELITE AND ECONOMIC LIFE

Carlisle's vision of the colony as a commercial centre in the West India trade system was rigorously implemented by his Governors. Land was allocated mostly to colonists with known financial and social connections in England. The result of this policy was that a small number of prominent men soon engrossed the vast majority of arable land, and were well placed to impose their social and political power on the colony. In Hawley's

Council of 1639, for example, were William, his brother, Thomas Hothersall, James Drax, Richard Leonard, Daniel Fletcher, Richard Peers and William Perkins. These men were also the officers of militia regiments which added to their social status and respectability; Hothersall and William Hawley were captains.

As a new colonial elite, there were many issues in England on which they were divided. Most of them had been involved in the quarrels between King and Parliament on different sides, and had come to Barbados hoping to repair lost fortunes or make new ones. In spite of these differences, which were hardened by war and intolerance, they were able to achieve a large measure of social unity in Barbados which contributed to their profitable colonisation. Richard Ligon, who arrived in 1647 and published his history of the colony in 1657, was astonished by the level of socio-political solidarity among the planter elite. He noted that they were 'loving, friendly and hospitable one to another, and though they are several persuasions yet, their discretion ordered everything so well, as they never were any fallings out between them'.[3] Gentlemen's agreements and other non-legal methods were used in order to remove or reduce differences arising from English politics. Ligon noted that they 'made a law amongst themselves, that whosoever nam'd the word Roundhead or Cavalier should give to all those that heard him a shot and a turkey, to be eaten at his house that made the forfeiture'.[4] Furthermore, he added, many planters would deliberately make the forfeiture so as to occasion a social gathering.

Partly because of these political and constitutional developments, Barbados emerged in the mid-1640s as perhaps the most attractive colony in the English New World. This economic achievement was largely the result of planters' ability to borrow Dutch finance capital as well as their willingness to re-invest small profits in labour, machinery and new lands. Their readiness to shift investments into the production of alternative crops when required, was also an important factor. It was this sensitivity to market requirements, and commitment to profiteering by farming, which distinguished them from their Spanish predecessors in the West Indies.

From 1627, colonists went about the task of producing tobacco, the most profitable New World agricultural staple on the European market. In 1623, Virginian tobacco reaching England was worth one-and-a-half shillings per pound, and in 1625, three shillings per pound. This price level was lucrative and incited 'tobacco fever' among the Barbadians. Within a year of settlement, they exported to London, along with planters at St Kitts, 100,000 pounds in weight of tobacco which was sold at nine pence per pound. At this stage, Barbados was described as a colony 'wholly built on smoke', as tobacco was its only export crop.

By August 1631, the London tobacco market was glutted, and prices fell sharply. The Virginians opted for a policy of output control and price fixing. The English government, in sympathy with these their first American colonists, imposed a ban upon domestic production in an effort to keep up prices. Imperial restrictions were then imposed on Barbadian producers. An order of the Privy Council in 1631 directed the planting of tobacco to be limited in St Kitts and Barbados 'until such time as more staple commodities may be raised there'. The Barbadians, however, ignored this order, and by the end of the decade their volume of tobacco exports was still rising while those of Virginia and St Kitts were falling. Opposition to the imperial ruling was based upon the argument that the Virginians, whose political lobby in the metropole was more influential, had persuaded the monarch to adopt a discriminatory policy against West Indian interests.

While the conflict between the Barbadians and the Virginians ensued, the former were aware that the future of their colony could not depend upon tobacco cultivation. It was now well known in Europe that Barbadian tobacco was close to being 'the worst that grows in the world'. The first shipment which Henry Winthrop sent to London in 1628 was described as 'very ill-conditioned, foul, full of stalks and evil coloured'. Though tobacco smokers themselves, the Barbadians preferred to import Virginian and Spanish brands. By the early 1630s they had shifted from tobacco to cotton cultivation – a staple in great demand in Europe and fetching high prices on the London market.

The move towards cotton production assisted in maintaining moderate profit levels. When Sir Henry Colt visited the island in 1632 he noted that the 'trade in cotton fills them all with hope'. By 1635, however, the more creditworthy planters were dominating its production and marketing. In May 1636, Peter Hay, the resident proprietary agent, was instructed not to allow the leading planters to engross the cotton industry, but to 'encourage every planter to plant it, for Barbados' cotton of all is esteemed best . . ., and is a staple commodity that will ever be worth money'. Two years later profit levels were reported as impressive, and the colony once again experiencing boom conditions.

High cotton prices in Europe attracted other English planters in the Eastern Caribbean into its production. By 1639 the London market was over-supplied, and prices fell rapidly. The collapse was sudden and unexpected, and many marginal planters were ruined. In 1640 Peter Hay informed the Proprietor: 'This yeare hath been so baise a cotton yeare that the inhabitants hath not maide so much on cotton as will buye necessaries'. The price of high-quality cotton fell by 50 per cent between 1635 and 1641.

For the Barbados planter it meant the search, once again, for another staple in order to maintain the colony's economic viability. It was at this stage that a few innovating planters began to experiment with the large-scale production of indigo, which was in increasing demand for the making of dyes used in textiles manufacturing. Between 1640 and 1642, Barbadian indigo sold at profitable rates both in London and in the English mainland colonies, especially New England. By 1643, there was over-production and prices in Europe fell sharply. This prompted the proprietary agent to state that 'unless some new invention be found out to make a commodity', the colonists would be reduced to subsistence, and the commerical worth of the island lost. Sugar was the commodity which saved the colonists and their merchant allies during the mid-1640s.

WHITE INDENTURED SERVANTS

The production of tobacco, cotton and indigo depended upon the labour of thousands of British indentured servants. The English at Barbados, unlike the Spanish in the Greater Antilles, found no supply of Amerindian labour to enslave. In addition, at this stage of colonisation, the English were not financially able to use black slavery as the primary labour institution. The initial intention of planters was to rely upon indentured servants, and if Indians and the more expensive blacks could be obtained cheaply and reduced to slavery, so much the better.

The situation was the same in Barbados as it was in Virginia. More than half the whites who came to Barbados during the 1630s and 1640s were indentured servants. These people, in return for a passage to the colony and subsistence on arrival, signed contracts to serve employers for periods of up to seven years. Individuals under 21 normally served for seven years, and those over that age, five years.

The planting careers of Henry Winthrop and Thomas Verney can be used to illustrate the importance of indentured servants within the early plantation economy. Winthrop arrived in Barbados during the tobacco boom of July 1628, while Verney arrived in 1639. Winthrop had emigrated to Barbados during the Courteen administration, and on arrival agreed to work an estate for three years at an annual wage of £100. In October 1628, he informed his uncle, Thomas Fones: 'I do intend, God willing, to stay here on this island called Barbados, in the West Indies, and here I and my servants to join in the planting of tobacco.' Henry soon realised that in order to make the best of his tobacco plantation, he needed 'every year some twenty three servants'. He considered the importation of a male servant from England, at a cost of £5–6 for the passage and £10 annually for food, clothes and shelter, money well spent. On the arrival of his first crop in London he wrote to his father requesting more servants.

Winthrop was typical of Barbadian colonists, rushing to make a quick fortune. He was also a shrewd entrepreneur and a survivor. When Carlisle took full control of the island in 1629, he abandoned his commitment to Courteen and aligned himself with Carlisle's faction. He managed to obtain some credit which was used to expand his plantation which was now well stocked with servants imported from Bristol. By 1630, he was a leading tobacco planter and one of the twelve magistrates on the island.

The planting experience of Thomas Verney illustrates that without an adequate supply of servants the objective of profit-making was extremely hazardous. Thomas was the young son of Sir Edmund Verney, and an embarrassment to his respectable family. He was described as adventurous in a reckless way, and seemed to conform to the commonly stereotyped personality of the disinherited younger son. In 1638, he turned up in Barbados, recommended by the Earl of Warwick. On arrival, he wrote to his mother (his father having dismissed him as a useless spendthrift) stating that he had resolved (by the grace of God) to lead a new life in Barbados.

Within three weeks, Verney had obtained a plantation of 100 acres, bought 'at reasonable terms'. He was instantly elevated into the property-owning elite. Following this purchase, he sent an invoice to his father which listed the commodities needed in order to make use of a plantation. The invoice was headed with a request for 'twenty able men servants, whereof two to be carpenters, two of them to be unskilled labourers strong enough for working in the fields'. Such a labour force was certain to produce high clothing costs, and Thomas asked for two extra servants, 'a weaver that can weave diapers and the other a taylor'.

Thomas soon ran into trouble with his servants. Some fell sick from overwork, and others he had to auction on the open market because he could not afford to maintain them. In June 1640, he wrote to his father asking if he could, with the help of the warden of the Bridewell prison, obtain 100 servants for his estate. Thomas was either trying his hand at servant trading, or was repaying his debts on the island with servants, as was customary. His father refused him both labour and capital. In September, Thomas informed his brother that 'the next year I shall not have so much credit, unless my father is pleased to send me over a good supply of servants that I may pay that which I am indebted in the country, which if I do not pay I must lye and starve in prison . . .'. In December, Thomas was imprisoned for non-payment of debt by Governor Huncks. He obtained bail, but was forced to leave the island – the ultimate penalty for a disgraced man. Such, then, were the varied life experiences of young planters coming to terms with early plantation culture in Barbados.

Verney also showed that planters quite freely bought, sold, gambled away, mortgaged, taxed as property, and alienated in wills their indentured servants. These practices were governed not by English labour customs and traditions, but by a loosely defined concept – 'the custom of the Country' – which was the law and deciding force in the colony before a comprehensive master-and-servant code was established in 1661. Through the manipulation of this concept, Barbadian planters developed a system of white servitude which was peculiarly New World. The servant was accountable to his master for the total time embraced under his indenture. The result was that servants could not legally leave their plantations without a pass signed by the master, which in effect meant that the total control element so characteristically demonstrated in black slavery was applicable to white servants. Also, planters were keen to establish that the servant was not a free person under contractual obligations, but primarily a capital investment with property characteristics – factors which were contradictory to the concept of social freedom.

Constraints of race and culture, none the less, played an important part in limiting the degree of harshness of Barbadian servitude. In spite of the oppressiveness of their social lives, servants were not slaves, and could not have been enslaved. Both masters and the imperial government would have had great difficulty in legitimising the reduction of indentured servants to the kind of perpetual slavery imposed upon blacks. Most servants in these years came to the West Indies voluntarily, and planters needed the servant trade for their own survival. Their limited use as 'property' had already contributed to an anti-West Indian attitude among the English poor, with negative implications for supply, and was partly responsible for the political crisis in the white community – evidenced by the aborted servant insurrections of 1634 and 1647.

The terms of servants' contracts did in fact give them rights, such as the right to complain to local magistrates over excessive maltreatment at the hands of their masters, receipt of a freedom-due of £10 or 400 lb of cotton after the termination of their contracts, and adequate food, clothing and shelter as defined by the customs of the colony. These rights were rarely effectively exercised, as masters who sat on the Council, Assembly and Judiciary, suppressed them so that they did not adversely affect their property right. For example, in 1640, when two Barbados servants lodged complaints against their master, Captain Thomas Stanhope, for maltreatment, after examination the local magistrate found them to be malicious and had them publicly flogged, thus removing any legal threat to the planters' right to treat their property as they wished within the wide limits of the 'custom of the country'. Planters expected such decisions from the judiciary and held the view that since they paid a property tax on their servants, their disposal and use of them was no concern of the wider community.

AFRICANS AND INDIANS

The introduction of Africans as slaves into Barbados at the beginning of colonisation was not part of a formulated policy. Captain Henry Powell had obtained ten Africans at some point between Guiana and Barbados in 1627; these were the first blacks to be enslaved on the island. The following year, Henry Winthrop noted that the island's population consisted also of a few 'slave negeres'. Black people, then, were among the party of colonists who first settled Barbados in 1627.

Between 1627 and 1645, blacks remained a small minority. In the 1630s they did not exceed 800 in number. White servant labour was cheaper, and most planters did not purchase blacks. In 1627, Captain Henry Powell also landed a group of thirty-two 'Indians' from Guiana. It was agreed that they would live 'as free people' while teaching the English the art of tropical agriculture, and regional political geography. With the collapse of the Courteen Proprietorship, and the emergence of Lord Carlisle's plantocracy, these conditions were not recognised, and their status changed to that of involuntary bondage. In 1629 Winthrop stated that the island was also populated with '50 slaves of Indians and blacks'.

The early socio-legal status of blacks and Indians is unclear for some historians. It was not until 1636 that the Barbadians, or more specifically Governor Henry Hawley, issued a proclamation that henceforth all blacks and Indians brought to the island, and their offspring, were to be received as life slaves, unless prior agreements to the contrary existed. As a result, some scholars have suggested that in the pre-1636 period blacks were not necessarily slaves in the sense of being chattel or real estate, but that a range of interpersonal relationships existed, some of which were indeed temporary servitude as opposed to indefinite slavery. The opposing view has it that the English refrained from formulating a system of laws which defined slaves in the early period, probably because they did not consider this important as the number of non-whites was small. They nevertheless had clearly devised a pattern of labour use which was undoubtedly chattel slavery. According to Richard Dunn, for example, early Englishmen in

Barbados immediately 'categorised the Negroes and Indians who worked for them as heathen brutes and very quickly treated them as chattels'.[5]

Male Indians were generally employed in the fishing industry, and females in the households. Few Indians performed field work, but most blacks did. Indians were seen by the English as useful intelligence allies in their political conflicts with Spain and France. Though they were used as slaves, the English tended to see them as a 'special' people with certain privileges which blacks did not enjoy. But their numbers were too small to make any impact upon the colony's labour force. According to Ligon, planters found them 'more apt to learn anything, sooner than the negroes'.[6] This he linked to the fact that the Indians had more of the shape of the European than the negroes. He also stated that the Indians were given certain social privileges while the blacks were reduced to 'absolute slavery to their masters'.

Some Indians were imported under indenture. For example, in 1648 an Indian by the name of Hope was imported from New England to serve in Barbados for ten years 'according to the orders and Customs of English servants in the said Island'. No such contracts have been found for blacks as hereditary life slavery was the established pattern from the beginning. The Hawley proclamation of 1636 merely gave constitutionality to custom. Ligon stated that during the 1640s the social structure of the island consisted of masters, servants and slaves. The slaves and their posterity, he noted, were subjected to their masters for ever, while the servants were subjected for just five years.[7]

CHAPTER THREE

Sugar and slavery
1644–1692

SUGAR REVOLUTION

Sugar cane was introduced into the colony's agriculture in the mid-1630s. During this time it was not used for the manufacture of sugar. It was grown mainly for the feeding of cattle and for the making of manure and fuel. The rise of the sugar industry was to await a series of domestic and international circumstances. In the former category, one important development was the planters' perception that there was a satisfactory resolution to the problem of land tenure by the early 1640s. When Philip Bell was appointed Governor in 1641, he opened the issue of land tenure for discussion in the Assembly, and in 1643 legislation was passed in the form of 'An Act for the settling of estates and titles of the inhabitants of this island'. This Act satisfied planters' demands for freehold ownership and hereditary tenure.

International political forces also affected Barbadian socio-economic development during the mid-1640s. It has been argued that the Brazilian civil war between Portuguese settlers and their Dutch commercial overlords, which escalated during the early 1640s, gave the Barbadians the long-awaited opportunity to break into the sugar market with a commanding position. The civil war did cause a supply crisis on the European sugar market, since Brazil supplied at least 80 per cent of the sugar which reached Europe. The defeat of the Dutch during the 1640s is considered an important watershed in the rise of the English sugar industry. Unable to capture Brazil, Dutch merchants have been credited with assisting struggling English colonists with capital, technology, markets and credit lines. As the principal suppliers of African slaves to the New World, and established shippers of colonial produce to Europe, their economic relationship with English colonists was a logical response to their Brazilian dislodgement.

Dutch merchants saw the potential of Barbados as a market for slaves and sugar-making machinery. By financing sugar planters, these merchants expected a derived demand for slaves which the English could not supply themselves as they had no secure slave-trading base on the West African coast. As leading slave traders they desired to replace indentured servants with slaves everywhere they could. Being in large part Jewish, many Dutch merchants in Barbados were not allowed, by law and custom, to contract white servants – the result of the exportation of English anti-semitism to the colony. Logically, therefore, they conceived indentured servitude as inconsistent with their New World economic and social interests.

By 1645, Barbadian planters believed that they had found, at last, a truly profitable staple, one which was free from short-term price fluctuations. The economic prosperity brought by this commodity was immediate. In 1645, George Downing observed that if 'you go to Barbados, you shall see a flourishing Island', fully recovered from the crisis in tobacco and cotton production. By the early 1650s, Barbados was described as the richest spot in the New World, and colonial officials boasted that the island's value, in terms of trade and capital, was greater than all the English colonies put together.

Ligon captured the nature of this economic explosion with references to planters' expectations. He related the case of Thomas Modyford, son of the Mayor of Exeter, who arrived on the island in 1647. Modyford bought a plantation of 500 acres and provided it with a labour force of twenty-eight English servants and a larger number of slaves. He took 'a resolution to himself not to set face in England, till he had made his voyage and employment there worth him a hundred thousand pounds sterling; and all by this sugar plant'.[1] Modyford's optimism was, indeed, justified; by 1657 he had made a fortune and was appointed Governor in 1660. In the early 1660s he expanded his interests into the newly acquired Jamaica, and became Governor of that island in 1664. At his death in 1679 he owned one of the largest plantations in the West Indies.

James Drax arrived on the island during the tobacco boom of the late 1620s with a capital stock of £300. By 1654, Drax was the richest planter in Barbados (if not the West Indies) with an estate of 700 acres and 200 slaves. Both Drax and Modyford represented the optimism and success of the Barbados planter elite, who saw the opportunity to rapidly accumulate capital at an unparalleled rate in the West Indies. In the second half of the century, when it became fashionable to grant English titles to prominent planters, these men among eleven other Barbadians were knighted, a symbol of their colonial success and the achievements of mercantile capitalism.[2] Drax was knighted by Cromwell in 1658, while Modyford was made a baronet by Charles II.

le 1. *Estimated sugar imports (tons) to England, 1651–80*

	Barbados	Jamaica	Leewards
	3,750	—	—
5	7,787	—	—
~3	7,176	—	1,000
1669	9,525	500	1,679
1672	—	522	—
1676	—	1,154	—
1678	—	2,259	—
1680	—	3,563	—

Between 1628 and 1640, land values were relatively low and a small capital stock could get a planter a substantial estate. In the 1630s, £200 could purchase a 100-acre plantation stocked with indentured servants. After 1643, when sugar had proven lucrative, the price of land increased rapidly until the mid-1650s. By 1670, all the colony's good arable land was under sugar cultivation. In 1676, Governor Atkins noted: 'As for the lands in Barbados I am confident there is not one foot that is not employed down to the very seaside.'[3]

The Barbadians dominated the Caribbean sugar industry in these early years. They exported some 15,000 tons in the good years from the 1650s to the 1670s – about 65 per cent of all sugar exported from the region (see Table 1). By the early 1700s they began to lose their supremacy to the Jamaicans and Leeward Islanders, and complained not so much about their marketing skills, but about diminishing soil fertility, rising costs, insects and drought. By the turn of the century, however, they were still the leading sugar exporters in the English West Indies. Between 1698 and 1700 the value of their sugar trade averaged about £316,000 per annum as against Jamaican exports of £201,400 and the Leewards exports of £192,000. But between 1690 and 1705, their share of West Indian commerce to England had fallen by about 40 per cent, and by 1715 their sugar output was surpassed by Jamaica and the Leewards.

The wealth of the planter class was visible everywhere – at home, in London, and on the mainland. An observer who compared Barbados in 1643 and 1666, noted that 'the island in 1643 was not valued one seventeenth so considerable as in 1666; the negroes not being in 1643 above 6,400 were in 1666 above 50,000; the buildings in 1643 were mean, with things only for necessity; but in 1666, plate, jewels, and household stuff were estimated at £500,000; their buildings very fair and beautiful, and their houses like castles'. Such developments were said to have made the popular colony of New England look like 'a very poore country' indeed. Barbados, therefore, made the transition from a struggling frontier community to a wealthy sugar economy within half a century.

RISE OF THE PLANTER CLASS

Until recently it was generally accepted that a powerful and cohesive planter class did not develop until the advent of large-scale sugar production; also, that society in the pre-sugar era was composed mainly of hundreds of small yeoman farmers who were displaced by the market forces released by large-scale sugar cultivation and slave labour. The sugar-planter elite was conceived as a new crop of entrepreneurs who arrived from England during the late 1640s and did not therefore experience the hardships of the tobacco and cotton years.

This view, however, has been moderated by recent scholars who have shown that the sugar magnates of the 1650s were mostly men who had arrived in Barbados during the earliest years. Evidence has been produced which shows that many of the large sugar estates were formed by the amalgamation of smaller ones, and that many marginal farmers sold out, and were pushed out, by their wealthier neighbours. But many of the more successful sugar estates were also formed by the opposite process – the subdivision of large properties into more manageable units of 300–500 acres. For example, the 4,500 acres of land in the possession of Henry Hawley in 1640, most of it in the St Philip parish, was divided into several successful sugar plantations by 1650; among these were Three Houses, Bayfield, Fortescue, Thickett, Vineyard, Golden Grove, Wiltshire, Mapps and Bayleys.

Elite planters like James Drax, Richard Peers and James Holdip were all large-scale farmers before the advent of sugar production. Other prom-inent families such as the Alleynes, Farmers, Dottins, Gibbes's, Maycocks and Rouses, who have survived into the present century, were all substantial landowners before 1643. In terms of size and continuity, the 700-acre estate which was owned by the Drax family in the St George parish from the 1640s, and which was owned by the family into the 1980s, is probably the most remarkable. Some families that owned large estates in the 1650s continued to be sugar producers into the mid-nineteenth century, which illustrates an important characteristic of the island's landed elite.

Much of the land consolidation which produced the planting elite in fact occurred after the first phase of sugar cultivation. It is during the period 1650–65 that the evidence of reduction in the number of landholders becomes substantial. According to John Scott, a Restoration adventurer in the Caribbean, the number of landed proprietors in the colony diminished from 11,200 to 745 between 1645 and 1667. Although these data given by Scott are now considered to represent an exaggerated view of the process of consolidation, he accurately recalled one Captain Waterman, whose estates, Springfield and Cambridge, totalled 800 acres in the 1660s, but had once been forty separate holdings.

By the 1660s, the planter class was fully formed and its internal socio-economic divisions were identifiable. In 1673 the President of the island submitted a list of the seventy-four 'most eminent' planters to the Colonial Office. The acreage of these planters ranged from 200 acres to 1,000 acres. In all, they held 29,050 acres out of a total of 92,000 acres of farm land. More than two-thirds of the colony's arable land was thus held in units of less than 300 acres. John Pierce headed the list with 1,000 acres and Robert Haskett came next with 900. Henry Drax and John Waterman each held 880, while Sir Peter Colleton held 700 acres. Holding less than 501 acres each were such prominent families as the Gibbes's, Farmers, Walronds and Yeamans.

According to the 1680 census, the 175 biggest planters, who constituted 7 per cent of the island's property holders, controlled 54 per cent of all landed property and 60 per cent of all the slaves. This census understates the full holdings of these planters, and therefore their full share of the colony's property might well have been nearer 60 per cent. The majority of these planters in 1680 were second- and third-generation colonists. Just about 48 per cent of them had been in the colony since the 1630s, and only about 20 per cent or so had arrived after the sugar boom of the 1650s. This characteristic of the plantocracy tells much about its socio-political attitudes, especially in terms of its self-identity.

From the 1640s, the plantocracy, strengthened by the massive accumulation of capital generated by the sugar industry, began to conceive its economic interests in clear class terms. Prominent planters used their dominance of colonial political institutions in order to develop socio-political profiles that reflected that class consciousness. In general, they were not prepared to allow political disputes in England, for example, to undermine their class authority and interest. Neither were they prepared to allow proprietary power to undermine their perceived right to manage the colony's affairs in a manner that suited them.

From the 1640s, the planter elite, with minority dissension, was determined to ensure that the colony enjoyed a maximum degree of self-government within the imperial structure. This meant, therefore, the adoption of a neutral position and an independent line on the conflict between King and Parliament. The colony had prospered, also, under a free trade policy mainly with Dutch merchants, and was prepared to continue along that line in spite of imperial opposition. Indeed, it was evident, during the late 1640s, that some prominent planters would rather push for home rule and independence than relinquish their freedom of trade and rights to self-government.

News of the execution of Charles I by Parliament in January 1649, however, threw the Barbadian plantocracy into disarray. They had managed to maintain a policy of non-interference for nearly a decade, and had not racked the colony with Cavalier–Roundhead conflict. All along, men like James Drax, Thomas Noel and John Bayes had controlled their feelings of support for Parliament, but could do so no longer, and decided to challenge the neutralist stance of the colony. But none was prepared to see the colony's self-government subjected to rule by parliamentary decree.

Royalist sympathisers, however, such as Humphrey and Edward Walrond, Thomas Modyford and William Byam, expressed their opposition to parliamentary authority, and advocated that colonists should reject the mercantile principles of Cromwell, and practise free trade as formerly. As royalist opinion among the plantocracy moved in favour of 'independence' from the Commonwealth, few persons expressed the principle of the King's right to rule. Parliament considered offensive the political stance of the empowered royalist planter faction, and resorted to a military operation to subdue the colony. Planters, both Roundheads and Cavaliers, were described by Parliament as rebels and insurrectionists who had to be crushed.

On 7th May 1650, the General Assembly of the colony voted to receive Francis Lord Willoughby as Governor, a move which confirmed that Cavaliers had succeeded in breaking Roundhead political power. The Willoughby government wasted no time in deporting many Roundheads from the colony and confiscated their properties. Parliament was distressed by these developments and dispatched a military fleet under the command of Sir George Asycue to subordinate the colony. For three months, Asycue blockaded the colony, as his force of 860 men lacked the military power to conquer the royalists' militia. Finally, on 11th January 1652, the colonists, feeling the pressures of commercial insulation, agreed to accept the terms of Asycue's delegation.

Barbadians considered the terms of agreement favourable to themselves.

They agreed to recognise the rule of Parliament, and its representative Governor, Daniel Searle, in return for continued self-government, free trade, and a restoration of confiscated properties. With this agreement, planters got back to their task of producing sugar, even though it was clear to many that Parliament had no intention of honouring the agreement to allow them free trade with the Dutch. This agreement, known as the Charter of Barbados, represented for the planter class imperial constitutional recognition of their right to rule themselves, and a confirmation that propertied Englishmen overseas were also entitled to the same political freedoms that they enjoyed at home.

The Restoration Government of Charles II attempted to curtail many of the political rights which Barbadians won during the Commonwealth. By means of a series of trade laws, attempts were made to bring the Barbados economy more fully under the control of the metropole. Planters were then required to send their sugar and other cargoes to England in English ships, and purchase their slaves only from English traders. In return, the mother country offered them protected and guaranteed commodity markets.

In response to these mercantile provisions, the Barbadians petitioned Charles II for the annulment of the Earl of Carlisle's proprietary patent. This was done, and Barbados became a Crown Colony. Francis Lord Willoughby was sent out as the Royal Governor to strengthen loyalty to the Crown, as he had done during the turbulent years of 1650 to 1652. Using his influence among leading colonists he persuaded the Assembly in 1663 to grant to the King a permanent $4\frac{1}{2}$ per cent duty on all exports from the island in order to finance the royal administration. The Barbadians considered this levy as part of the cost which they paid for self-government, and the right to control their own finance and taxation policies. On the whole, they believed, according to Dunn, that they had 'struck a pretty good bargain with Charles II'.[4]

Secured in the legitimacy of their authority, and the legality of their landholdings, the plantocracy extended their domination of the colony's political and social institutions. They dominated public life and all civic organisations which conferred social status and respectability. In addition, they fashioned social ideologies so as to ensure that elitism was confined to white Anglo-Saxon Anglicans. In spite of an official policy of religious tolerance, Catholics, Jews and non-conformist Protestants were discriminated against and kept away from all seats of political power. Quakers were expelled from the colony and Irish Catholics not welcomed. All civic officers, such as councillors, assemblymen, judges, magistrates, jurors and coroners were drawn frm the upper ranks of the planter class who were white and Anglican in religion. Petty officers were drawn from the lower sections of the landed community who qualified on these racial and religious criteria.

During the 1660s, also, the plantocracy was able to add the finishing touches to their aristocratic inclinations. Between 1658 and 1665, five of them received knighthoods or baronetcies, and at least another dozen were so honoured in the remaining years of the century. This symbol of imperial recognition also conferred tremendous social respect within the colony, and added to the sense of achievement within the class.

In contrast, many smaller planters were forced to emigrate from the colony as economic conditions became less favourable. This factor contributed greatly to the decline of the white population during the second half of the seventeenth century. It also became an issue of imperial concern, as militia regiments declined in size. During the 1660s at least 3,000 small planters and white labourers emigrated to other Caribbean islands and the mainland colonies. Also, between 1670 and 1675 another 4,000 to 5,000 whites departed, with some 2,000 emigrating in the year 1670. While members of the planter elite obtained their honours and returned to England as absentees, less successful planters sought out alternative colonies where they could pursue their dream of making a fortune and obtaining the highest social status.

Other developments in the late seventeenth century combined to weaken the hand of the planter class and reduce their status within the West Indian empire. The colony experienced a series of natural disasters, such as the locust plague in 1663, the Bridgetown fire and a major hurricane in 1667. Drought in 1668 ruined some planters and excessive rain in 1669 added to their financial problems. Yet the Barbadians were optimistic about their future prospects, and continued to invest in sugar and slaves.

Uncertainty, however, did set in after one of their sugar fleets was captured by the Dutch in the Anglo-Dutch War of 1672–74. By 1680, none the less, the island was described as being in a flourishing condition in spite of international rivalry in the region. The years 1675 to 1688 were a period of peace, and it was during this time that the sugar planters in Jamaica and the Leeward Islands made great strides. By 1720 Barbadians were no longer a dominant force within the world's sugar industry. They had been surpassed by the Jamaicans and the Leeward Islanders. The colony, moreover, ceased to be the 'brightest gem' in the imperial crown of New World trade.

Barbados, therefore, had lost its lead position within the region after a period of fifty years, and its absentee planter elite also gave way to other regional elites as metropolitan representatives of the sugar and slavery culture. In 1700, for example, John Pollexfen, a member of the Colonial Office, wrote that the planter class of Barbados received annually from their estates £300,000, while the Crown secured a revenue from the island of £70,000. Jamaica was far more valuable to the Crown, with annual revenue gains of £600,000 of which £200,000 was in bullion. By 1713, while the Barbadian planters annually exported goods to the value of £309,000, exports from the Leewards were annually valued at about £437,000 and Jamaica £322,000. These data indicate the extent to which Barbados and its planting elite had been superseded by regional counterparts in the sugar industry at the beginning of the eighteenth century.

AFRICANS AND SLAVERY

The dominant traditional interpretation of the origins of slave society and economy in Barbados is the climatic theory, which stressed the physical inability of whites, and the ability of blacks, to work efficiently on tropical plantations. Partly related to this theory is the fact that planters preferred black to white labour for racist, cultural or other non-economic reasons. In 1926, Vincent Harlow in his *A History of Barbados* noted:

the planters discovered that labour of Negro slaves, accustomed as they were to intense heat and sudden cold, was more efficient . . .; consequently the British labourer . . . gave place to the Negro. It was the triumph of geographical conditions.[5]

Eric Williams, in 1944, developed an incisive critique of the climatic theory. He showed that the economic history of Barbados between 1627 and 1650 illustrates that planters were quite satisfied with the productivity of white labourers, and their primary complaint was that the supply was never really adequate. He concluded that the rise of black slavery was not the triumph of climatic or geographical conditions, but of market forces.[6]

A price and cost analysis of slavery and servitude shows that

1 prior to the Restoration (1660), indentured labour was cheaper than slave labour, hence its general adoption by Barbadian planters;

2 the tendency towards the growing efficiency of the slave trade between 1650 and 1660 allowed the slave to become a satisfactory economic substitute for the servant during this period;

3 not until the mid-1660s, when adverse forces affected the servant market,

drastically reducing supply and pushing up costs, did slave labour gain a clear cost advantage over servant labour.

The displacement process had accelerated during the 1650s, but this merely suggested that planters had perceived correctly these trends in the two labour markets, and were able to absorb, in the short term, the higher marginal cost incurred by black labour because of the extraordinarily large profits generated by early sugar production.

The level of demand for servants during the 1640s was estimated at about 2,000 per year. In 1652, the demand was estimated at 3,000 per year, and in that year there were some 13,000 servants on the island. Between 1645 and 1650, at least 8,000 white workers arrived in Barbados. These were a mixture of voluntary servants, political refugees and transported convicts and rogues. In England, overpopulation was seen as the main reason for the social distress and economic dislocation which produced the pool of potential emigrants. The majority of servants who arrived had no ready contracts with specific planters, but were recruited and their contracts sold by merchants on the open market.

During the century, the cost of bringing servants to the colony increased, but at no stage did it exceed £8 sterling per servant. The market price of prime indentures varied minimally according to skill, sex and nationality. In general, merchants aimed to sell each servant indenture at twice the capital outlay involved in bringing it to market. Age and skills were not critical factors on the primary market as most servants were between the ages of 16 and 30, and most artisan skills were not directly applicable to sugar production. Planters were prepared to pay marginally more for good Scottish servants, but cared less for Irish Catholics. The fifty-six servants aboard the *Abraham*, for example, who were sold in January 1637, went for a mean price, male and female, of £7 sterling.

During the 1640s and early 1650s, as the demand for servants rapidly increased, so did their prices. By the mid-1650s, servants were being sold in Barbados at between £10 and £14 per head. This inflation in servant prices placed considerable financial pressure upon small and middle-rank planters, most of whom were already heavily indebted to merchants. In 1661, the Governor informed the Colonial Office that the 'price of servants', among other commodities, 'being doubled what they were must ruin the planters'. He pleaded for an increase in supply in order to reduce price levels, but it was not forthcoming. During the 1660s, prices continued to increase, while the length of service was being rapidly reduced.

By the late 1670s, after many unsuccessful attempts by the planters to increase the supply of servants, the Council and Assembly decided upon a legislative path in order to stabilise prices. In 1678 the first of a series of laws was passed, entitled, 'An Act to encourage the Bringing in of Christian Servants'. In 1682 another Act was passed which led to local government's direct involvement in the servant market in an attempt to regulate prices. The Act provided that if merchants brought 'good servants' to the colony and were unable to dispose of them within ten days, the Treasurer would purchase them at a rate of £12. 5s. per head. These servant indentures would then be re-sold to planters at a rate of £13 per head. The fifteen shillings' difference was to cover the cost of administering the facility, plus a fee for allowing the planters to pay in credit instalments.

In 1688, this price level was changed. The Treasurer was now instructed that since planters consistently complained about the high costs of servant labour, he was to subsidise prices by re-selling servant indentures at the rate of £10 per male and £10. 10s. per female. By 1690, merchants were rejecting these prices. They petitioned the Assembly, stating that the war against the French, which made their business riskier, and rising recruitment costs in England, required a significant price increase. By 1696, the Treasurer was paying servant traders £18 per head.

Meanwhile, the price of slave labour became progressively lower between 1627 and 1680 (see Table 2). Between 1630 and 1650, slave prices in Barbados were generally some 200–300 per cent higher than servant prices. The limited data available for most of this period suggest an estimated mean price of £35 per slave. These were the years when the Dutch merchants, operating largely from Pernambuco in north-east Brazil, had a virtual monopoly of the Barbados slave market.

In the post-Restoration period, however, significant changes took place

Table 2. *Estimated Barbados slave prices, 1638–45*

Year	£ sterling
1638	40.88
1639	44.15
1640	30.03
1641	36.72
1642	39.75
1643	20.54
1644	18.03
1645	20.98

in both the slave and servant markets. These changes were substantial enough to give slave labour a marginal cost advantage over servant labour, thus reversing the economic pattern of the previous thirty years. This change in the price/cost ratios of servant and slave labour took place quite rapidly. In addition, during this period an anti-emigration movement was popularised in England, fuelled by the writings of political economists and economic pamphleteers, and supported by the State. These writings, still operating within the confines of demographic analysis, now argued that England was underpopulated, and the emigration of every servant to the colonies represented a drain upon its resources; hence the trade was seen as contrary to the economic interests of England. During the 1660s, for the first time in the seventeenth century, merchants were brought before the courts and tried for kidnapping and inveigling servants away from the realm.

More importantly, the Navigation Acts of 1660 and 1661 made it illegal for ships to take servants from Scotland to the colonies without first stopping at an English port and registering the cargo. This had the effect of driving Scottish merchants out of the servant trade, thus taking the Scottish labour market out of the orbit of the Barbadian planter. In addition, Jamaica emerged after the 1660s as the most attractive destination for British servants going to the West Indies. No land was offered to servants in Barbados, and little opportunity existed for them to acquire land after their period of servitude expired. The Jamaican planters offered indentured servants contracts of two to four years, plus up to twenty acres of land at the expiration of their servitude. In fact, Barbados after 1660 was the least attractive of the West Indies colonies from the perspective of the potential servant, and hence the larger proportion of servants going to the West Indies after 1670 went to Jamaica and the Leeward Islands. It was specifically at this juncture that the English merchant class began to organise joint stock companies with royal charters to break into the African slave trade.

According to Philip Curtin's census of the African slave trade, about 263,700 Africans were imported into the English West Indies between 1640 and 1700. Of this total, Barbados received some 134,500, Jamaica 85,100 and the Leewards, 44,100.[7] While the black population rose throughout the seventeenth century, the number of whites, which reached a peak about 1660, fell slowly up to 1700, and then remained relatively stable for the rest of the slavery period (Table 3). The reduction of the white population was due mainly to the crisis of indentureship, which resulted in a high level of ex-servant emigration. The 1679/80 islandwide census gave data for both

Table 3. *Barbados population
estimates, 1655–1712*

Year	Whites	Blacks
1655	23,000	20,000
1673	21,309	33,184
1676	21,725	32,473
1684	19,568	46,602
1712	12,528	41,970

Source: R. Dunn, *Sugar and Slaves*, p. 87

white servants and black slaves on a parish basis. These data illustrate the pace at which black slaves had replaced white servants on the island. Most servants employed on plantations by this time were overseers, artisans, book-keepers and other non-field occupations. They represented the labour elite of the plantation economy, but soon began to experience severe competition from the emerging slave artisan group.

Tracing the African origins of slaves in early Barbadian society, as indeed elsewhere, is complicated by the fact that most information on the slave trade relates to the port of departure rather than the catchment area from which slaves originated. In addition, planters and slave traders alike simplified the slave trading world of West Africa and in the process lost much of the details concerning ethnicity. For example, they would refer to Coromantee or Coromantine slaves as an ethnic type shipped from Ghana, when in fact linguists have now shown that, as a term, it refers to a wide range of peoples, most of whom spoke basically Akan languages, such as the Ashanti or Fanti. It is therefore relatively easy to establish the ports from which slaves departed for Barbados, but it is a more difficult task to establish their ethnic type.

Richard Ligon stated that most slaves in Barbados during his time (1647–50) were fetched from 'Guinny and Binny', 'Angola' and the 'Gambia River'.[8] This range covers virtually all of the West African coast. The contemporary data show that, in the period 1640–70, most slaves being sold in Barbados were sold by Dutch merchants. Research on the Dutch slave trade shows that in this period, most slaves were taken from the Angola region, Ghana, Togo and Dahomey, and the overwhelming majority from the first region. Handler and Lange concluded that the evidence from the slave trade itself indicates that during the period of the most intensive trade to Barbados, the Gold Coast and the Bight of Benin (including the modern areas of Ghana, Togo, Dahomey and western

Nigeria) supplied most of the slaves shipped by British and Dutch slavers.[9]

Between 1673 and 1700, most slaves sold in Barbados were supplied by the Royal African Company. The agents for this company generally stated that they supplied mostly 'Coromantine', 'Whydah', and other Gold Coast Africans. In 1657, Governor Atkins reported that the majority of slaves in Barbados were 'Coromantine'.[10] Hughes, in his eighteenth-century natural history of the island, noted that 'Coromantee' slaves were seconded by 'Whydah' slaves.[11] Whydah was also a collective term that embraced people as diverse as the Dahomeans, Popo or Gun.

Taking all of these difficulties into consideration, it is possible to make the generalisation that most blacks brought to Barbados during the seventeenth century were from the Ga, Ibo, Ashanti, Ewe, Edo, Fanti, Adangme, Dahomey and Yoruba peoples. During the eighteenth century, these groups rapidly intermixed, and ethnic divisions quickly became muted. By 1817, only 7 per cent of black Barbadians were African-born; the vast majority were creoles, most of whom had lost any claim to ethnic exclusiveness.

CONTROL OF SLAVES

Planters in Barbados kept African slaves subordinated by an effective deployment of militia regiments, supported by imperial troops and navy. These forces were strengthened by a complex legal machinery. Legal forces were designed to regulate slaves' social behaviour, within and outside the production process, as well as to police their daily movements.

The first comprehensive slave code for Barbados was the 1661 'Act for the better ordering and governing of Negroes'. This slave law, according to Richard Dunn, 'legitimised a state of war between blacks and whites, sanctioned rigid segregation, and institutionalised an early warning system against slave revolt'.[12] It formed the legal basis of slave–planter relations and represented an attempt to legally structure the social order of the plantation world. The Act was amended in 1676, 1682 and 1688. In the preamble of the 1661 Code, the slaves were described as 'heathenish', 'brutish', and a 'dangerous kind of people', whose naturally wicked instincts should at all times be suppressed. It provided that masters should feed, clothe and accommodate the slave within the 'customs of the country', while on the other hand, it provided that slaves found guilty of certain crimes, other than those of a public nature, would be punished by being branded, whipped, having their noses slit, or by having a limb removed.

For crimes of a public nature, such as rebellion, slaves were capitally punished. In such cases, the island's Treasurer compensated slave owners for their loss of capital. In addition, the Act of April 1688 declared slaves as 'real estate' as opposed to mere chattel; this meant that slaves were legally tied to plantations, and could not easily be alienated from them in probate settlements. No legal provisions were made for the Christianisation of slaves; they were generally conceived by the Anglican Church as intellectually unable to comprehend the concept of the faith and the Christian vision.

In the 1688 Code, clauses covered almost every area of the slave's social existence. This was the most comprehensive revision of the 1661 Act, and it remained in place throughout the eighteenth century. It provided that no master should give his slave leave to go off his estate unless a signed ticket was given to the slave stating the time allowed for return. Any white who found a slave on his property without such a ticket and did not apprehend him was liable to forfeit ten shillings sterling to the Treasurer, half of which was paid to the informant. In addition, it became lawful 'for all masters, overseers, and other persons whatsoever, to apprehend and take up any Negro, or other slave that should be found out of the plantation of his master . . . at any time, especially Saturday nights, Sundays, or other Holidays, not being on lawful business, or with a letter from their master, or a ticket, or not having a white man with them'.

The 1688 Code also stated that slaves were not lawfully allowed to 'beat drums, blow horns, or use other loud instruments', and their houses were to be 'diligently searched . . . once every week'. Any white who entertained a 'strange' negro, upon conviction was to forfeit £2. 10s. A series of punishments was provided for slaves who (1) traded in stolen goods; (2) struck a Christian; (3) ran away; (4) burnt canes; or (5) stole provisions. In addition, whites were liable to fines for improper policing of slaves, assisting slaves to escape, murdering slaves, or exposing them to seditious doctrines. On the other hand, slaves received limited legal protection, as the Act recognised the need to 'guard them from the cruelties and insolence of themselves, and other ill-tempered people or owners'. Clause 6 provided that 'all slaves . . . shall have clothes once every year, that is to say, drawers and caps for men and petticoats and caps for women'.

Slaves were real estate and therefore could not own property – the basis of social mobility. In addition, the laws emphasised that owners were able to receive compensation within the courts for the destruction of such property. Under the 1688 Slave Code, a master could wilfully kill his slave and be liable only to a £15 fine. If, however, his slave died while being punished, and it could be established that no malice had been intended, then there would be no fine under the law.

Blacks were not allowed to give evidence in court against whites until the early nineteenth century, and whites rarely came to the legal assistance of blacks. If a master wilfully killed the slave of another, he was fined £25 upon conviction. An additional payment of double the slave's value was also to be made in compensation to the owner. It was not until 1805 that the murder of a slave by a white became a capital felony in Barbados. On the other hand slaves could be punished by death for striking or threatening a white person, or stealing property.

These were the essential features of the world which was constructed by slave owners in Barbados during the seventeenth century. The 1661 Barbados Code was later applied, almost clause by clause, to Jamaica in 1664 by its new Governor, Thomas Modyford, an old Barbadian planter. The Antigua Slave Code of 1702 was also modelled on the 1661 Barbados Code. Barbados, therefore, showed the rest of the English Caribbean not only how to manage profitable sugar plantations, but also how to legally control their slaves.

AFRICANS AND REBELLION

Africans resisted their enslavement in Barbados from earliest times. They organised rebellions, made continuous attempts to run away, and engaged in a wide range of limited day-to-day anti-slavery actions. There were aborted rebellions in 1649, 1675 and 1692. The sophistication of the organisation and range of objectives of these plots increased in time, so that the 1692 event was considered by contemporaries to have been the most complex, comprehensive and far-reaching of all. Between these periodic plots the full panorama of resistance can be identified. Taken together, this tradition of persistent slave resistance and planter reactions constituted a most noticeable feature of early Barbadian political culture.

During the 1640s when the black population began to increase rapidly, the fear of slave rebellion was evident everywhere within the white community, even in its architecture. Ligon made some important observations on this issue. He noted how the planters built 'their houses in a manner of fortification', with elevated cisterns to 'throw down hot water upon the naked bodies of their negroes'. This they considered as good a system of defence 'as any other weapon'. Their houses, he stated, looked more like small forts than villas. But this was not all. Planters assembled themselves from time to time in order to plan the various modes of communication necessary to prevent the rapid spread of slave uprisings.

The first recorded incident of an attempted collective slave rebellion was the aborted plot of 1649. It was organised by a small group of slaves at a time when a food crisis had thrown colonists into panic. Ligon noted that provisions were scarce and expensive, and slaves absorbed the harder share of the shortages. It has been suggested that the plot was within the tradition of the 'food riot', and was not intended to be a general political uprising. It was conceived, Ligon noted, by 'some of the high spirited and turbulent' slaves, and was confined to one or probably two plantations. It was not seen by all planters as a threat to the wider social order, but some were convinced that the real cause of the event was a desire by a few slaves to gain their freedom.

The plot was a small-scale affair, but what it revealed was that the slaves had quickly arrived at the stage where they were prepared to make collective military decisions. At this juncture the Assembly began to discuss the idea of integrating all indentured servants into the local militias. A ticket system was established whereby masters were required to give their slaves a signed pass in order to legitimise and control their movements off the plantations. Increased slave policing and the expansion of militia forces, therefore, resulted from the failed insurrection.

The colonels of the militia were given frequent instructions to 'search the houses of slaves from time to time' and to recover any weapons, arms, or instruments of war. These orders were renewed frequently between 1650 and 1660. Colonel John Higginbottom particularly was given special orders on more than one occasion to search and interrogate slaves suspected of armed rebellion. The number of blacks executed at law for insubordination escalated. The result, according to one observer, was that 'the planters of Barbados make no conscience of killing their slaves – dogs and them being in one rank in their opinion'.

The refusal of slaves to organise rebellions during the 1650s and 1660s did not mean that they had lost their desire to be free. Increased planter repression forced a large number of slaves to perceive marronage as a more attractive option. During this period there was a marked increase in the number of reports referring to the activity of runaway slaves hiding out in the woods and gullies about the island. Some of these runaways were mere deserters with intentions of returning to their estates. Others had no intention of returning, and linked their marronage with hostile acts towards the white communities. The rebels were said to be behaving in a 'rebellious and arrogant manner', 'making a mockery of the law, and attempting to draw other slaves into their design'. During the mid-1650s, Governor Searle, after hearing this alarming report, ordered Colonel Higginbottom to pursue 'these runaway negroes and if he [should] meet with any of them to cause them forthwith to be secured . . . but if they refused to peaceably submit themselves, then use his utmost endeavour to supress or destroy them'.

In June 1657, Captain Edward Thompson reported that his militiamen had found 'divers rebellious and runaway negroes lying in woods and other secret places in and about the plantations having of late committed divers murders, robberies, and other fellonies'. Once again, Council expressed its determination to ensure that these runaways were eradicated. This time, Governor Searle ordered the Provost Marshal:

> to make search and find out or discover such negroes as do stand forth in rebellion, committing such crimes and . . . apprehend them, and then convey them to the common gaol that they may be proceeded against according to law.

Marronage, none the less, appeared to have grown in magnitude, and after receiving more petitions, the Council allotted a special day whereupon commissions were granted to 'divers men' for a 'general hunting . . . of the great number of Negroes that are out in rebellion . . .'.

The 1675 aborted revolt

The white population fell from 23,000 in 1665 to 21,309 by 1673, while the black population rose from 20,000 to 33,184 in the same period. In May 1675, a fully fledged plot by slaves to overthrow the planters and seize control of the island was unearthed by the militia. Governor Atkins noted that the aborted revolt interrupted all public affairs. His investigative committee suggested that the organisers of the revolt were almost exclusively Coromantee men, who were described as 'the greater number from any one country, and a warlike and robust people.' Slaves from other ethnic groups were also involved, and it was almost totally an affair of African-born slaves.

The revolt was not spontaneous; its planning, according to the Commissioners, was 'cunningly and clandestinely carried and kept secret even from the knowledge of their own wives'. Women were not identified as involved in the organisation of the revolt. The rebels had been planning the insurrection for about three years, said the Commissioners, and a large number of plantations across the island were involved. It was not limited to any one parish or group of slaves, but was an islandwide conspiracy.

Obtaining freedom by force of arms was the first objective. After they had seized control of the island, the rebels intended to establish an Asante-style monarchy under Cuffee, who was described as an 'Ancient Gold Coast Negro'. Cuffee was to be crowned King of Barbados on 12th June, and enstooled on a 'chair of state' – the symbol of political leadership within Akan culture. It is possible that old Cuffee was the mastermind behind the revolt, and as a respected elder would assume political authority over his fellow rebels. The specific details relating to the leadership and organisation of the revolt are still unavailable. But the random execution of the so-called leaders, with no specific reference to old Cuffee's execution, suggests that the leaders might have hidden well their identities.

The revolt was discovered eight days before the intended date of implementation on Captain Hall's plantation in the north-western parish of St Peter. A domestic slave by the name of Anna (or Fortuna) overheard a young rebel apparently trying to recruit a reluctant slave into the scheme, and informed her master who, with Governor Atkin's commission, organised an inquiry. The Commissioners revealed that the plot was 'far more dangerous than was first thought'. About 110 slaves were arrested by the militia companies for participation in the conspiracy. A court martial was convened by the Governor under the '1661 Act for the governing of slaves', and the trials proceeded. It was disclosed by rebels under torture how the alarm was to be sounded at different parts of the island simultaneously to signal the rising, and that the slaves in the dead of night were to cut the throats of their masters, burn the canes and eliminate all the white males within two weeks.

On preliminary investigations, seventeen slaves were found guilty and executed; six were burnt alive and eleven beheaded – their bodies being dragged through the streets of Speightstown 'and were afterwards burnt with those that were burnt alive'. When one of the conspirators was being urged to confess the full nature of the plot, he refused and stated, 'If you roast me today, you cannot roast me tomorrow', and urged the executioner to proceed. Five of the men arrested (probably the prime leaders) committed suicide before the trial; another thirty-five were executed before the Governor was satisfied that leaders were fully rooted out. On 24th November, Fortuna was freed by order of the Assembly 'in recompense of her eminent service to the good of [the] country in discovering the intended plotted rebellion of the negroes'.

Resistance continued, and in 1686 Governor Stede was informed that the creole slaves were drawing some of the 'Irish nation' into a design to destroy the English interest. The Governor quickly ordered the constables of seven parishes to 'search the negroes' houses within their parishes for arms and ammunition, to secure the arms and such negroes as shall be suspected of an intention to rebel; there being signs of an insurrection of negroes'.

One alleged objective of the plot was to kill all planters and keep their wives and white servants as slaves. A large number of slaves was rounded up within a few hours. The Governor, after making a thorough investigation into this 'combination of Irish servants and Negroes', found no evidence to convict the Irish servants. In 1688, however, the Assembly passed an Act 'for the Good Governing of Negroes', and provisions were made for the complete disarmament of the Irish.

The 1692 aborted rebellion

The slaves did not give the planters much time or opportunity to improve their internal defence system. They began once again to organise a general conspiracy to defeat the whites and take control of the island. The plan was exposed in January 1692, but the political shrewdness of the slaves was demonstrated. The rebels were aware that England, and therefore her colonies in the region, were at war, a condition which weakened the island's defence system. What the militia unearthed was a comprehensive plan of action, designed to defeat the whites at the moment of their greatest vulnerability. The planning of the revolt showed great judgement on the part of the slaves, more so than earlier attempts, and it was 'cunningly managed'. The Assembly's commission of inquiry noted that several slaves were in the leadership, but identified four men – Hammon, Ben, Samson and Sambo – as the most prominent. The ringleaders were described as slaves from the artisan elite. Their privileged positions on the estates were emphasised, and this fact, more than any other, horrified the planters.

Three months prior to the date of implementing the revolt, the rebels had formed themselves into a military force comprising four regiments of foot and two of horse, in the traditional English manner of military organisation. The horses were to be taken from their masters' stables by the elite slaves, mostly rangers, watchmen and artisans, who had access to the facilities. The revolt was intended to be general, bringing the entire island under black control. Though the Assembly's investigation showed the planning to be centred mainly in the St Michael, Christ Church and St James parishes, some of the identified rebel organisers came from plantations in the St Andrew, St Joseph and St John parishes.

The confession of a rebel slave reveals a great deal about the aborted revolt. First, it was initially scheduled to occur in May 1689, shortly after a major expedition had left the colony to defend the Leewards against the

French. The assembled army, however, did not depart as scheduled, and in June a substantial English naval fleet docked at Carlisle Bay. This put an instant halt to the rebels' designs. The revolt was rescheduled for the following year but another fleet arrived in Barbados after an attack upon Guadeloupe. This strengthened local defences and forced the rebels to defer their attack. In late 1691, the rebels agreed that they would strike to coincide with the departure of the fleets to Martinique. During the confusion caused by the changing of dates, however, Ben and Sambo were arrested and, under torture, confessed to being privy to an insurrection.

The strategy of the rebels was to initiate the revolt in the plantation zones, and then move towards Bridgetown where they would capture the forts and assume control over shipping and communications. They had infiltrated the white militia structure by involving in their plans a black armourer who worked in the Bridgetown magazine. This armourer was to supply the rebel forces on their arrival at the fort with 400 barrels of powder, 300 small arms and 160 swords. The next stage of the rebels' plan was to gain access to the weapons stored at Needham fort. The strategy here was to gain the support of six Irishmen.

Slaves within the Bridgetown gaol were to be released to join the rebellion, and all ships in the harbour burnt so as to avoid the early communication of news of the rebellion. All the forts on the island were to be taken with the assistance of the slave artisans who were employed in their construction. Weapons were to be taken and the rebels were to prepare themselves for the defence of the island from outside attacks. Having defeated the militia forces, the next objective was to kill the Governor and militia officer, Colonel Salter, and then declare themselves rulers of Barbados.

The trials of the rebels took place between 10th and 22nd October that year. The report of the court martial was submitted to the Governor on 3rd November. Between 200 and 300 slaves were arrested, but fewer were tried at the court martial. An anonymous account of the conspiracy stated that the rebels aimed to execute the Governor and all the planters, seize control of the island, and 'to set up a new governor and government of their own'. How and where the plot was discovered is not stated within the contemporary data. There is reference only to a slave informant. After Ben and Sambo were arrested, Hammon was captured while apparently urging the two prisoners not to confess. Ben and Sambo were immediately put to death, while Hammon confessed under the promise of a reprieve. His confession, which implicated Samson as a primary leader, did not save his life. He was tried and executed, along with ninety-two other slaves.

CHAPTER FOUR

Slave society and economy, 1688–1807

DEMOGRAPHIC TRENDS

Between the passing of the 1688 slave code, which outlined the legal structure of societal relations, and the ending of the slave trade in 1807, Barbadian society underwent a rapid process of creolisation which had profound implications for the nature of social life. So striking was this development that scholars have argued that the outstanding social features of the island in the eighteenth century were its settled nature and advanced formation of a Barbadian identity. The frontier aspects of the previous century quickly disappeared, and the original forest cover was replaced by fields of sugar cane. Moll's map of 1717 clearly indicates the densely settled nature of the island. By 1800 the island had a density of almost 600 inhabitants per square mile. By contrast, Jamaica's population density in 1713 was 14 persons per square mile, and a hundred years later had reached 75 persons per square mile. Antigua recorded a density of 107 per square mile in 1708, which rose to 236 in 1774.

More demographic data are available for the white than the black community, which makes it easier to be more assertive about this racial group. In 1684, when the white population was counted by parish church wardens, the sex ratio was 55.8 per cent male and 44.2 per cent female. It shifted slowly over the remainder of the seventeenth century, largely under the influence of high levels of poor-white male emigration. When the 1715 census was completed, white women outnumbered white men by about 1 per cent. The female majority continued to rise during the first half of the eighteenth century, reaching a peak of 57.6 per cent in 1748, then levelling off at around 52 per cent for the remainder of the slavery period (see Table 4).

The female majority in the colony's white population had significant effects upon the nature of slave owners' social culture. Not only were white family structures more developed in Barbados than in other colonies, but contemporaries were convinced also that it had some positive repercussions

Table 4. *Barbados population estimates, 1630–1780 (in thousands)*

Year	Whites	Blacks	Total
1700	15.4	50.1	65.5
1710	13.0	52.3	65.3
1720	17.7	58.8	76.5
1730	18.2	65.3	83.5
1740	17.8	72.1	89.9
1750	17.2	78.8	96.0
1760	17.8	86.6	104.4
1770	17.2	92.0	109.2
1780	16.9	82.4	99.3

Source: J. McCusker and R. Menard, *The Economy of British America, 1607–1789*, p. 153

upon many aspects of the slaves' daily lives. During the 1780s, William Dickson believed, for example, that the white female majority tempered the brutish frontier mentality of planters and integrated white men into developed family structures – which, he believed, tended towards the gradual amelioration of the slaves' condition. Certainly, of all the major slave societies, the size and rate of growth of Barbados' mulatto group remained small during the eighteenth century. Also, many free-coloured women might have found that their inability to gain high levels of respectability by becoming the wives, lovers and mistresses of prominent white planters had a great deal to do with the large number of white women in the society.

THE WHITE ELITE

During the eighteenth century, the landed elite considered itself an aristocracy that had mastered the art of government and economic management. Interlocked to a large degree by marriage (among prominent creole families), it considered its exclusive elitism a hallmark of its right to rule. Families believed that their ability to trace ancestry to the frontier years of the 1630s and 1640s was in itself a criterion of pedigree, and as such they developed a suspicious and discriminatory attitude towards newcomers. As an elite, which continuously received recruits from below, its members' expressions of self-identity contained many elements of contradiction. They were proud of their English ancestry and held firmly to what they understood to be English values and systems of public protocol, and yet many of them were loud advocates of their Barbadian origins. They looked forward to their trips to England and basked in the cultural experiences it offered, yet they were increasingly being received as distant cousins who had been amputated from the trunk of civilisation. They dressed in the finest English clothes that were wholly unsuited to the tropics and yet were angered easily by metropolitan claims that they were mimics of a culture they had lost.

As an elite, their socio-political power was based upon the ownership of successful estates. Control of these planting enterprises allowed them to dictate the pattern of economic activity on the island, and to ensure that their social authority was stamped upon all civic institutions. In 1721 they stripped all non-whites of the right to vote or give evidence in courts against whites. The concept of white racial supremacy was therefore their guiding instrument. In the process they aspired to live as English country gentlemen in spite of the fact that many of them were as alien to the details of English culture as their slaves. Although by the end of the eighteenth century they were confident in the quality of their Barbadian life, they continued to use English symbols and values as standard references. As a result, their intellectual and cultural subordination to England remained complete into the nineteenth century.

As a ruling class, sugar planters were confident in the security of their material culture, and used their economic power to exercise a distinct conservative socio-political dominance over the society. They developed no specific socio-political ideology other than racism, and unlike their mainland cousins, few of them could seriously contemplate an end to their colonial status. Yet, in spite of their preference for British rule, and recognition that successful absenteeism was the noblest of ends, many advocated a commitment to the island which transcended mere material interest.

The leading families in the eighteenth century are identifiable by the following names:

Adams	Ford	Jordan	Salter
Alleyne	Frere	Lyte	Skeete
Applewhaite	Gibbes	Maycock	Terrill
Beckles	Gibbons	Maynard	Thornhill
Best	Gittens	Osborne	Walker
Bishop	Haynes	Peers	Walrond
Brathwaite	Hinds	Pinder	Walters
Carrington	Holder	Powell	Waterman
Cumberbatch	Hothersall	Rous	Weeks
Dottin	Husbands	Salmon	Yeamans

Members of these families dominated the Assembly, and were appointed to the Council; they also filled posts in most civic institutions. The Alleyne family, for example, produced a number of prominent politicians during the eighteenth and nineteenth centuries. As prominent slave-holders they subscribed to the ideas and values of the system, and none of them emerged as anti-slavery activists. Many were lawyers and clergymen by profession, and none were distinguished as writers, scholars or philosophers. Their pursuit of an English education meant that no worthy facilities for learning, apart from the Codrington Theological College, existed in the colony. As such, the social elite was noted for its wealth, political power and attachment to conservative English values, but not for matters of a creative or intellectual nature.

Traditionally, it has been argued that the planter's ultimate objective was to establish in the colony an income-earning property which would enable him to achieve social and political standing in the mother country. On becoming an absentee owner in England, he would entrust his estate to the care of managers and attorneys, who also possessed similar aspirations. This perception of the planter class, however, has been receiving much criticism in recent years. The evidence unearthed by Ronnie Hughes, for example, suggests that the degree of absenteeism was not on the same scale as it was in, say, Jamaica, though many of those estates which remained in the hands of the same family over the eighteenth century tended to be absentee owned.[1] Byde Mill plantation, for instance, was owned by absentees from c.1660 to 1846 and passed by inheritance throughout that period. Also, Drax Hall estate, which was consolidated by Sir James Drax during the 1640s and remained within the family into the twentieth century, was continuously absentee owned from c.1720 to 1846.

It has not been disputed that many of the prominent planter families were absentee owners for periods during the seventeenth and eighteenth centuries. William Hilliard, Sir Peter Colleton, Fernando Gorges, John Peers, Edward Thornburgh, Sir Paul Paynter, Henry Drax, Sir John Bawden and James Kendall, sugar magnates of the seventeenth century, for example, were absentees. In England they formed the 'Committee of Gentlemen Planters' which functioned as a major political lobby to further the colony's economic interests.

But these prominent men were a minority within the planter class, and during the eighteenth century there was no wholesale absenteeism. In the early years of the nineteenth century, absenteeism did increase significantly, but this trend was the result of many estates falling into the hands of English merchant companies, in themselves a form of absentee ownership.

Though some of these merchant companies were Barbadian in origins, the majority were located in English towns such as Bath, Bristol, Liverpool and London. Prior to 1820, Lascelles and Maxwell, and later Lascelles and Daling, English companies, were substantial owners of Barbadian estates, and held mortgages on many. Other English merchant companies that owned Barbadian estates prior to 1807 were Bond and Ryland, Barrow and Barrow, Irlam and Higginson, Thomas Daniel and Sir William Baker.

The extent to which sections of the planter elite had developed a patriotic consciousness was tested most vigorously during the period of the American Revolution which adversely affected the plantation economy and strained relations between imperial authority and the Assembly. A significant part of the planter elite was sympathetic to the American revolutionary cause and was among the first to establish a fund for the sufferers of Boston. Though this faction failed in July 1774 to persuade the Assembly to adopt an anti-English position, it was clear none the less that leading colonists saw English attitudes to the Americans, and the colonial question in general, as threatening to their political autonomy. As a result, the Assembly took measures during this period to demand even greater control over the executive power of the imperial Governor. It was Sir John Gay Alleyne, a popular leader of the planter elite, and Speaker of the Assembly during the period of the American War, who was most responsible for articulating the principles of Barbadian political autonomy, and made a significant contribution to the theory and practice of political representation within the Barbadian context. He was described as the chief opponent of the 'King's interests', who endeavoured to place Barbadian rights at the centre of the political arena by robbing the Crown of executive power.[2]

While sections of the planter elite publicly criticised imperial power, and asserted their right to full and free control over the expenditure of public money, and in the field of taxation, others expressed an unswerving loyalty to the Crown and English interest. So while the radical sect, led by Sir John Gay Alleyne, attempted to persuade the Assembly to adopt a non-cooperation stance in relation to Britain and its colonial policy on the United States, there was also a powerful group of loyalists who saw themselves as Englishmen overseas rather than Barbadians. None the less, during this time the planter elite was frequently accused by administrators in the London colonial office of harbouring a republican ideology, and seeking to place all executive power under the control of the Assemblies and reducing imperial governors to nominal heads. By the end of the war, the Assembly had removed executive power over expenditure of public revenue. Though in theory the Governor's right to issue all public monies was still upheld, in practice this was not the case. The outcome of the American War, then, was that the planter class succeeded in strengthening its constitutional power within the colony at the expense of the Crown by taking a firm position on the question of colonial rights.

The tendency for political and legal structures within the colony to be dominated by wealthy planters, therefore, continued into the late eighteenth century. Merchants who resided in Bridgetown and sat on the Assembly or Council, or held high posts in the judiciary or militia, were also substantial plantation owners. Merchants such as Dudley Woodbridge, Othneil Haggatt, Thomas Harrison, Hamlet Fairchild and Samson Wood, were also substantial plantation owners who sat on the Council and Assembly.

Even the prominent lawyers were substantial plantation owners. Such men as Henry Beckles and John Beckles, both Attorney-Generals, were prominent landowners. Anglican clergymen were also an important element within the plantocracy. The Reverends Carter, Brathwaite, Duke, Gittens, Brome, Maycock, Holder, Pilgrim, Terrill, Pinder and Gibbes, contributed to the formation of family fortunes from sugar and slavery. The Hon. Rev. John Brathwaite, councillor, owned several estates, among them Three Houses, Palmers, Oldbury, and Rock Hall. In short, most men of respectable professions were either within the plantocracy, on its fringes, or aspired to join it.

Located beneath the planter elite in the social structure were hundreds of smaller farming families who traditionally have been described as the yeomanry. Owning up to 40 hectares (100 acres) of land, many of these families were not substantial slave owners; nor were all of them engaged in sugar cultivation. In the southern and northern ends of the colony, where these families tended to congregate, lands were not well suited to sugar. In these areas during the eighteenth century, many planters were cotton producers. Families such as the Rocks, Agards, Boyces, Coziers, Thornes, Connells and Griffiths were well known as 'cotton' growers. Those who were engaged in sugar were rarely able to own their own mills, and tended to make arrangements with their wealthier neighbours to have their cane milled.

POOR-WHITES

By the end of the eighteenth century the social structure of white society was fully formed, and one of its distinguishing features was a heterogeneous class of wage labourers, peasants and unemployed 'vagrants'. The origins of this group lie in the formative stage of colonisation when white indentured servitude was displaced by black slavery. Most ex-indentured servants during the seventeenth century did not succeed in acquiring quality land; as such the labour system of white servitude served the primary purpose of creating a wage proletariat rather than reproducing the planting community.

In general, these labourers were unable to find steady, well-paid employment; many resorted to the socially degrading poor-relief facilities, and some attempted the isolating backcountry, earth-scratching sub-sistence farming. The more fortunate earned a living by serving as plantation militia tenants, an occupation which entailed the constant policing of plantation slaves, retrieving runaways and suppressing rebels. In most cases, militia tenants were allocated 'little odd skirts of land' on the plantations under a form of military tenure. Living in close proximity with plantation slaves, the wives of these tenants, invariably also from poor-white stock, came under the influence of the vibrant huckstering and proto-peasant culture of the slaves. They were often seen on the way to market walking many miles, loaded with the produce of their spots, 'which they exchanged in the towns for such European goods as they could afford to purchase'. Both male and female, Dickson noted during the 1780s, were engaged in marketing, and made 'a practice of buying stolen goods from the negroes, whom they encourage to plunder their owners of everything that is portable'.

By the beginning of the nineteenth century, most rural poor-whites, with the exception of plantation militia tenants, inhabited small villages located in the remote, less favourable 'rab' lands of the St Andrew, St Lucy, St John, St Joseph and St Philip parishes – areas that the planter class had rejected as unsuited to sugar cultivation. These communities were quite distinct, and visitors to the island finding them rather slave-like in appearance, frequently commented upon their squalor and insanitation. One such visitor was Dr George Pinckard. He toured the West Indies with the military expedition of General Abercromby during the 1790s, and in his published notes on Barbados are accounts of poor-white settlements. He described their material condition as follows:

Besides the great number of hospitable mansions found on the plantations, in the different parts of the country, many humble dwellings attract the notice of the traveller . . . They are the cottages of a poorer order of white people – of obscure individuals, remote from the great class of merchants and planters, and who obtain a scanty livelihood by cultivating a small patch of earth, and breeding-up poultry, or what they term stock for the markets. They are descended from European settlers, but from misfortune, or misconduct, in some of the race, are reduced to a state far removed from independence.[3]

In some instances, Pinckard stated, their condition was 'little superior' to that of free negroes in the countryside, and was beneath that of the established urban free coloureds and free blacks. He described their houses as 'small huts or cabins' in which large families live, located 'amidst the mountains, apparently shut from the world, and but seldom exposed to the intrusion of strangers'. One household he visited in the backlands of Mount Hillaby was six generations removed from an English settler. This family 'were poor, like the others, and compelled to labour much in full exposure to the sun'. In all, Pinckard visited three such households, of which members were fifth- to sixth-generation settlers. 'Only the abode of poverty', he stated, '[they know, and] have been compelled to use a diet very similar to that of the Africans'. Yet they remained fiercely attached to the colony, rather than to the mother country, and would commonly confirm this by stating that they are 'neither Charib nor Creole, but true Barbadian'.

In 1788 colonial officials asked Barbadian planters whether the poor-whites could take up the labour deficit on the sugar estates occasioned by the possible abolition of the slave trade, and the answer they received was affirmative. Planters knew that in the formative years of sugar cultivation, 1644–50, white servants working in field gangs were the backbone of the industry. Indeed, on some sugar estates, gangs of poor-whites were still to be found in the cane fields during the second half of the eighteenth century. This fact posed no ideological problem for planters or their managers, who had long accepted that 'sugar and white labour' carried no fundamental contradiction – in spite of black slavery.

Planters believed that poor-white labourers were social failures and degenerates who deserved no paternal sympathy or special consideration. Though, in their dominant political ideology, the principle of 'race first' was clearly articulated, it was not dogmatically applied at the lower levels of society, unless the integrity of the entire structure was endangered. That is, planter elitism was not offended, but confirmed, by the existence of a white working-class culture of poverty on the periphery of the plantations.

During the 1780s, however, Joshua Steele, a prominent planter and member of the London Royal Society of Arts, took measures to rehabilitate unskilled poor-whites, whom he considered a major social problem. A labour survey conducted in the 1780s revealed that the 'mechanical trades and occupations' were 'almost extinct' among this group, and dominated by blacks, both slave and free. To reverse this de-skilling process, Steele was instrumental in the establishment of the Society for the Encouragement of Arts, Manufactures and Commerce in 1781. This organisation, dedicated to the provision of industrial employment for white labourers, functioned against the background of rapidly rising vestry poor-rates for the relief of whites. The previous year, for example, the returns for the parish of St Peter showed a total of 94 white persons, from a total of some 1,340, in receipt of poor-relief – a parish with a relatively small poor-white population.

In his campaign to assist poor-whites, Steele made references to the comparative material living standard of free coloureds, free blacks and elite slaves. These whites, his findings indicate, represented the lowest levels of material life within the free community. Generations of unemployment, he stated, had removed from their consciousness the desire to labour, and as such they had to be persuaded by the offer of respectable and regular work; in this way they could be reminded that the possession of 'shoes, stockings or any more clothing than a ragged shirt or shift, with an Osnaburg breeches or petticoat', are worth labouring for. Their habit of begging 'from house to house for victuals' and finding 'some hovel to lie under a night' could be broken, he added, but respectable conditions and terms of employment had to be provided.

Steele proposed that manufacturing industries, using local materials, be established so as to create artisan employment. Cotton goods, for example, could be locally manufactured using the homegrown cotton which many small planters produced. Rather than importing cheap cotton items for slaves and poor-whites alike, an indigenous industry could meet market demands. Such a proposal, however, ran counter to the long-established dictates of mercantilism which insisted upon a division of production, assigning to colonies the role of raw material exporter, and that of manufacturer to the mother country. That not even a nail was to be made in the colonies was already a well-known dictum of English New World colonisation, which in the previous decade had encouraged the mainland colonists into revolutionary opposition. Some success was attained in providing work in the partially revived pottery industry and in fort construction, but the sum result of this initiative was disappointing.

The Society also pressed for legislative action in a bid to expand the employment range for white labourers. A bill was brought before the House in 1783 which aimed to encourage planters and merchants to employ the 'profligate' whites who lived by 'vagrant beggary' and other forms of 'indolence'. The bill was passed, but it had little positive effect upon either unemployment level or poor-law rates. Legislative efforts were repeated during the 1790s, but to no avail, and in the early 1800s a colonial official visiting the island noted that in 'no other colony is the same number of unemployed whites' to be met as in Barbados.

Dickson, though a close friend of Steele, did not share his enthusiasm for the upliftment of poor-whites. His *Letters on Slavery* published in 1789, and a larger book, *Mitigation of Slavery*, which appendixed letters by Steele, published in 1814, elevated him as the leading literary authority on eighteenth-century slavery in Barbados. He dealt at length with the problem of white unemployment, but did not perceive it as constituting an ideological crisis for white society. For him, any policy which attempted to elevate white labourers by means of systematic discriminatory action against hardworking and thrifty free blacks and free coloureds was neither morally correct nor in the interest of the colony. Instead, he argued that societal advancement depended upon the upliftment, emancipation and integration of blacks. Poor-whites, he implied, had had their opportunity and wasted it, while non-whites should be encouraged in their energetic pursuit of betterment. He described them as lazy, vicious and irresponsible:

The extreme ignorance of many of the poor white Barbadians, cannot justly be attributed to the want of opportunities and instructions, for there are schools in every parish, which I believe, were constructed for their betterment. Nor are the clergy blamable for that ignorance. The free Blacks and Coloureds attend the schools and regularly attend divine service. The poor whites very seldom enter a church, except to observe elections and attend funerals, and are then, generally, in a state of intoxication.[4]

The outstanding defender of poor-whites, after the failed efforts of Joshua Steele (who died in 1796) was John Poyer, a white creole historian, and intellectual pro-slavery idealogue. Elsa Goveia, in her classic review of British West Indian colonial historiography, stated in relation to Poyer's 1808 *The History of Barbados*: 'There is one point to which he returns again and again – the need for encouraging the poorer whites. . . .' She suggested that for Poyer the elevation of poor-whites was a critical aspect of the general defence of slavery. The slave system, Poyer wrote, rested upon the 'natural' principle of white racial superiority, and hence the existence of blacks above whites within any of its structures represented a fundamental ideological contradiction which, if not resolved, could erode the very conceptual apparatuses which held it together.

THE SLAVE COMMUNITY

Population structure

Two distinguishing features of the black population during the eighteenth century were its female majority and its advancing rate of creolisation. No other English Caribbean sugar colony developed a similar sex ratio for this period. The first official reference to the sex structure of the slave population was provided by Governor Sir Jonathan Atkins in 1673. It shows that slave women had already outnumbered slave men. This population report stated that the colony was inhabited by 33,184 black slaves. Of these, 30.8 per cent were men, 35.9 per cent women and 33.3 per cent children; altogether, 48.4 per cent male and 51.6 per cent female. The female majority was not sustained for long, as the 1676 population report showed that of the 32,468 slaves, 16,121 were female and 16,346 were male; that is, 49.6 per cent and 50.4 per cent respectively. It is not possible to establish the rate at which the sex ratio grew, nor at what precise stage females acquired a sustained majority, but by the early eighteenth century the gender balance had settled down to a ratio of about 48 per cent male and 52 per cent female.

Barbadian planters attempted to balance males and females in their slave purchases, and succeeded in reversing on their estates the overwhelming male bias established within the Atlantic slave trade. On the plantations by 1740 more women worked as field-hands than men. There were fewer skilled women than men, though many female artisans, such as seamstresses, could be found on most estates. Potential for the technological training of male slaves inflated their prices in the same manner that females' fertility constituted an important element in their price levels. Planters expected that female field-hands would at some time produce at least two healthy children, the value of which would partly compensate for the differential which existed with male prices.

Slave women performed the same field labour as men. They worked together in the same gangs from sun-up till sun-down. Though women were less strong physically than men, slave owners believed that field cultivation required more stamina than strength, and in this regard, recognised that women were already accustomed to agricultural tasks. These factors, then, meant that planters were encouraged to reject a sexual division of labour among field cultivators based upon production or productivity differentials.

From the mid-eighteenth century, not only was the Barbados slave population predominantly female (Table 5), but it was also overwhelmingly creole (as opposed to African born). Between 1750 and 1834, it had a larger percentage of creole blacks in the population than any other sugar colony in the West Indies. It was common for contemporary commentators on slavery to argue that creoles possessed a more amenable psychological profile than the African born, and that this affected the nature of their daily experiences. Dickson believed, furthermore, that this stereotype affected in important ways the overall nature of master-slave relations. Creole slaves, he added, were likely to be treated better materially and socially than Africans. Life options, limited though they were for all slaves, seemed greater for creoles than Africans as a result of the pervasive anti-African attitudes held by Europeans, and free-coloured slave owners.

The impact of rapid black creolisation during the eighteenth century upon the slave community was profound. It meant that African culture in Barbados came under greater internal pressure as a result of the diminishing percentage of African recruits. That creole slaves would respond to planter stimuli in rejecting things African cannot be dismissed as unlikely. The social culture of Africans was degraded by the white community, and blacks were penalised for adhering too closely to it. Blacks responded in two basic ways to this intense social pressure. First, by taking underground those elements of culture which could survive without public display. These include aspects of religion and philosophic world views. Obeah, for example, survived underground in spite of legislation which outlawed its practice as a social ritual or religious construct. Second, by openly assimilating European-derived elements of the creole culture so as to achieve social and material betterment.

Table 5. *Sex structure of the slave population in Barbados, 1801–32*

Year	Male		Female	
	No.	%	No.	%
1801	29,872	46.5	34,324	53.5
1817	35,354	45.6	42,139	54.4
1823	36,159	45.9	42,657	54.1
1829	37,691	46.0	44,211	54.0
1832	37,762	46.3	43,738	53.7

Source: J. Handler, *The Unappropriated People*, p. 24

Barbados mulatto girl of the eighteenth century. From a print by Agostino Brunias.

In spite of these anti-African pressures, creole blacks were able to enhance and defend many aspects of their ancestral heritage. The creative arts, mortuary practices, language and social philosophy of the post-slavery period illustrate that even where the traditional African forms were not present, the spirit, feel and content of cultural life survived, though diluted and metamorphosed. Dr George Pinckard gave an example of the prejudiced attitude held by Europeans at the end of the eighteenth century towards Afro-Barbadian and African social culture:

They assemble, in crowds, upon the open green, or in any square or corner of the town, and, forming a ring in the centre of the throng, dance to the sound of their favourite African yell. Both music and dance are of a savage nature, . . . their songs which are very simple, [are] harsh and wholly deficient in softness and melody . . . While one negro strikes the Banjar, another shakes the rattle with great force of arm, and a third sitting across the body of the drum, as it lies lengthwise upon the ground, beats and kicks the sheepskin at the end, in violent exertion with his hands and heels, and a fourth sitting upon the ground at the other end, behind the man upon the drum, beats upon the wooden sides of it with two sticks. Together with the noisy sounds, numbers of the party of both sexes bawl forth their dear delighting sound with all possible force of lungs, . . . a spectator would require only a slight aid from fancy to transport him to the savage wilds of Africa.[5]

Frederick Bayley, who visited Barbados during the 1820s, stated how the blacks, to the annoyance of whites, would 'sit up during the greater part of the moonlight nights, chattering together, and telling "nancy stories"'. He added, furthermore: 'A nancy story is nothing more or less than a tale of ghosts and goblins, which pass with the negroes by the appellation of Jumbees." He then commented on the slaves' 'grand day of jubilee, which they call "crop over"'. During the late eighteenth century, he added, 'it was common [on crop over] to see the different African tribes forming each a distinct party, singing and dancing to the gumbay, after the rude manner of their native Africa'. He added that the festival had now been made less African, with the fiddle and tambourine being used instead of drums, while 'black and white, overseer and book-keeper mingle together in dance'.[6]

African culture, then, in becoming Afro-Barbadian, absorbed elements of Euro-creole ideas and practices. This was undoubtedly a rational response to the circumstances of power inequality. But by virtue of its majority representation, black culture emerged as the dominant popular form and survived as the national norm into the modern era.

During the early nineteenth century, especially after the abolition of the

Table 6. *Distribution of African-born slaves in Barbados, 1817*

Parish	Numbers	% parish slave population
St Michael	2,252	12.30
Christ Church	680	6.85
St Philip	724	7.64
St John	212	3.87
St Joseph	160	4.64
St George	384	5.67
St James	148	3.86
St Thomas	199	3.84
St Andrew	138	4.06
St Peter	329	5.36
St Lucy	270	4.93
Total	5,496	Island % 7.10

Source: CO 28/86, Public Records Office

slave trade in 1807, the percentage of African-born blacks in the colony's population declined steadily. According to the 1817 census, there were only 5,496 African-born blacks in Barbados, a mere 7.1 per cent of the total slave population (Table 6). In 1832, the year before the Emancipation Bill passed through Parliament, this figure had dwindled to a mere 2.9 per cent. This constituted a total of some 2,364 Africans, about 1,229 of whom (51.9 per cent) were females. As a percentage, this was the lowest African demographic component for any English Caribbean colony. The African percentage was highest in the new frontier colony of Demerara/Essequibo, and next to Barbados at the other extreme were St Kitts and Nevis – the other two matured plantation economies.

Slave control and resistance

During the eighteenth century, the insurrectionist practices of slaves gave way to patterns of behaviour characterised primarily by limited protest and the seeking of socio-economic concessions from masters – both within the labour regime and in socio-cultural life. No armed rebellions or aborted rebellions were recorded in Barbados between 1702 and 1815. Yet the eighteenth century was the period when slaves in the other islands seem to have intensified their militant struggle for freedom. This development had much to do with the fact that Barbadian planters moved into the eighteenth century with perhaps the most developed internal military system in the

English West Indies. With large militia regiments, plantation militia tenants, and frequent visits from imperial armies and naval fleets, the white community was able to establish and maintain a powerful islandwide system for the day-to-day control of slaves.

The apparent success of the planters' defence system, as evident from the refusal of slaves to confront collectively their masters with arms, allowed the white community to become overtly complacent about the security and legitimacy of its rule. The most immediate result of this confidence in their collective military strength was that individual planters were able to relax and liberalise their plantation control systems, so that, in general, planter–slave relations became increasingly less marked by acute levels of tension and fear.

The system of slave control was further supported by topographical and geographical features. The vast network of roads which were built to facilitate the movement of goods to and from the sugar plantations also allowed the militia to function with comparative efficiency. According to Karl Watson, the ability of regiments to traverse this flat and open country with relative ease had obvious negative implications for overt slave uprisings. In addition, the dozens of forts and magazines which were strung out along the coast served not only to protect the planters from French invasion, but also acted as sentinels against their enemy within.

The image that emerges of the colony in the eighteenth century, therefore, is one of effective slave control. In 1789, Governor Parry informed the Colonial Office that the 'militia is very strong', and *The Barbados Mercury* (a local newspaper) of 24th November 1787, quoted Sir John Gay Alleyne, Speaker of the House of Assembly, as saying that the 'militia, the natural strength of this island, is fully equal to her internal defence if properly brought into the field, and led to action'. Also, in 1802, Governor Seaforth informed the Colonial Office that the militia was in a 'very respectable state', perfectly adequate for 'the safety and tranquility of the colony'.

Dickson was particularly fascinated by the refusal of slaves to organise violent rebellions during the eighteenth century. He suggested that in the period after the 1770s, whites on the island no longer had an acute fear of blacks: 'I must do the Barbadians the justice to say that their general behaviour shows but little of that corporal dread of the blacks which seems to pervade some of the islands.' He rejected, however, the planters' view that this must be explained in terms of the good treatment of the slaves by their masters. For him, the explanation rested within the dynamics of the highly creolised nature of the society – its demographic, topographical, economic and military structures. He offered the following reasons for the absence of slave revolts:

1 The colony is the oldest sugar producer in the region, and the majority of the slaves are creole; these slaves are less aggressive in their responses to enslavement than African-born slaves.
2 These slaves are more exposed to the Christian religion than in the other islands, which has a pacifying effect upon them.
3 There is a large white female population which, unlike elsewhere, tempers white male aggression and produces a more civil social outlook.
4 The colony's topography and geography are less conducive to 'marronage' than other West Indian islands.
5 Planters grant more socio-economic concessions to their slaves than their counterparts in other islands; hence slaves appeared to have more 'liberties'.
6 Because of the size and organisation of the white community, the day-to-day discipline and control of slaves is more effective.
7 There is far less absentee landlordship than elsewhere, and the social culture and outlook of the white elite are more conducive to social stability.

For these reasons, Dickson added, it was logical that blacks would reject the approach to freedom which called for violent struggle and opt instead for socio-economic betterment within the system by means of non-violent protest – not losing sight of the opportunity for full legal freedom. The pursuit of upward social mobility and ultimate freedom by manumission, therefore, became the dominant response to the slavery system. This response to slave relations assisted the development of a highly stratified social order within the slave communities which might have assisted planters in strengthening their social dominance. By the 1750s, a relatively privileged elite of slaves, free blacks and free coloureds, was clearly identifiable in Barbados.

Planters soon realised that by granting slaves concessions such as access to stable sexual partners, a home, a plot of land, easy travel and some control over their children, most would behave in a manner conducive to social stability and high levels of productivity. Edward Brathwaite has noted, for example, that creole slaves, like most people wholly involved in settled agricultural routines, tended to be conservative, with a dislike for change and an attachment to places or persons with whom they had identified themselves. For the docile, there was the whip; for the venal, there were bribes and gifts or the offer of a better position.

Furthering the capacity of whites to control slaves was the tendency of the latter to identify strongly with the particular estates on which their parents and grandparents were born and buried. This enhanced among them a sense of lineage, of belonging to an ancestral world which was important and difficult to shatter or reject by violent resistance. There were those creole slaves who loved their island, and resisted white attitudes which attempted to render them rootless and transient. Nothing disturbed them more, according to Dickson, than to be told that they were to be transported to another island. In such situations, he noted, it was common for them to respond: '. . . here we are born, and here are the graves of our fathers. Can we say to their bones, arise and go with us into a foreign land?' When news of a victory over the French arrived, for example, 'the negroes . . . were almost frantic with joy'. Dickson continued: 'The very slaves in Barbados are inspired with something called loyalty. The same kind of contempt of the French, which actuates the bosom of our soldiers . . . has taken possession of those of the negroes.' It is possible that this development in consciousness contributed to creole slaves not taking full political advantage of crises facing white society. During the French War of the 1790s, when militias were greatly weakened and the Imperial troops were off fighting, slaves did not rebel. Neither did they take advantage of dislocations caused by natural disasters which exposed slave-owners' defence. As evidence of this, Dickson intimated that during the great hurricane in 1780, which put the 'whites entirely in the power of the blacks the negroes remained peaceably with their owners; and shewed no signs of a spirit of mutiny'.

Given these social, political and military developments, the most persistent attack by slaves upon planter authority was the act of running away. The colony's physical landscape did not permit marronage on a grand scale, and running away consisted largely of individual responses to situations of impending threat or great tension, which provided at best a few months' respite from the rigours of the system – though some slaves managed to stay at large for a number of years.

In 1728, for example, the manager of Codrington plantations indicated that 'runaways were frequent' and that great expense was incurred in their retrieval. In 1726, Thomas Wilkie wrote to the Bishop of London informing him that it was still possible for Barbadian 'negroes . . . to run away from their masters into the woods for months together before they can be found out'. But as the remaining wooded areas of the island were converted into sugar-cane fields, only three marronage possibilities existed for slaves. They could seek temporary shelter on another plantation;

'disappear' in the crowds in Bridgetown; or flee to one of the neighbouring colonies. Advertisements for runaways placed in local newspapers show that all these forms of marronage were persistent features of slave resistance.

On the plantations there was also considerable resistance in the area of working conditions. Slaves used their collective force in the production system in order to establish agreeable working conditions within the confines of their enslavement. Invariably, this meant dogged opposition to overseers who sought to reverse earlier concessions which were seen by the slaves as rights. When overseers proved too efficient, intelligent and strict, slaves resorted to collective tactics by thwarting their plans and deliberately misunderstanding their orders. In some cases they demanded the removal of plantation personnel. For example, in June 1738, a large gang of slaves on the Codrington plantation put down their tools, marched off the plantation without the overseer's permission, and journeyed some fifteen miles into Bridgetown to make a collective complaint to the plantation attorney concerning the overseer's management of the estate. The nature of their protest was clear. They demanded that the book-keeper on the estate be replaced; that they be given more leisure time, more and better food and clothing; and that the estate should in future have 'no more than one white and one black overseer'. They were not persuaded to return to work until their case was heard in full, and when it was, they returned with much excitement 'as if they had gained a conquest'. Not all of their demands were met, and the two spokesmen for the gang were publicly flogged. Sometimes they won and other times they did not, but this early form of collective bargaining was part of their strategy for betterment.

In addition to pressing for labour reforms, slaves also sought considerable socio-cultural autonomy. In the early eighteenth century, for example, some masters gave plantation slaves much latitude in the ceremonial burial of their dead. Slaves considered this a right to be defended, and commonly used it as an instrument of mass protest against both individual planters and government authority. In cases where blacks were either murdered by whites or executed at law, the legal system did not permit any form of slave protest. Slaves, however, registered their disapproval by mass attendance at these funerals. Such burials were greatly ritualised with much honour paid to the deceased, which whites correctly perceived as a deliberate affront to their authority.

Resistance also took place in the economic area of the social order. Blacks had brought with them from West Africa a strong inclination for marketing, and sought to establish their own commercial patterns. They planted ground provisions and raised poultry which they sold to each other and also to some whites. Sunday was their trading day, and by the mid-eighteenth century the Sunday markets were popular economic institutions.

Initially, slaves were encouraged to produce foodstuffs in their house gardens, an activity which planters saw as contributing to the estates' self-sufficiency in foodstuffs. From the 1690s, however, discussions were being held in the Assembly concerning the need to control or eradicate 'Black Merchants'. Laws were passed in 1708 and 1733 which aimed to prevent whites employing their slaves or other blacks in selling or bartering. These laws indicate that the commercial activities of the slaves were causing considerable concern to the administrators of the island. The 1733 Act, in particular, emphasised the competition to white small farmers posed by slave hucksters.

In spite of these legal sanctions, slaves continued to play an important role in the marketing system. Indeed, the volume of trading increased, both in Bridgetown and on the country roads. In 1779 another Act was passed 'to prohibit Goods, Wares and Merchandizes and other things from being carried from House to House or about the roads or streets in this island, to be sold bartered or disposed of . . . from the Traffic of Huckster slaves, Free Mulattoes and Negroes'. In this Act, however, the Assembly recognised its inability to eradicate the commercial activities of slaves, who resisted in spite of the constables' frequent raids upon their houses in search of goods, and opted instead for control of these activities. A clause was inserted in this Act which allowed 'Country Negroes' to sell firewood and horsemeat 'and such stock and other things as usually are and may be legally sold to them, and purchasing or taking in return salt provisions and necessaries not purchased in the open streets or in crowds, but in houses or shops in an orderly manner'.

Again, slaves ignored the legislation, and the number of hucksters who sold their goods in the streets of Bridgetown increased. A minor victory for the slaves came in 1794 with the repeal of the 1779 Act which had been found 'rather injurious to the . . . inhabitants of the several towns, as well as to persons residing in the country'. The slave hucksters were still not content and continued to resist rigorously their confinement to a market established for their specific use. In June 1811 the Assembly heard how 'Roebuck [a central Bridgetown street] was as much crowded as ever by country negroes selling their goods there . . . to the great nuisance of . . . all persons who had occasion to pass through that street'.

After much discussion the Assembly decided that stocks would be fixed in the market where the clerk might confine disorderly negroes and flog them for misbehaviour. The intensity of conflict between slave hucksters and constables in the market place did not diminish, and the Court of Grand Sessions in 1811 was informed that the market had become 'a public flogging place to the great disgust and annoyance of all who go there to buy and sell'. Eventually, the slaves' economic culture survived these legislative assaults by the political elite, and by 1830 it had become a most visible feature of Bridgetown.

The black family and its survival

In 1723, a slave from the Codrington estate named Jupiter, in an attempt to gain his freedom, took flight from the estate, and the island. He was accompanied by another slave named Churo, both of whom were reportedly seen somewhere in the Leeward Islands. The following year, however, Jupiter returned to Barbados and handed himself over to the estate manager, in spite of the severe punishments which awaited him. The manager, in assessing the nature of this unusual case, thought it necessary to state that Jupiter was 'much rejoiced at the opportunity of getting back to his wife and children'.

Jupiter's decision to abandon his precarious freedom for the comparatively greater pleasures of kinship suggests a perspective on family relations among slaves which differs radically from that commonly advocated by contemporary commentators. There is an abundance of evidence to illustrate that Jupiter's behaviour was not phenomenal. These data show the development of black family structures and kinship relations, and how they adjusted over time to the changing nature of plantation conditions.

John Pinder, a local clergyman, commented in detail upon the marital patterns of slaves during the early nineteenth century. He believed that slaves were willing to accept Christian marriage, but their owners refused to recognise such relations as legitimate and sacred. In 1819, Pinder stated: 'There is no such thing, as far as I can find, as promiscuous concubinage among them . . .; the slaves marry by agreement; sometimes alas! the men have two and even three wives.' No woman, however, was allowed to have more than one husband. For most Africans, polygamous family structures were part of their cultural tradition, and men and women had no reason to believe that this norm should not continue. Ligon noted that during the early seventeenth century slaves formed unions in which partners referred to each other as wife and husband. These 'families', however, were not given any legal identity by white society.

It was common for both African-born and creole slaves from different estates to enter marital unions and live separately. Though planters hoped that families would be confined to single estates, inevitably some slaves sought partners on the outside. Men generally kept one resident wife, while others were located throughout the colony. Given the polygamous nature of these family structures, and the existence of laws to control slave movements, planters believed that they were in a position to manipulate the slaves' domestic lives. Certainly, black children at birth took the legal status of their mothers, and slave children were the exclusive property of their mothers' owner.

The spatially disintegrated nature of many slave families did not preclude their ability to offer protection and care for members, even when such behaviour was outlawed. Families protected and harboured their runaway kin in defiance of the law. For example, the following advertisement appeared in the *Barbados Globe* in 1829 for a runaway slave:

Reward of $5 for Amelia:
Suppose to be harboured by her father or his connections. This man has a sister or some family connections near Canewood-Moore estate, and no doubt his daughter meets with a welcome reception there . . .

Likewise, Mary Jane, an unmarried woman, who ran away in 1831, was suspected of being harboured by her family, which included her mother, who lived at Collymore Rock, two brothers, one named John Henry who lived near Coverly in Christ Church, and the other named James Williams who lived near Lowthers, and 'other relatives and connections at Newton and Seawell' plantations.

Slaves' responses to the Christian nuclear family structure became increasingly favourable over time, and by the end of slavery in 1838 it was a common part of the social culture of the black communities. In 1819, for example, the Reverend John Pinder stated that slave women would regularly come to him and demand right to the banns. This kind of experience had convinced him that the desire for monogamous unions was preferred by creole slave women, many of whom were now prepared to resist the polygamous family tradition. Many slave owners, by the end of the eighteenth century, were also prepared to sponsor a nuclear family sanctified by the Anglican Church, among their slaves. In 1825, for example, the management of Codrington plantation was encouraged to promote Christian marriage among slaves by holding forth 'such further inducements as a superior habitation, and additional comforts of clothing and security of the customary inheritance of their legitimate children, if belonging to the estate, and any other privileges . . . as may appear . . .

expedient'. An estate attorney, Foster Clarke, also recommended to all slave owners during the 1820s that 'every mother having six children born in lawful wedlock' should be exempted from further work on the estate.

Although there was no law against it, few Christian marriages of slaves were performed in the colony before 1825. Some ceremonies were conducted by the Reverend W. M. Harte of the St Lucy parish, who was subsequently persecuted by his parishioners for his apparent support of slaves' demands for civic respectability. One slave couple apparently insisted upon being addressed as Mr and Mrs, to the great irritation of whites who did not believe that slaves should enjoy this conferment of social honour. On 17th April 1827, Harte's parishioners passed a resolution which embodied the following accusation: 'endeavouring to alienate their slaves from a sense of their duty, by inculcating doctrines of equality inconsistent with their obedience to their masters and the policy of the island'. Christian marriage, then, was perceived by whites as one way of removing the label of 'heathen' from blacks, and thereby uniting the two races at a level of equality within the ideological climate of the church. There was, therefore, much resistance from the white community, and the number of blacks taking banns remained small in the final years of slavery. None the less, in the decade before the Sunday and Marriage Act of 1826, by which the Established Anglican Church sought to promote baptism and marriage among slaves, such marriages were already commonplace.

But long before the 1826 legislative provision, slaves had been accustomed to cohesion and continuity in their family life. To some extent, this has to do with the relatively high level of stability in estate ownership which reduced the incidence of separation of slave families. Most estates in the colony in 1826 were owned by the same family fifty years earlier, so that generations of slaves were born, raised and died in the same plantation villages. This sense of continuity in slave life certainly allowed for the emergence of grandmothers and great-grandmothers as matriarchal figures on estates, empowered with tremendous moral and social authority in the slave yards. Slaves, then, by the end of the eighteenth century, could speak firmly about family lineage and traditions.

FREE BLACKS AND FREE COLOUREDS

Free blacks

By the end of the seventeenth century, there was a small number of blacks in the colony who were legally free (Table 7). The presence of this group

Table 7. *Free-black population of*
Barbados, 1773–1829

Year	No.	% free non-white population
1773	78	36.4
1825	1,760	46.0
1826	1,905	46.8
1827	1,947	46.9
1828	1,989	46.8
1829	2,027	46.7

Source: J. Handler, *The Unappropriated People*, p. 21

illustrates the slight degree of flexibility in slave owners' racial ideology as well as the need for rationality in social organisation. Freedom for slaves could be granted as a gift from their owners. There were several ways in which this could be done: they could be manumitted by Acts of the legislature for their 'good conduct' at times of planned or actual slave rebellions, or by will and deed, which were the most common forms that existed in the colony. Between 1650 and 1725, a total of 5,522 wills which have survived and have been recorded, were registered; in these wills 132 testators manumitted 201 slaves.

It is sometimes difficult to distinguish the evidence which relates to free blacks from that which concerns the free coloureds – persons of mixed racial ancestry. Both groups were lumped together for legislative consideration. The civil disabilities which the free coloureds suffered were also applicable to free blacks, who were a minority within the free non-white population. For example, in 1721 legislation passed to strip the free-coloured propertied community of the franchise also applied to free blacks. In 1773, 63.6 per cent of the free non-white population of St Michael was 'coloured' which illustrates the minority status of the free blacks. Over the last fifty years of slavery, the number and proportion of free blacks increased. During the 1820s, at least 47 per cent of the freed non-white population was black.

Free blacks tended to gravitate towards the towns where they made a living mostly as petty hucksters, tradesmen and tavern attendants, though some did become prominent within the business community. Always under suspicion of entering into illicit activities with slaves, free blacks never developed a distinct social identity, and political agitation for an extension in civil rights was reported as an initiative of the free coloureds.

The legislature persistently expressed opposition to the practice among slave owners of freeing their old, infirm or useless slaves, who commonly drifted into the towns and made a living by beggary. Laws were passed designed to ensure that manumissions were granted only to slaves who would not become a charge upon the poor-relief funds of the vestries. These provisions were not effective and the general result was that the status of many free blacks was not much removed from the degradation of slave-like conditions. For many freedmen manumission did not result in an improvement in material conditions. Yet slaves craved freedom, and pursued it by all means possible.

Free coloureds

Richard Dunn has noted that from the seventeenth century, white men in Barbados 'slept with their slave women and sired mulatto children'. Such children, by virtue of their mothers being slaves, were born into slavery, and referred to as coloured. Black motherhood, then, by implication was conceptually and legally tied to the perpetuation of slavery. This matrifocal legislative approach to slave reproduction ensured that black maternity could not be separated from the forces of enslavement. But these coloured offspring also had to be accounted for socially, to remove any possible claim to their white father's property by inheritance, especially when they were freed. White slave owners wanted to ensure that their property could not become the basis of any coloured people's ascendancy within the socio-economic structure, so legislative provisions, as well as social ideologies, were shaped in an effort to attach the stain of racial and genetic inferiority to non-whites. By the early eighteenth century, a small community of free persons of mixed racial ancestry existed in the colony, and soon became a target for the legislature.

Political efforts to reduce the free coloureds to second-class inhabitants, with fewer civic rights than whites, began in 1721. In that year an Act was passed which specified that for inhabitants to have the right to vote, be elected to public office, or serve on juries, they had to be 'free holders', male, Christian, citizen of Great Britain, white, and own at least ten acres of land, or a house having an annual taxable value of £10 local currency. The racial qualification remained in force until 1831, and was the prime basis of free-coloured and free-black civic disability. In addition, the law stated that they could not give evidence against whites in courts, which severely hampered their ability to enter commercial or agricultural businesses, and was the most keenly contested aspect of the discriminatory legislative machinery.

In the formative decades of slave society, when social ideologies were not yet fully constitutionalised, sexual relations between black men and white women were recorded as no extraordinary social occurrences. An account of the colony in 1683 mentioned the existence of 326 'mulatto' inhabitants, some of whom were free. In the St Michael parish register for 4th December 1685, for example, a marriage is entered between 'Peter Perkins, a negro, and Jane Long, a white woman'. The 1715 census shows that they had a son. During the eighteenth century, however, as the slave society matured, the role of racial ideologies became more important to the white elite as tools of social control, and reports of such relations became less frequent in official documents. During the eighteenth century, planters tended to refer to all persons of mixed racial ancestry as coloured, unlike Jamaicans, for example, who paid social and official attention to all the various possible types of inter-racial mixtures.

Some whites preferred to have their coloured progeny legally freed, and made arrangements for their manumission – with and without their slave mothers. In general, these coloured persons cherished their freedom, the most valuable social asset in slave society, and sought to distance themselves from their slave ancestry which white society defined as the undisputed mark of racial inferiority. For this social group, then, their black mothers were generally seen as a disability, while their white grandmothers tended to see them as a disgrace. Living between these two psychological worlds the free coloureds developed a unique perspective on society (see Table 8).

Most white males who manumitted their coloured children did not free their black mothers. On the estates, it was not uncommon for planters or

Table 8. *Estimated free-coloured population*
of Barbados, 1748–1828

Year	Number	% total free non-white population
1748	107	63.6
1773	136	54.0
1825	2,066	53.2
1826	2,169	53.1
1827	2,201	53.2
1828	2,259	53.3

managers to free their coloured children on their reaching adulthood, while their mothers continued as slaves in the fields or in the households. These children were not always the result of voluntary sexual relations; rape, duress, and other forms of coercion featured commonly in these contexts. Instances where white males made provisions for black women who mothered their children were few, and generally those in which there was some emotional intimacy; in such cases it was common for white fathers to accept social responsibility for their 'illegitimate' family. Generally, white fathers of coloured children were socially anonymous, and the material condition of such children was not bettered by paternal influence. As such, the majority of coloured children remained slaves, and the free coloureds represented no more than the tip of the coloured population.

One of the most outstanding men within the business community of Bridgetown during the mid-eighteenth century was Joseph Rachell, a free-coloured merchant, who had large and extensive concerns. In the early nineteenth century, London Bourne, also free coloured, was a wealthy Bridgetown merchant. He was described as 'one of the wealthiest merchants in Bridgetown'. He owned 'many businesses at home and abroad', and in 1837 he owned three stores and was reputed to be worth between $20,000 and $30,000. Both Rachell and Bourne were born into slavery and manumitted as young men. The rise of prominent free-coloured family dynasties such as the Belgraves, Collymores, Bournes, Mapps, Hinds and Montefiores should not, however, be studied without careful reference to the fact that most coloured people were still plantation slaves.

William A. Green has argued that as Barbados was the most mature slave society at the end of the eighteenth century, the prejudice against the black skin was more intense than in other British colonies. During the 1800s, Elizabeth Fenwick, who carefully observed Barbadian white racism and its subtype, 'colourism', found that the 'boundary' which separated the races was 'impassable', though some of the coloureds were 'fair, light haired people' with wealth and education. Since the free coloureds, who aspired to be merchants and planters, were pro-slavery, many enslaved black women endured the condition of seeing their free coloured progeny defend slavery with the same intense vigour as their white fathers.

For the free coloureds, the 1816 revolt was their most testing moment, during which they were forced to take a firm position on the slavery question. Only a handful of free coloureds supported the slaves. Some of these, according to an Assembly report, joined the black rebels probably because they had slave children whom they wanted freed. One of them, Joseph Franklyn, who was believed by many whites to be a leading provocateur, was born a slave and freed at the age of 21 by his father, an estate owner, while his mother Leah remained a slave on the estate. He resented and rejected white arrogance, and found companionship among blacks. But those free coloureds who fought against the slaves were commended by white society for their 'determination to do their duty by the country', and 'devotion to the interest of whites'.

It was also during the revolt that the free-coloured elites articulated their acceptance of the ideology of white racial supremacy as a social principle, with all that implied for their black heritage. In 1817, the free coloureds were given a major concession by the white legislators for their loyalty – the right to give evidence in courts against whites. It was in their acceptance memorandum that they expressed support for the white supremacy ideological structure of the slave society. In the letter to John Beckles, Speaker of the House, they stated:

We are sensible that in a country like this where slavery exists, there must necessarily be distinction between the white and free coloured inhabitants and that there are privileges which the latter do not expect to enjoy. It affords us general satisfaction to find that our conduct upon the late unfortunate occasion [rebellion] has met with the approbation of the legislature.

In addition, they assured the House that as a group they would at all times 'give proof of loyalty and sincere attachment to the King and constitution and risk our lives in the defence and protection of our country and its laws'.[7]

Not only were the free coloureds opposed to the armed liberation of blacks, but also to their imperial legislative emancipation. At no stage did they consider that the black sections of their families, including their mothers, were worthy of general emancipation. From the beginning of the nineteenth century when imperial legislative action was tending towards the amelioration of slaves' conditions, they adopted a stern pro-slavery position. In an 1803 petition addressed to the Assembly, they argued: '. . . we have all our lives been accustomed to the assistance of slaves . . . Many of our children who are now grown almost to the years of maturity have from their earliest infancy been accustomed to be attended by slaves . . . Surely death would be preferable to . . . a situation [of slavelessness]'. When in 1831 they gained full civil rights, on par with whites, they joined the vanguard of the anti-emancipation movement in a manner comparable with their behaviour during the 1816 slave revolt.

Thome and Kimball, who observed the emancipation process in 1837, wrote: 'The majority of them are either indifferent, or actually hostile to emancipation. They have no fellow feeling with the slave. In fact, they have had prejudices against the negroes no less bitter than those which the whites have experienced towards them.'

ECONOMIC TRENDS

By the end of the seventeenth century the super profits which were generated by sugar and slavery had come to an end. The expected process of competition caused by the entry of most other islands into large-scale sugar production reduced prices considerably and brought profits to more modest levels. The decline was rapid in Barbados where falling yields and soil exhaustion became the daily concerns of the planter class. These forces accelerated the trend towards the elimination of small planters and at the same time strengthened the grip of the sugar-planter elite over the colony.

The prosperity of the seventeenth century did not prepare most planters for the difficult years ahead (Table 9). Exports to England dropped sharply in both volume and value during the first few years of the eighteenth

Table 9. *Barbados and British West Indies sugar production, 1700–79 (tons)*

Year	West Indies total	Barbados % share
1700–04	19.467	41.91
1705–09	17.729	46.69
1710–14	22.697	33.33
1715–19	31.691	34.28
1720–24	31.644	25.15
1725–29	42.875	23.77
1730–34	44.199	16.66
1735–39	41.170	14.86
1740–44	39.038	17.63
1745–49	39.383	15.78
1750–54	44.276	14.99
1755–59	55.247	12.91
1760–64	66.334	13.05
1765–69	70.436	11.36
1770–74	84.179	7.91
1775–79	72.998	5.50

Source: D. Watts, *The West Indies,* p. 288

century, and caused considerable alarm within the sugar industry. In 1700, for example, 14,411 hogsheads of sugar were exported to England at a value of £350,000 while in 1701 exports of 11,524 hogsheads were valued at only £110,000.

Many planters explained the decline of the economy in terms of losses at sea during war, very high duties paid on exports and high levels of slave mortality. Others thought that the decline of cotton and ginger production was a contributory factor. But they were all concerned that the early eighteenth century saw only 220–230 ships arriving yearly as opposed to near 400 during the 1680s. The yellow fever epidemic in 1703 coupled with low export levels and drought did little to raise optimism. In addition, the war with France between 1689 and 1713 which affected shipping, aggravated economic uncertainty.

War conditions created a shortage of investment funds on the island. The trade with the Spanish had hitherto brought in pieces-of-eight to purchase slaves, and this was now cut off. New Englanders who supplied foodstuffs, timber and other items were now insisting on cash payments owing to the cheapness of sugar, and in 1706 Barbadians resorted to the use of paper money backed with sugar as security. The shortage of money continued until the end of the Seven Years War (1763) and sugar at market prices was everywhere accepted as money.

During the War, foreign sugars were imported into Barbados and re-exported as local produce. This caused much hardship upon local planters and a tariff of 12s. 6d. per cwt was imposed to protect the Barbadian planter. For reasons of self-interest, planters welcomed the Peace of Utrecht in 1713 which ended the War with the French. Immediately, the colony experienced a short-lived boom. In 1714 and 1716, exports of sugar to England rose above the 1700–1705 average, and planters spoke of the long-awaited return to prosperity. By 1718 decline was once again evident, and exports in 1719 were only half of the 1716 quantity. During 1721 and 1722 export levels continued to fall, and the ruin of marginal planters was widespread. Rising numbers of emigrants to Carolina and Pennsylvania illustrated the crisis within the sugar economy.

The Barbadians immediately recognised that the expansion of world sugar supplies, occasioned by a phenomenal increase in production at French St Domingue, Martinique and Guadeloupe, was responsible for their economic depression. In addition, competition from Jamaica, Antigua and St Kitts could not be underestimated. St Kitts succeeded in doubling its exports of sugar between 1710 and 1728, and redoubling them during the 1730s. The decade 1730 to 1740 was, however, one of grief for sugar cultivators in Barbados. A slump in prices was caused by excessive sugar supplies, and the sugar industry began to contract. Net emigration of whites from the colony continued. That Barbados was the only West Indian colony which was reported well stocked with slaves attests to the general lack of growth within the economy.

On 13th August 1731, a hurricane struck the island and caused extensive damage to its infrastructure. Money for rebuilding the sugar-producing facilities was scarce, and in 1733/34 drought caused severe hunger and many fatalities among the poorer whites and slaves. The passage of the Molasses Act in 1733, which was designed by Parliament to assist planters by placing a levy on foreign sugar imported into British colonies, was of little benefit, and Barbadians began to agitate for direct trade with European markets. During the 1740s, the sugar crop declined further to an average of 13,948 hogsheads. Though colonists were allowed direct trade with Europe by the 1739 Sugar Act, it had little impact upon the local economy.

One important adjustment made by Barbadian planters to offset the adverse effects of falling prices was in the marketing of 'clayed' as opposed to muscovado sugar. Their clayed sugar was in good demand for the making of preserves and much was made of the distinction between it and muscovado. Richard Pares states that claying seems to have originated in Barbados, and most planters took the view that the additional cost of production was compensated for by higher returns. The result, Pares added, was that they had produced 'a sugar which could compete, though not always with success, against sugar refined in Europe'. The extensive use of the claying process could explain in part why Barbados, unlike other West Indian colonies, produced considerably less sugar in the forty years after 1735 than in the forty years before. The evidence suggests, however, that clayed sugar did not do consistently better than muscovado, and that it was also subject to peculiar movements in English demand.

The price of sugar improved marginally during the mid-1740s, but low production levels in Barbados meant that earnings did not increase appreciably. White emigration continued, with the size of the white community falling to less than 16,000 – half its level a hundred years earlier. Between 1750 and 1768, the economy experienced moderate levels of prosperity. The Seven Years War caused some concern since it led to an inflation in insurance and freight costs. These problems, however, were minimised by English military attacks upon the French which severely damaged the sugar industries at Martinique and Guadeloupe. Barbadians responded to the war by expanding production, and during the 1760s high export levels, and good prices, brought a long-awaited sense of the 'good times' to the colony.

Prosperity was short-lived. On the eve of the American Revolution, which caused severe dislocations within the Barbadian economy, an Act was passed (1766) which permitted English creditors to legally seize the property of Barbadian debtors and dispose of it as they wished. The revolution itself caused a drastic reduction in the volume of trade between Barbados and the United States – cutting off some vital supplies of foodstuffs for slaves and materials for the sugar industry.

By the mid-part of 1776, sugar planters were pleading with England for financial assistance. They argued that the economy needed some protection from the free market, and if this could not be done then direct financial aid from England would be of great value. A petition to the King on 9th September 1776 stated that the colony could not become self-sufficient in foodstuffs and therefore needed assistance with its food import bill. Reports of slaves starving and praedial larceny were commonplace, and fear of slave uprisings was discussed in the Assembly. Attempts to supply the colony with food from England were not effective, owing to the prevalence of American privateers within the region. Food shortages were the result, and many contemporaries made references to the poor, both black and white, 'dropping down in the streets, or silently pining and expiring in their cottages'.

The prices of most provisions in the colony escalated between 1774 and 1776. During this period the price of flour moved from 15s. to 37s. 6d. per cwt; Indian corn from 2s. 6d. to 13s. per bushel and saltfish from 12s. 6d. to 40s. per quintal. In 1776, the Council and Assembly addressed the King, stating: 'We have, sir, near 80,000 black and 12,000 white people daily to support. Our ground provisions (the internal resource) have failed for want of seasonable rains; the stock of provisions on hand will not last many weeks, and we are without hope of future foreign resources.' The following year the Assembly described the colony as 'decaying and impoverished' and stated that 'credit has ceased and trade very low'. England did respond, though rather slowly, by sending out supplies which arrived in early 1778; these included large consignments of flour, beans, peas and fish, which alleviated considerably the despair of inhabitants.

The crisis of subsistence created by the war was further aggravated by the hurricane which struck the island on 10th October 1780. Damage was extensive and costly. The Assembly estimated it at £1,350,564 – inclusive of 2,033 slaves, 211 horses and 6,606 cattle killed. The number of white people who died as a result of the catastrophe has been estimated at between

700 and 1,000. Buildings in Bridgetown were flattened, though Speightstown, the second town, fared better. Slaves were left houseless as their little wooden structures were easily swept away by the winds. The English government voted £80,000 for the relief of inhabitants, and private citizens in Britain also made a substantial charity contribution.

According to Otis Starkey, 'the economic position of Barbados at the end of the war (1783) was poor, and a number of planters left the island rather than undertake to repair the damage done by the hurricane'. During the late 1770s, many planters had placed greater acreage under corn and other food crops in order to free themselves of the food market, and these crops were destroyed. Money for rebuilding was therefore scarce, and repairs moved ahead slowly. There were also outbreaks of yellow fever and smallpox which increased mortality levels during the reconstruction; these outbreaks struck hard at the white regiments stationed in St Michael; among these imperial soldiers the mortality rate averaged 185 per 1,000 between 1795 and 1805, and 413 in 1796. This development threatened English control of the island, and planters came to expect the possibility of attack by French troops.

During the last quarter of the century, not only were planters placing greater emphasis upon the cultivation of food crops, both for cash sales and the feeding of slaves, but there was a widespread shift into cotton cultivation. There were three main reasons for this development. First, the revolution in the cotton textiles industry in England created a great demand for raw cotton which, with the hostilities with the United States, a principal supplier, could not be adequately met; second, for planters with small capital and marginal lands it was an attractive crop once the demand was there; third, it was a good cash crop that could be planted on marginal lands, leaving quality arable regions for sugar and food provisions. In 1779, a patent was issued for the construction of a windmill for ginning cotton, and another in 1786 for a machine for removing seeds.

During the early war years, 1789 to 1794, the price of sugar rose rapidly, enhanced by the slave revolution in St Domingue, the largest producer of sugar in the Caribbean. While the revolutionaries prepared to establish the black republic of Haiti in 1804, Barbadian planters shifted back their marginal lands to sugar. With high prices after 1795, and some relaxing of trade with the United States, prosperity returned to the sugar industry of Barbados (Figure 2). It was also a period when two new varieties of cane were introduced to the island – the Otaheita (from Tahiti) and the Bourbon, from the French Indian Ocean island colony of Bourbon. With these canes, planters increased yields, and obtained bumper crops, though

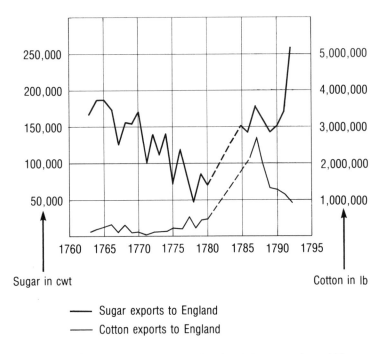

Source: O. Starkey, *The Economic Geography of Barbados,* 1971 edn, p. 102

Fig. 2   Barbados sugar and cotton exports to England, 1760–95

they did not ratoon as well as creole canes and were said to exhaust the soils more rapidly.

In mid-1799, financial crisis in Europe led to the collapse of sugar prices, and wholesale prices in London markets fell from 68s. per cwt to 41s. by December that year. After 1801, prices fluctuated widely as a result of the Anglo-French War which altered the imperial balance of power in the West Indies. The victory of Lord Admiral Nelson at Trafalgar, and the military success of English troops in the West Indies, led to a stabilisation of sugar markets as supplies reached Europe with greater ease. White Barbadians hailed Nelson as a hero and erected a statue to symbolise the English triumph over the French in the region.

CHAPTER FIVE

Abolition, rebellion and emancipation, 1807–1838

SLAVE TRADE AND ABOLITION

Barbados was the only major West Indian sugar plantation colony which succeeded in eliminating an economic need for African slave imports before the slave trade was abolished in 1807. This labour supply condition was a result of a positive natural growth performance among the slave stock towards the closing years of the eighteenth century. By 1800, most major sugar plantations were producing their own slave labour by 'breeding' as opposed to 'buying'. For these slave owners, this was a major economic and social achievement, not only because it was cheaper by this time to reproduce slaves naturally as opposed to buying them from Africa, but also because there was a widespread social preference for creole slaves.

During the last quarter of the eighteenth century, planters actively sought to establish a comprehensive incentive package directed specifically at fertile slave women. Planters recognised that female slaves were the majority in field gangs, but also had to consider the impact of reproduction upon labour productivity in general. It was necessary for fertile women to be treated differently if pro-natalist policies were to be successful, not only by lessening work loads, but also in providing better diet and material care. Such incentives, planters hoped, would encourage women to perceive procreation in a more positive manner.

Slave owners had no direct evidence to prove that slave women had been consciously imposing constraints upon their fertility, even though they believed this to be the case. It was never suggested that slave women practised sexual abstinence (gynaecological resistance), though it was widely believed that some women possessed a deep-rooted hostility towards childbearing in slavery. Slave owners, then, proposed to minimise the degree of female indifference and resistance to child rearing by systematically offering pro-natalist socio-material incentives. This ameliorative thrust was the last of a series of measures by which planters attempted to maintain and reproduce an adequate workforce. It is uniquely important because it was the one policy that entailed reform in the treatment of slaves. For the planter, however, such reforms to the slave system were simply the means to an economic end – the breeding of slaves.

Logically, then, the so-called 'amelioration' of the late eighteenth century can be defined as a system of thought and practice by which money that would have been otherwise spent on hiring and buying unseasoned Africans was used to improve the lot of existing slaves in order to induce them to breed their replacements. This policy development, and its underlying ideas and concepts, were carefully tested and evaluated. From the 1770s Barbadian planters contributed to an upsurge in literature which addressed specifically aspects of slave reproduction. Most writers, many of them posing as experienced authorities on slave management, sought to encourage slave natalism, and conceived it as expressive of progressive management. In addition, they stressed that a successful slave reproduction policy was the most effective strategy to undermine the credibility of those abolitionists who argued that slaves were ill-treated on the estates.

The most influential of these works was published in 1786, entitled 'The Following instructions are Offered to the Consideration of Proprietors and Managers of Plantations in Barbados'. Published in London, it was written by a combination of prominent absentee and resident Barbadian planters – Edwin Lascelles, James Colleton, Edwin Drax, Francis Ford, Rev. John Brathwaite, John Walters, William Thorpe Holder, James Holder, Philip Gibbes and John Birney. Printed in bold, capitalised letters in the introduction is their central thesis: 'THE INCREASE IS THE ONLY TEST OF THE CARE WITH WHICH THEY ARE TREATED.' This work called for a systematic approach to the matter of 'slave breeding' within the context of a 'good treatment' policy.[1]

Planters were encouraged to implement a series of pre-natal policies to assist pregnant women to deliver healthy babies. Emphasis was placed on the need to protect fertile women from undue physical stress. In addition, much was made of the need for post-natal facilities in order to assist lactating mothers in reducing the high level of infant mortality. These policies meant the marginal reduction of working hours for pregnant and lactating field women, and improved material care. In effect, the authors recommended a significant reshaping of slave women's experiences as plantation labourers.

Since a high level of infant mortality was considered a principal factor in the poor demographic performance of the slave population during the early eighteenth century, most planters recognised the need for post-natal policies which took into consideration not only the care of infants, but also their mothers. Edwin Lascelles urged slave managers to take particular care that mothers did not return to the fields too soon after birth, for in his opinion available mortality evidence showed a direct correlation between the health of mothers and infant longevity.

By the end of the eighteenth century the offer of financial incentives to slave women as a stimulus to reproduction was a feature of plantation management. During the 1780s, according to Dickson, 'a small matter in money' was given to successful mothers and midwives. He did emphasise, however, that this was not yet 'the ordinary practice'. By the 1790s, evidence from the account books of large estates, such as Newton, Drax Hall, Colleton, Mount Gay, and Lowthers, suggests that slave women were offered financial incentives for reproduction. At Drax Hall and Mount Gay, for example, women were paid 6s. 3d. for 'bringing out' a child. At Newton and Seawell, the sum of 6s. 6d. was paid to successful slave mothers. Slave midwives also received some financial consideration.

Some plantations were more successful than others. For example, on 26th July 1797, Sampson Wood, manager of Newton plantation, informed his employer: 'I encourage the slaves to breed as much as I can, [but] if we increase as we have done, I am afraid in a few years, we shall have too many.' Rare indeed, however, was the sugar estate in the Caribbean at the end of the eighteenth century on which management feared an over-supply of labour as a result of natural reproduction.

By 1800, most large Barbadian sugar estates were in a position to ensure future labour supplies by natural increase. Metropolitan lobbies for the abolition of the slave trade, which succeeded in 1807, caused no sleepless nights in plantation great houses. Indeed, the colony became an important re-exporter of slaves, and its entrepôt business flourished during the closing years of the African slave trade. In addition, many prominent planters who had expanded their economic interests into the newly acquired colonies of Trinidad and Guiana envisaged that infrastructural developments there could be carried out by slaves from Barbados.

So confident were the Barbadian slave owners that they would solve the labour supply problem by natural reproduction before the Abolition Act that few of them gave their moral and active support to abolitionists. Not only were Africans in diminished economic demand, but they were considered as socio-political undesirables since it was widely believed that they were more likely to explode into violent anti-slavery action than creole slaves. In 1806, for example, Robert Haynes, a prominent planter-politician from a long-established creole family, stated: 'I sincerely rejoice at the abolition of the slave trade', and he wished it had 'been totally abolished twenty years ago'. In this view he expressed the sentiments of many influential slave owners.

In 1814 the abolitionists' lobby, insisting that Africans were being sold clandestinely in the islands after the 1807 Abolition Act, proposed that all slave owners in the colonies should prepare registers of their slaves. By this means, Parliament hoped to monitor West Indian slave populations in order to detect illegal entries of Africans. The Barbados Assembly objected to the assumptions of the proposed legislation and rejected the bill after a heated and prolonged debate. John Beckles, Speaker of the House, accepted the fact that some colonies suffered a severe labour crisis after the 1807 Abolition Act, and resorted to illegal labour supply methods, but argued fiercely that Barbados should not be included among this group. In a frontal attack upon the logic and ascribed hidden agenda of the bill, Beckles referred to the strong anti-African sentiment which existed in white Barbadian society, and the overwhelming planter preference for both creole slaves and natural reproduction. He received full support from Robert Haynes, who explained to the anti-slavery lobbies that blacks were reproducing at a healthy rate because of their improved material and social conditions. In a letter to Thomas Lane, absentee owner of Newton estate, he stated: 'What more can any set of men require to convince them of our preferring to breed slaves in preference to purchasing them?'

BUSSA'S REBELLION

From the slaves' point of view, attempts to ameliorate the hardships of slavery during the late eighteenth century were motivated by slave owners' narrow economic interests and not by humanitarian considerations. From the beginning of the nineteenth century slaves appeared increasingly anxious and restless – the result of their perception that the possibility of obtaining imperial legislated freedom was, unlike all previous times, fairly good. Abolitionist discussions in England seemed serious and fruitful, as was evident in the 1807 Slave Trade Abolition Act. There was also the example of self-liberation set by Haitian blacks which, though difficult to assess accurately, cannot be under-rated in terms of its psychological impact upon all Caribbean slave communities.

Many Barbadian slave owners stated that in the years after the slave trade legislation, blacks seemed unusually aggressive, and were visibly refusing to be cooperative. This was especially so among the artisans and domestics, those elite slaves who considered themselves closer to both full freedom and political information. During the House of Assembly debate of 10th December 1810, it was noted that 'the increase of arrrogance and vice among slaves', particularly those in Bridgetown who were more aware of the activities of Mr Wilberforce, 'has occasioned, nay demanded, punishment'. For the first time since the early eighteenth century, serious discussions were taking place among planters concerning the 'relaxed state of the police and the effects which it produces amongst the slaves'. From 1804, when the Haitian revolutionaries declared their independence from France, Assembly debates focused increasingly upon this apparent insolent attitude among slaves. There was, however, no suspicion of the possibility of an armed rebellion of slaves. It was generally thought that a tightening of control systems was all that was necessary in order to ensure the tranquillity of the traditional order.

On Easter Sunday, 14th April 1816, Barbados experienced its only slave rebellion. It was the first of the three major slave uprisings that took place in the British Caribbean between the abolition of the slave trade in 1807 and general emancipation in 1838; the other two rebellions occurred in Demerara in 1823 and Jamaica in 1831/32. Most accounts suggest that it began about 8.30 p.m. in the south-eastern parish of St Philip, and quickly spread throughout most of the southern and central parishes of Christ Church, St John, St Thomas, St George and parts of St Michael. Minor outbreaks of arson (but no skirmishes with the militia) also occurred in the northernmost parish of St Lucy. No fighting between rebel slaves and the militia forces was reported for the eastern and western parishes of St Andrew, St James and St Peter. In geo-political terms, more than half of the island was engulfed by the insurrection.

The rebellion was short-lived. Within three days it was effectively quashed by a joint offensive of the local militia and imperial troops garrisoned on the island; included among the latter were the black slave soldiers of the 1st West India Regiment. Mopping-up operations continued during May and June, and martial law, which was imposed about 2.00 a.m. on Monday, 15th April, was lifted eighty-nine days later on 12th July. The death toll was very unevenly balanced between blacks and whites. Governor Leith's report of 30th April stated that it was 'impossible with any certainty to state the numbers who have fallen; but about 50 however are at present conjectured to be the amount'. He also estimated that the number executed under martial law was about 70, and that many prisoners remained in gaol pending trial. By 21st September he had revised his estimates to 144 executed under martial law, 70 sentenced to death, and 123 sentenced to transportation.[2]

The anonymous author of an account of the insurrection (written most probably in September that year) suggests that the Governor's figures represent a gross underestimate of the total fatalities, and that 'a little short of 1,000 slaves were killed in battle and executed at Law'. Colonel Rycroft Best, commander of the Christ Church parish militia, stated that his men alone killed forty rebels in battles during Monday and Tuesday, 15th and 16th of April. The reason, according to Colonel Best, why many more had to be executed in the field was because 'the numbers not only implicated but actively employed' were great. In addition, he stated that many of those tried had to be executed because 'they were all ringleaders'.

Only one white militiaman was killed in battle, Private Brewster, of the St Philip parish militia. Several whites were seriously injured in combat, and many of the elderly died of 'fatigue' caused by the rebellion. In addition, during the clashes between slaves and the imperial troops at Bayleys and Golden Grove plantations on the Tuesday morning, two of the 150 men of the West India Regiment were killed. Damage to property was estimated by the Assembly's investigative committee at £175,000. Twenty-five per cent of the year's sugar-cane crop was burnt, as arson was used extensively by rebels, both as an instrument to undermine the economic base of the planters, and to convey logistical signals to their scattered contingents.

Slaves had organised an islandwide conspiracy to overthrow slave owners and to obtain their freedom. The Governor, the Colonels of militia and the Commandant of the imperial troops, were all convinced that this was the case. They denied that the rebellion was limited in nature, or directed specifically against a section of the island's planter class. Neither did they believe that the revolt was simply a form of protest action by slaves designed to gain the further amelioration of their social and labour conditions. According to Colonel Best the Monday night was to be the beginning of an arsonist attack upon the slave-owning community; canes and buildings were to be burnt to the ground. During the panic caused by this action, the Tuesday and/or Wednesday was for the 'murder of whitemen' across the island. One captured rebel who was tried by court martial confessed that they had intended slave owners to cry 'Water!' on the Monday night and 'Blood!' on subsequent nights. They wanted freedom, and the only way to get it, according to Nanny Grig, a woman slave at Simmons plantation, 'was to fight for it'.

Evidence produced by prominent members of the slave-owning community suggests that the uprising was sudden and unexpected. They generally believed that their slaves, not having attempted any insurrections since the minor aborted Bridgetown affair in 1701, were more prone to running away, withholding their labour in protest, and petitioning estate owners, attorneys and managers concerning conditions of work and leisure, than to armed insurrection. They claimed that their slaves were given 'liberties' which planters in the other islands could not dare even to consider.

The ability of most slaves to travel the island extensively in pursuit of social and economic activity was held by the planters as proof of the longstanding mildness of race relations and openness of plantation management. John Beckles, Speaker of the Assembly at the time of the insurrection, confessed that the slave laws did 'wear a most sanguinary complexion', and were a 'disgrace' to the island, but he affirmed that they were rarely applied, and in this sense they were largely 'dead letters'. Robert Haynes stated his attitude towards slaves on the eve of the revolt in a letter dated September 1816:

The night of the insurrection I would and did sleep with my chamber door open, and if I had possessed ten thousand pounds in my house I should not have had any more precaution, so well convinced I was of their [the slaves'] attachment . . .

This attitude seems to have been general throughout the white community. Governor Leith, in awareness of this long-held complacency, which he personally did not share, informed the Secretary for Colonies that slave owners had 'flattered themselves that the general good treatment of the slaves would have prevented them resorting to violence to establish an elusion of material right,' and that they 'had not any apprehension of such a convulsion'.

The slaves had been planning the rebellion since the House of Assembly discussed and rejected an imperial bill for a general slave census. The alleged primary leader within the folk culture – though this was not stated by the Assembly's investigative committee – was a slave by the name of Bussa (or Bussoe), an African-born man, head ranger at Bayleys plantation in the parish of St Philip. Biographical data on Bussa are unavailable, but certain inductive points may be raised. First, that an African-born man should be the prime leader of a predominantly creole rebellion is significant. In 1816 at least 92 per cent of the slave population was creole, and all the other leaders of rebel contingents were creole. Second, that an African should have achieved the status of head ranger suggests that he most probably was not a young man in 1816, since the slave trade was abolished in 1807, and in general it took at least ten years for Africans to acquire the language and managerial skills, plus their masters' confidence, in order to become the chief slave personnel on estates. The military leadership of Bussa in the rebellion can be partially established by looking at the general movement of the armed encounters. Rebel contingents assembled at Bayleys plantation on the Tuesday for the final showdown with imperial troops, which points to Bussa's central role as the revolutionary leader. Rebels from all over the island rallied to Bussa at Bayleys, and it was there that the rebellion was finally put down by imperial troops. Bussa, according to the late H. A. Vaughan, a local historian, met his death in battle ahead of his rebel contingent in St Philip.

The Assembly, however, reported that a free-coloured, propertyless man named Washington Franklin had encouraged the slaves to revolt, and referred to a slave confession in which it was stated that the rebels had intended to make Franklin the Governor in the revolutionary regime. There is no reliable evidence to attribute a leadership role to Franklin. It is more likely that the St Philip militia used the opportunity of the rebellion to execute Franklin, long considered an insubordinate individual by whites within the parish. He was arrested, tried for inciting slaves to rebellion, and hanged.

Confession data supplied by rebels suggest a decentralised form of leadership organisation. Each plantation actively involved in the insurrection was represented by a rebel group which had one dominant leader. These leaders, all male slaves, met frequently to discuss logistics and strategy. Jackey, a creole slave, head driver at Simmons plantation in St Philip, was chiefly responsible for the overall coordination of these groups. He convened planning meetings, most of which took place on his plantation, and reported to Bussa. The Assembly's report stated that he frequently invited the leaders of rebel contingents from plantations in St Philip, such as Gittens, Bushy Park, Byde Mill, Nightengale, Congo Road, and Sunbury, to his home in order to coordinate the details of the insurrection. John, a slave and ranger at Simmons plantation, was Jackey's chief messenger. According to the Report, John frequently took messages to rebel groups throughout the southern and central parts of the island, and also kept Bussa at Bayleys plantation informed. James Bowland, a literate slave belonging to the River plantation in St Philip, confessed that John had been in frequent touch with Bussa since March, and that he often took instruction to rebel groups in all the 'different parishes'.

In addition to these leaders, the mobilisation of the slave masses and the general spreading of insurrectionist propaganda were done by three literate free-coloured men, Cain Davis, Roach, and Richard Sarjeant. Davis held meetings with slaves on several plantations, such as River and Bayleys in St Philip, and Sturges in St Thomas. He propagated the view among slaves that their masters were opposing metropolitan efforts to have them freed, and that if they wanted freedom they had to fight for it, as Nanny Grig suggested.

The Assembly's report into the rebellion was finally published on 7th January 1818.[3] It reflected an opinion generally held by the planters that the rebellion originated in the campaign for slave emancipation led by Mr Wilberforce. Wilberforce was accused of having agents and spies in Barbados, who had informed the slaves that the process leading to their freedom was being obstructed by the planters, and that it was therefore up to them to assert pressure from their end by violent means. Furthermore, the report stated, the rebellion originated

solely and entirely in consequence of the intelligence imparted to the slaves, which intelligence was obtained from the English Newspapers, that their freedom had been granted them in England . . . These reports first took their rise immediately after the information of the proposed establishments of Registries in the British Settlements in the West Indies . . . and in the mistaken idea that the Registry Bill was actually their Manumission . . .; these hopes were strengthened and kept alive by the promises held out, that a party in England, and particularly Mr. Wilberforce . . . were exerting themselves to ameliorate their condition, and ultimately effect their emancipation.

A white Barbadian, referring to Wilberforce and other members of the African Institute as a 'dangerous crew', wrote a letter to the *Barbados Mercury and Bridgetown Gazette*, stating that they 'have pierced the inmost recesses of our island, inflected deep and deadly wounds in the minds of the black population, and engendered the Hydra, Rebellion, which had well nigh deluged our fields with blood'. The *London Times* suggested that the Rebellion was due primarily to the 'impolite' and thoughtless interference of Wilberforce in the political business of the Barbadian planters. It informed its readers that the revolt was led by slaves, some of whom could 'read and write'. These instigators, the paper noted, 'availed themselves of this parliamentary interference and the public anxiety it occasioned, to instill into the minds of the slaves generally a belief that they were already freed by the King and Parliament'.

The slaves, or at least the more informed among them, were aware, especially after the abolition of the slave trade in 1807, of Wilberforce's hostility to slavery. His success in 1807, and his ability to mobilise parliamentary support for the imposition of amelioration measures upon the planters, established him as a hero among West Indian slaves. By January 1816, the leaders of the rebellion, who according to the Assembly 'had gained an ascendancy over their fellows by being able to read and write', had obtained a reasonable amount of information concerning the political situation both in Barbados and in the London West Indian community. This information was obtained from local and English newspapers. In the confessions of Robert, for example, a slave from Simmons plantation, it is stated that Nanny Grig frequently read English and local papers, and informed other slaves on the developments in Haiti and in the metropolis.

The rebellion, as an isolated military event, was quickly suppressed, but the process of resistance continued. On 30th April, the Speaker of the Assembly stated that he hoped 'the fate of those deluded men who have fallen victims of their rashness and folly may be a salutary warning to those who have returned to their duty,' and that they may hereafter be 'impressed with this feeling that it is only by a faithful performance of it that they can look for that protection and those comforts which every master is desirous of offering his slave'.

The Governor was more forthright in his address to the slave population on 26th April. He informed them that slavery could be abolished only 'by a wise unremitting system of amelioration by which it will gradually produce its own reformation. By such means alone, and not by the attempting of a rash and destructive convulsion has slavery . . . happily changed.' In addition, the Governor continued,

I cannot omit to express my satisfaction at the good sense and feeling of so large a proportion of you who rallied around your masters and their families. I sincerely trust that the lesson of the rebels' defeat will save me from the painful task of using the ample power at all times in my hands to crush the refractory and punish the guilty.

In June 1816, none the less, a white visitor to Barbados describing the post-rebellion feeling among blacks, and outlining the dangers it posed for white society, stated that 'the disposition of the slaves in general is very bad. They are sullen and sulky and seem to cherish feelings of deep revenge.' Furthermore, he added, 'we hold the West Indies by a very precarious tenure – that of military strength only'.

In September, a small party of slaves were arrested for trying to organise a second insurrection. According to Colonel Best, 'as on the former occasion, the drivers, rangers, carpenters, and watchmen were chiefly concerned and few field labourers.' Furthermore, he added, they had convinced themselves that they were 'sufficiently numerous to become the masters . . . of the island'. According to Thomas Moody, this September affair, which originated in the parish of Christ Church, 'excited much alarm and uneasiness in the minds of the inhabitants'. The Governor dismissed it as the 'result of one or two turbulent men, disappointed at their failure, endeavouring ineffectually to reproduce insubordination'. The event, none the less, convinced planters that greater repression was necessary in order to keep slaves in subjection. Summing up the debate in the House concerning the crisis in slave control, John Beckles stated that the rebellious 'spirit' of the slave was

not subdued, nor will it ever be subdued . . . [it] behoves us to be upon guard, to keep a watch that we may not again be caught so shamefully unprepared. The comfort and happiness of our families require it – the safety and tranquility of the island call for it.[4]

IMPERIAL LEGISLATIVE AMELIORATION

Though slave owners established elements of the foundations for measures designed to reform the slave system between the 1780s and 1817, it was not until 1823 that so-called 'amelioration' became an official policy – and then it was initiated as the programme of the British Government. Prior to 1823, slave owners did implement some legal reforms so as to ward off increasing emancipation pressures. In 1805, for example, provisions were made to establish that whites could be capitally punished for the murder of a black, and in 1817, free blacks and free coloureds were given the right to give evidence in courts against whites. In spite of these limited legal adjustments, the abolitionist movement intensified its critique of the slave system, and forced Barbados planters, during the 1820s, into a hard-nosed defence of their slavery world.

Abolitionists in England frequently described Barbadian slave owners as perhaps the most conservative in the West Indies. They were considered always the last to reform their slave codes and to extend legal rights to slaves and free coloureds. As a result, when, in 1823, the British Government indicated that amelioration was indeed the prelude to a future general emancipation, and sought to impose reform measures upon the colony, the consequence was the development of an intense struggle with the local Assembly. Slave owners stubbornly refused to accept Parliamentary perceptions of amelioration, and suggested aggressively instead that they would accept such reform measures only if they were seen as one way to avoid the need for emancipation legislation. Parliament decided, therefore, that serious ameliorative measures would have to be firmly imposed upon the colony, in light of the Assembly's resistance, and began the formulation of a comprehensive reform bill.

In response, Barbadian slave owners proposed to use the positive growth performance of the slave population, among other things, as a propaganda instrument against the abolitionists' argument that the lot of slaves could only be seriously improved by legislative action. By linking 'growth' to 'good treatment', they sought to promote themselves as 'ideal' administrators and business managers in command of a paternalist social order. Sir Reynold Alleyne, a prominent politician from a long-established slave-owning family, and son of Sir John Gay Alleyne, was the leading articulator of this argument.

The 1823 development in the British humanitarian movement, which transformed the debate over amelioration of slavery in Barbados, has mostly to do with Thomas Fowell Buxton, the new theoretician of the parliamentary caucus. He drew Parliament's attention to another important equation: that slavery and Christian social thought were incompatible, and hence its members were duty bound, as guardian of a Christian culture, to abolish slavery immediately. Parliament was moved, but not to legislate; members were merely prepared to adopt resolutions promising reforms designed to make the lives of blacks less slave-like. Secretary of State for the Colonies, Lord Bathurst, immediately demanded that all West Indian legislatures implement the following reforms:

(a) the outlawing of the whip, especially in the case of women;
(b) the recording of all slave punishments;
(c) abolition of manumission fees;
(d) allowance of slaves to own property;
(e) allowance of slaves to purchase their freedom;
(f) abolition of slave-owner's right to separate families by sale.

Bathurst went to great lengths to impress upon the Barbados legislature in particular that if they failed to adopt these reforms, Parliament would have no choice but to impose them.

The receipt of these reform proposals by the Barbadians coincided with the news of the Demerara slave revolt, and fear that it might spread to their colony. Not surprisingly, slave owners used this opportunity to reject Bathurst's suggestions by adding that they represented dangerous concessions to blacks who were prepared to use Parliament's concern over their plight as the basis for their own militant agenda. This response was supported by Governor Henry Wade. Following their refusal to comply with Bathurst's demands, a memorial was sent by the Assembly to the Colonial Office which stated that his reforms were fanatical, prejudicial and unjust. The memorialists also added that 'neither threats nor persuasion' would ever induce them 'to put the finishing hand' to their 'political, perhaps natural existence'.

The Barbados legislature used the Demerara slave rebellion to advantage, but was somewhat concerned that Parliament would charge them with extreme recalcitrance following the mob demolition in 1823 of the chapel of William Shrewsbury, a reformist Methodist minister. Compromise was therefore sought, and this took the form of a proposal to pass its own reform bill. This measure was intended to appease Parliament, and at the same time to ensure that slave owners had effective control over their slaves and other properties.

The local bill was debated by the Assembly in 1824, its objective to 'consolidate and improve' the ancient legal machinery under which blacks had been governed. Three legislative concessions were granted to slaves:

(a) right to own property;
(b) right to give evidence in courts in all cases;
(c) reduction in manumission fees.

But three assurances were also granted to slave owners:

(a) that any white person who killed a slave in revolt should be immune from prosecution;
(b) death to any slave who threatened the life of a white person;
(c) any black without proper proof of the right to be free should be presumed a slave.

In 1825, this bill was consented to by the Council, and became known as the Consolidated Slave Law. It was received by an angered Secretary Bathurst, who made no effort to hide his vexation with the arrogance of the Barbados legislature. He rejected the law with the explanation that it was a shoddy political ploy which did not incorporate the serious spirit of reform embodied in his own proposals.

After a prolonged debate over Bathurst's reply, the Barbados legislature agreed to moderate their law. They insisted upon the slave-owners' right to flog slaves, but decided that the provision which protected all whites from prosecution for killing insurrectionary slaves should be removed. In its place, slave owners maintained the right to imprison slaves for unlimited periods, and to prohibit slave gatherings after dark and holding social functions without a legal permit. In 1826, Parliament accepted the revised Consolidated Slave Law under the recommendation of the new and more pro-planter Secretary for Colonies, William Huskisson.

The slaves, meanwhile, were showing signs of frustration over the failure of Buxton's leadership to deliver the 'freedom paper'. In awareness that their masters were in opposition to serious reforms and emancipation, they continued to impress upon the white community their demand for full legal freedom. The anger and tension which resulted from their military defeat in 1816 remained, and reports of their 'restlessness' came from all quarters after the Act of 1826. In May 1833, when the new Governor, Sir Lionel Smith, arrived at the colony, slaves from all over the island sought a meeting with him to discuss the state of emancipation plans. There were also rumours of a revolt planned for 1st January 1834, which disturbed some sections of the white community. By now, it was clear to both the local and imperial governments that slaves considered themselves as principal emancipation lobbyists.

EDUCATION AND RELIGION AS REFORMS

During the 1820s some slave owners and officials in the Colonial Office suggested that the exposure to Christianity and secular education of black slaves, free blacks, and to a lesser extent the free-coloured poor and poor-whites, could have the effect of reducing the degree of socio-political turmoil. The perception of religion and education by these groups as instruments for the promotion of good conduct among labourers represented a radical departure from the Barbadian tradition. From the seventeenth century, it was generally the belief among the ruling elite that Christianity and literacy would have the effects of increasing black awareness of the injustice of their enslavement, and would therefore lead to the development of an insurrectionist ethos. In 1676, for example, the legislature had made it a legal offence for whites to expose blacks to Christian instruction.

Anglican clergymen, themselves prominent among the plantocracy, were generally of the opinion that blacks were intellectually incapable of comprehending the vision of the Christian. In 1710 Christopher Codrington had bequeathed his two estates in the parish of St John to the Church of England with a stipulation that they should be used to provide, among other things, some Christian instruction for slaves, but the Barbados Government continued to oppose such social policies. Indeed, during the seventeenth and early eighteenth centuries, Quakers were harassed and expelled from the island for enticing blacks to their meetings.

The arrival of Moravian and Methodist missionaries in 1765 and 1788 respectively, highlighted local divisions over the role of Christianity and education for slaves. The former sect was considered by slave owners to be ideologically compatible with their interests since central to their theology was the principle of working-class obedience to social superiors. The Methodists, however, articulated what planters believed to be social equalitarian theological principles, and became the bitter enemies of the slave-owning community. Generally abused and more than once driven out, Methodist preachers would return to their mission among slaves and developed with them a religious programme which came closest, among all missionaries, to support for anti-slavery thought – if not practice.

Concerned with the need to transform the image of the Anglican Church among blacks, the legislature provided in 1797 for Anglican ministers to offer slaves some religious training, but not within the Methodist framework. According to Claude Levy,

the gentry in Barbados began to think that there should be a place for blacks in the Church of England, and in 1822 the Council and Assembly supplied funds to erect an auxiliary chapel to accommodate the expected overflow of black worshippers from the Cathedral at Bridgetown.

In 1824, Parliament decided that Anglican religious training should be part of the preparation for emancipation, and created the diocese of Barbados, the Windward and Leeward Islands. This diocese was headed by Bishop William Hart Coleridge, who made some impact upon the development of religious and education policy.

Education for slaves, however, was generally conceived as religious instruction. The many schools and academies which developed in Barbados between 1733 when the Harrison Free School was established, and 1826 when the Central School of Bridgetown for girls opened its doors, did not accept blacks, slave or free – though the children of some free-coloured planters and merchants obtained, on occasions, rather controversial entry. The free coloureds generally provided for their own children, and sometimes blacks were accepted. When the Colonial Charity School was opened in 1818 as a public institution, financed by the free coloureds and free blacks, it provided lessons for more than fifty free-coloured and thirty slave children.

The Methodists, however, pioneered the policy of teaching slave children to read and write, while the Anglican clergy supported the planters' views that slave literacy was socially dangerous. In October 1823, Methodist minister William Shrewsbury, who had published a pamphlet critical of the pro-slavery mentality of the white community, had his chapel destroyed by angry whites, and in 1827, St Lucy parishioners publicly abused their unorthodox Anglican minister, W. M. Harte, for 'inculcating doctrines' of racial equality in the blacks which were 'inconsistent with their obedience to their masters and the policy of the island'. Harte was taken to court, found guilty of a misdemeanour and fined one shilling, but was pardoned by George IV after making a royal appeal.

During the closing years of slavery, the number of schools increased substantially owing to significantly larger sums of money being invested in education and religion by the imperial government. The Anglican Church was active in this development, and increased its numbers of schools from 8 in 1825 to 155 in 1834. In all, there were some 213 schools in Barbados in 1834 – more educational institutions per square mile than any other British West Indian colony.

In spite of imperial efforts at 'amelioration', however, blacks benefited only marginally in the expansion of educational facilities. Charles Latrobe, the British Government official Inspector of Education in the colonies, stated that in 1834 less than five of these schools accepted blacks. He stated from his West Indian experience that in 'no island has the distinction of colour been kept up with regard to the degree observable in Barbados'. His views were supported by W. G. Sewell who stated in the 1840s that in Barbados 'all schools are under church influence and are necessarily imbued with church prejudices'. In the area of political rights, Jews, free coloureds and free blacks were not given the franchise until 1831. It was after full emancipation in 1838 that blacks were able to participate more meaningfully in the educational facilities of the colony.

THE EMANCIPATION PROCESS

The 1833 Act

During the late 1820s, the opposition of slave owners, white as well as coloured, did not reduce the intensity of the imperial campaign for the abolition of slavery. In 1832, when Parliament developed an abolitionist stance, it was aware that the imposition of emancipation measures would not be an easy task. In order to facilitate the process, however, Parliament brought Barbados and the Windward Islands under a common governor-generalship in 1833, headed by Sir Lionel Smith. The task of the new Governor on arrival in Barbados in 1833 was to win the confidence of the slave owners, give assurances to the slaves, and illustrate to both groups that emancipation would not lead to any worsening of economic conditions in the colony. In fact, Smith, in his first address to the Barbados legislature in May 1833, intimated that his intention was to be 'attentive to the interests of the people of both races'.

Smith's line of argument did not gain him many friends among planters, who remained, in general, opposed to imperial legislative interventions in their domestic affairs. In May 1833, E. G. Stanley (Lord Derby), Secretary of State for Colonies, introduced the Emancipation Bill into the House of Commons. By then, Barbadian absentee planters in London, more aware than their colleagues at home of the mechanics of the parliamentary procedure, had accepted the inevitability of emancipation by imperial legislation. Stanley's introduction of the bill was flavoured by his insistence that only by British legislation could slavery be abolished, as West Indian slave owners, especially the Barbadians, remained recalcitrant on matters of slave amelioration. Parliament, he argued, in fulfilling its commitment to the slave population, had no choice but to impose the emancipation process upon the colonies.

The Emancipation Act was clear in its intention; on 1st August 1834, all slaves, black and coloured under the age of 6 years, would be totally and unconditionally emancipated; furthermore, all slaves over the age of 6 years were also freed, but under the stipulation that they were to serve their former owners as apprentices for the period of twelve years. The perception behind the twelve-year period of apprenticeship was that it would allow slaves to become adjusted gradually to the state of freedom. Also, it would give slave owners sufficient time to restructure their economies and adjust their social values and ideologies to the presence of free wage labourers. The Act carried further stipulations that wages were not to be paid to apprentices, except for additional work conducted in their free time. Masters were expected to carry on the slavery-days tasks of providing material subsistence for apprentices (see Table 10). Recognising that slave owners were likely to intensify the degree of labour exploitation during this transitional period, the Emancipation Act provided for the establishment of a judicial agency to mediate the conflicts that might arise. These special justices, or stipendiary magistrates, were appointed and paid by the Crown. It was hoped that their imperial mission would free their decisions from planter influence.

Finally accepting the fact of the emancipation process, West Indian slave owners prepared to do battle with the Colonial Office over its legislative details. One of their first demands was for compensation for the loss of property which emancipation represented. In July 1833, Parliament was informed by the Barbados Assembly:

As England is avowedly the author and was for a long time the chief gainer [of slavery] . . . let her bear her share of the penalty of expiation . . . Let a fair and just indemnity be first secured to the owner of the property which is to be put to risk . . . and then the Colonists will cooperate in accomplishing a real and effective emancipation of the slaves. All wise and well intentioned emancipationists will hail this alliance, conscious that without the cooperation and instrumentality of the resident Colonists, their object can only be attained through rapine violence and bloodshed, destroying all the elements of civilisation and ending in anarchy.

This policy demand was aggressive. If England, the Assembly added, was repenting 'the parts she has had in establishing and cherishing a system which she now thinks is criminal', then let her pay the cost of the newly found humanitarianism in the form of a cash indemnity to slave owners and not in the form of an adjustment loan.

The slave owners, supported by the London-based West India Committee, won this battle, and Parliament agreed to pay in cash to planters £20 million compensation money instead of the previously stated £15 million in loans. This concession to slave owners angered many elements within the humanitarian movement who perceived the £20 million as proof of Parliament's capitulation to immoral slave-owning

Table 10. *Apprentices' scale of allowances and commutations in Barbados*

Allowances	Commutations
30 lb. of roots per week or 10 pints of guinea corn to all apprentices above 10 years of age; to all under 10, half the quantity	To all apprentices above 16 years of age, $\frac{1}{2}$ acre of land for raising provisions; to all under 16, $\frac{1}{4}$ acre of land
2 lb. of fish per week to all apprentices	£1. 5s. a year or 17 days free of work
1 jacket or penistone 2 shirts or shifts 2 petticoats or trousers 1 cap or kerchief 6 skeins of thread	In money for each full-grown man or woman, 2 dollars 8 bits; for a second size man or woman, 2 dollars; for an apprentice 10–16 years of age, $17\frac{1}{2}$ bits; for apprentices from 10 years of age down, 15 bits
1 blanket every 2 years	1 dollar

Source: C. Levy, *Emancipation, Sugar and Federalism,* p. 60

interest, though the point made by a few members that perhaps slaves should also be compensated for past injustices was not pressed very hard. The humanitarians, none the less, now demanded from Parliament that the apprenticeship period be reduced from twelve to six years for field workers and to four years for artisans and domestic servants. This demand was also granted.

According to Levy, Barbadian slave owners were eager to augment their share of the £20 million voted by Parliament, and were prepared to forgo their right to apprenticed labour altogether in return for a larger per capita payment. But the imperial government was unwilling to make any new concessions, because it believed that the island already enjoyed an advantage over the other colonies as a result of its abundant labour supply. This argument suggests that Barbadians, unlike the imperial government, were not fully committed to an apprenticeship period as a prelude to full emancipation. In this regard, they might have entertained the possibility of moving in full freedom for blacks in 1834, as the Antigua and Bermuda slave owners did. The amount they received by way of compensation for their loss of slave property was £1$\frac{3}{4}$ million (see Table 11).

Table 11. *Compensation for emancipation of slaves in British West Indies*

Colony	Number of slaves	Total compensation (£)	Average compensation per slave (£. s. d.)
Jamaica	311,070	6,149,955	19. 15. 1
British Guiana	82,824	4,295,989	51. 17. 1
Barbados	83,150	1,719,980	20. 13. 8
Trinidad	20,657	1,033,992	51. 1. 1
Grenada	23,638	616,255	26. 1. 4
St Vincent	22,266	550,777	26. 10. 7
Antigua	29,121	425,547	14. 12. 3
St Lucia	13,291	334,495	25. 3. 2
St Kitts	19,780	329,393	16. 13. 0
Dominica	14,175	275,547	19. 8. 9
Tobago	11,589	233,875	23. 7. 0
Nevis	8,815	151,006	17. 2. 7
Bahamas	10,086	128,296	12. 14. 4
Montserrat	6,401	103,556	16. 3. 3
British Honduras	1,901	101,399	53. 6. 9
Virgin Islands	5,135	72,638	14. 1. 10
Bermuda	4,026	50,409	12. 10. 5

Sources: Parliamentary Papers, 1837–38, 44:154; C. Levy, *Emancipation, Sugar and Federalism*, p. 55

Refused any further concessions by Parliament in terms of compensation money, Barbadian slave owners decided to slow down the process of local legislation for black freedom with the intention of frustrating Parliament and asserting the strength of their dominance over their domestic constitutional affairs. As late as September 1833 they had not legislated emancipation, and the following month Governor Smith, showing excessive restraint, politely suggested that it was time for the legislature to implement Parliament's policy. The legislature refused to act, and towards the end of the year Governor Smith could only remind it that the compensation money allocated for the colony could only be obtained upon Parliament being convinced that it had performed its duty satisfactorily. It was in April 1834 that the legislature passed the bill instituting the Apprenticeship System as from 1st August 1834, and therein abolishing slavery.

Many aspects of the Barbados Act did not please Parliament, but it consented to the law in order to facilitate the speedy movement of the emancipation process. Planters retained full control of the police system and justices of the peace, two law and order agencies which Governor Smith was convinced would be used indiscriminately against apprentices. While Smith spoke of the 'unbending spirit of the planters', they in turn referred to his hasty and ill-informed attempts to undermine the foundations of their socio-economic world.

Governor Smith, meanwhile, took every opportunity to inform the Colonial Office that planters' refusal to apply the 'spirit of the new order' to their proceedings, and their determination to consolidate political, military and judicial power at the expense of apprentices, were likely to result in social unrest. In full awareness that any violent uprising of labourers would have to be effectively suppressed, Smith took the decision to dispatch several units of imperial soldiers to Bridgetown on 1st August, emancipation day. He took this precautionary measure as a show of imperial strength, and to impress upon the minds of blacks that emancipation was not a revolutionary measure, but a social reform. Apprentices were then told by Smith that 'the law is strong', and all those who did not work, 'the law will punish'. He had hoped to mark 1st August as a thanksgiving holiday, but the legislature, still not warming to the emancipation process, rejected his suggestion.

Emancipation day, then, though not representing true emancipation as far as apprentices were concerned, was a peaceful one. In Trinidad, there were riots in Port-of-Spain, and rumours of disturbances in the countryside as apprentices voiced their protest to the provisional freedom. Threats of disorder were also reported in Essequibo (British Guiana), and some unrest also occurred in St Kitts and Montserrat. Governor Smith, however, had the pleasure of informing the Colonial Office that on emancipation day Barbados was 'never more tranquil' though apprentices had verbally expressed their disenchantment with the restrictive conditions imposed upon their freedom.

APPRENTICESHIP AND 1838 EMANCIPATION

A survey of the slave population revealed that on 1st August 1834, 83,150 persons were freed – a labour force that would remain in excess of the economic needs of the sugar economy. Of those who became apprentices, 52,193 were categorised as praedials and 14,732 as non-praedials. The remainder were classified as children under 6 years who were fully freed, and 'worn out' and infirm persons. This meant that in terms of apprentices per square mile Barbados had a total of 501, while the closest figures to that density were recorded for Antigua and dependencies, 269, and St Kitts, 290. With this concentration of labourers on the island, most planters knew, in spite of their politically motivated statements to the contrary, that if they could maintain effective socio-political control of apprentices, the labour market would function in the interest of the plantation sector.

The Colonial Office was not satisfied with the provisions found within the Barbados legislation for the functioning of the Apprenticeship System. Planters remained hostile to the idea of imperially imposed emancipation, and as in the 1824 House of Assembly debate on the Colonial Office's ameliorative policies, made no attempts to suggest otherwise. They made no concessions to labourers but attempted to tighten their grip over the labour market. They implemented a series of measures designed to ensure that the level of conflict between themselves and apprentices over terms and conditions of work would increase rather than decrease. For example, they transferred non-praedials to the fields and so attempted to extend their apprenticeship to 1840 rather than 1838. They also insisted that many elite workers, such as boilermen and carpenters, should serve as apprentices until 1840.

In addition to these manoeuvres, the food rations offered apprentices remained among the most meagre in the West Indies in spite of the fact that they alone were experiencing expansion of sugar production and general economic buoyancy. Under criticisms from Secretary Thomas Spring-Rice, Stanley's replacement at the Colonial Office, the Barbados legislature amended their Emancipation Act in November, a mere three months after the Apprenticeship System had begun functioning. Their adjustments were minor:

(a) stipendiary magistrates could not investigate conditions in all prisons;
(b) watchmen and cattle tenders had their hours of work reduced to the standard 45 hours per week (5 days of 9 hours, excluding Saturday and Sunday);
(c) non-praedials would still be transferred to the fields for insubordination, though they would still be freed in 1838.

By 1835, when Lord Glenelg took over at the Colonial Office, the tone of discussions about the functioning of the Apprenticeship System was undergoing substantial changes. Glenelg, under the guidance of James Stephen, attempted to intimidate Barbadian planters by suggesting that the Apprenticeship was more about slaves slowly becoming free men than about slave owners adjusting to a wage labour system. He implied, furthermore, that it should be terminated prematurely as a just concession to workers. Robert Bowcher Clarke, considered the liberal-minded Assemblyman among the planter elite, sought to defend the Assembly's right to maintain legislative control over the Apprenticeship System. He recognised, none the less, that it was a system which by design bred discord between apprentice and planter, and suggested that its survival was not necessarily in the colony's long-term interest. As Solicitor-General for the colony, Clarke was positioned to assert intense pressure upon the legislature; as a result he sought to show the House that it would do the colony no harm by embracing the perspective of Lord Glenelg.

The reports of Crown-appointed special (stipendiary) magistrates suggest that it was not uncommon for apprentices to be given inadequate food rations, driven to work beyond normal time without proper rest periods, and punished with imprisonment for offences that would have been ignored by many planters during the slavery era. Furthermore, they point towards the deterioration of work relations on estates, the widespread abandonment by planters of the paternalist ideology which was considered part of their traditional authority, and the hardening of judicial attitudes towards workers. Meanwhile, planters complained about the insolence, insubordinate and lawless social manner of apprentices, in addition to their slack attitudes towards work, duties and civic responsibilities. In spite of these attacks upon the character of apprentices, the volume of Barbados sugar exports increased from an estimated 17,234 tons in 1835 to 23,679 tons in 1838.

Apprentices, however, not surprisingly expressed in no uncertain terms the desire to obtain their full freedom by self-purchase before the dates set by law for final emancipation. But few of them were able to achieve this end. The fragmented data show that during the first year of apprenticeship some 907 apprentices were freed – the vast majority of these were cases of employers voluntarily surrendering their legal rights in labourers. The fact that over 70 per cent of these voluntary discharges of apprentices occurred in the Bridgetown area suggests that the sugar planters showed less compassion on the question of black freedom than their urban counterparts. Furthermore, only about forty apprentices, most of whom were from Bridgetown, were able to purchase their freedom during this year, which suggests that the plantation sector proved relatively more rigid in its responses to emancipation. Apprentices willing to purchase their freedom were often forced to resort to all manner of trickery so as to obtain a low valuation from Justices – sometimes by faking infirmity, sickness and old age.

Undoubtedly – and this point has been stressed by historians – it was the 14,000 children under the age of 6 who were fully freed in 1834, that added greatly to the number of social destitutes in the colony. Parents were not keen to offer their children's labour to plantations, and employers responded by abandoning any responsibility for infants within their sphere of influence. Workers struggled to provide for children during the apprenticeship, and since planters took up responsibility only for those they employed, the dependent part of the black family felt the pinch. The result was that the level of infant mortality, on the decrease during the final years of slavery, began once again an upward path. Reverend Thomas Parry took up the campaign against this aspect of the apprenticeship before becoming Bishop of Barbados, but recognised that his efforts bore little fruit.

In the early part of 1836, the questions of child abandonment and rising mortality became focuses around which criticisms of the Apprenticeship System revolved. Governor Smith went on the offensive and abused planters for not accepting their social responsibility to the defenceless, and for using children as pawns in the bargaining process between themselves and adult workers. In order not to give the imperial government such an excuse to abolish the Apprenticeship System, planters encouraged their legislature to pass an act which made it unlawful for the plantations to apprentice children or for parents to offer their children as apprentices. With this issue behind them, planters settled down to making a positive evaluation of the apprenticeship. Their economy had not suffered as a result and they felt assured of a future supply of cheap, reliable landless labourers to work their estates.

By early 1838, the Colonial Office seemed determined to abolish completely the apprenticeship that year. It was persuasively argued in Parliament that planters were making a mockery of this transition period by preserving some of the worst aspects of their slave management, and were threatening to show the futility of the Emancipation Act of 1833. In Barbados, Governor MacGregor did well to convince the legislature that it should abolish the system, and that it should support the general plan of action outlined by Glenelg. His argument rested on the notions that labour would continue to be plentiful, and that it would assist planters to establish some measure of moral authority over labourers.

The Solicitor-General, Robert Clarke, was also quite eloquent and brilliant in the articulation of these ideas. He was instrumental in persuading the House to recognise that the creation of 'a happy and contented . . . community of free men' depended upon a speedy abolition of the system of apprenticed labour. Also, that a future order of social cohesion and political stability, which such an abolition would enhance, was infinitely more valuable to all Barbadians than the extra units of sugar production which planters sought to extract from the apprentices. Bishop Coleridge added to this campaign, and pleaded with the legislature to exercise vision on the matter. In May 1838, the Barbados legislature passed a law for the complete emancipation of all apprentices to take effect on 1st August that year – two years earlier than was provided for in the 1834 law of emancipation. On 2nd June, Governor MacGregor issued the statement given in Figure 3.

Some planters, however, continued to express fears of a labour shortage arising from a workers' boycott of their enterprises. Many blacks believed that the circumstances under which freedom would be attained – hardships in obtaining land and acceptable wages – would still ensure their socio-political subordination to employers. In spite of the widespread recognition that material living standards would fall owing to inadequate wages, many saw freedom as the opening of considerable possibilities – such as migration, family constitution and educational development. Discussions of the possibilities of social unrest were commonplace, especially within the Governor's circle; yet once again, as on 1st August 1834, this did not happen.

Final emancipation day passed quietly and peaceably. No riots or reports of serious disturbances occurred. Many blacks attended church services in

BARBADOS.

His Excellency Major General Sir Evan John Murray MacGregor, Bart., Companion of the Most Honorable Military Order of the Bath, Knight Commander of the Royal Hanoverian Guelphic Order, Governor and Commander-in-Chief in and over the Islands of Barbados, Saint Vincent, Grenada, Tobago, St. Lucia, and Trinidad, &c. &c. &c.

[L. S.]
E. J. M. MacGregor,
Governer.

A PROCLAMATION.

WHEREAS it hath pleased Almighty God, great in Council and mighty in Works, whose eyes are open upon all the Sons of Men, disposing and turning them as seemeth best to his Godly Wisdom, to incline the Legislature of this Colony to terminate altogether, by a Public Act, the System of Apprenticeship, and thus to accomplish, before the period prescribed by Law, the entire Emancipation of a large portion of its Inhabitants: And whereas it is of the Lord's blessing on human agency that great undertakings are brought to a happy completion; and that therefore it is our bounden duty, on the present eventful occasion, openly to acknowledge in all thankfulness of heart His gracious interposition, and to implore the continuance, over this Land, of His providential guidance and protection: I do hereby, by and with the advice of Her Majesty's Privy Council, set apart the First Day of August next, as a day of Solemn Thanksgiving and Devout Supplication to Almighty God, and do require that it be duly observed in all Churches, Chapels, and other places of Public Worship throughout the Land, as becometh a considerate and Christian People.

Given under my Hand and Seal this second day of July, One thousand eight hundred and thirty eight, and in the second year of Her Majesty's Reign.

GOD SAVE THE QUEEN!

By His Excellency's Command,
C. T. CUNNINGHAM,
Col. Sec.

Fig. 3   Proclamation terminating the apprenticeship system in Barbados, issued 2nd June 1838

the morning, and took part in festive activities for the remainder of the day. The militia and imperial soldiers were out in force to ensure that blacks did not heave off their chains with any turbulent behaviour. Barbados, then, did not begin its history as a constitutionally free society with an experience of violent conflict. The inequality of power distribution, however, remained such that Governor MacGregor considered it necessary to issue a proclamation on 13th August that year in order to reassure blacks that it was 'absolutely impossible that any of them can be compelled to revert to their past condition, either as apprentices or slaves'.

ECONOMIC TRENDS

Twenty years after the American Revolution, Barbados was annually exporting more sugar to England than it was in the twenty years before. The value of these exports was also increasing steadily. Planters rarely spoke of economic decline, though they were obviously aware that profit margins were no more than modest and markets more competitive. The 1807 slave trade abolition sent no negative tremors through their economy, though the American embargo and the outbreak of war in 1812 did. Planters had good grounds to believe that their trade would be adversely affected by American pirates.

One major response to the reduction in food supplies during the American Revolution was the allocation of greater amounts of plantation lands to the planting of food crops, which meant that only minor production adjustments were required in 1812 in order to ensure adequate food supplies. In that year the first Agricultural Society was formed by planters. Among its objectives was the improvement of land utilisation techniques, increase of labour productivity, and the enhancement of crop diversification. The Society claimed some success by suggesting that the increased production of sugar after the American and Napoleonic Wars had more to do with improved techniques (plough) and greater fertilisation (guano) than with a reduction in acreage under foodstuffs.

Having recovered from the destruction of crops and equipment that was a feature of the Bussa Rebellion (1816), the price of sugar on the world market began to decline from the artificially high levels at the time of the Napoleonic War. The 1820s was a period of decline and discomfort for sugar planters, though the adverse economic trends should not be used as the basis of a 'fall of the planter class' thesis. Economic indicators were certainly negative, but planters did not believe that they were experiencing any long-term structural decline. It is true that planters produced calculations which showed that the 1831 average price of sugar of 28s. 8d. per cwt was 6d. below the average cost of production including freight, but plantations remained economically viable. Most large estates were still able to cover their costs and make modest profits. An average range of profit of 4 to 8 per cent was common during the depressed 1820s, but there was evidence throughout of increasing productivity. This trend, planters believed, illustrated that their plantation operations were still attractive propositions. As a result, according to J. R. Ward, they 'still sought to maintain their capital and go on making sugar' with confidence in the future.

Barbadian sugar planters, like their counterparts in other West Indian colonies, attributed the depressed conditions of the 1820s to falling prices resulting from the introduction of low-cost East Indian, Cuban and Brazilian sugar to the European market. Also, their market position was aggravated by the reduction in their traditional tariff preference. In addition, by the 1820s they were fully convinced that their colony could not produce sugar as cheaply as their major competitors whose lands were more fertile and extensive. Even the colony of Trinidad, which was acquired by the English at the end of the 1790s, produced a crop in 1825 which was 12 cwt per slave as opposed to Barbados' $4\frac{1}{2}$ cwt per slave.

The early 1830s saw the intensification of the depressed conditions of the 1820s. Though legal trade was allowed with the United States in 1830, a development hailed by the Barbadians, the evidence of pending emancipation led to a reduction in confidence by metropolitan moneylenders, and planters experienced a reduction in credit levels that year. The hurricane of 1831 which was dubbed 'The Great Hurricane' added to this dismal condition by taking the lives of some 1,590 slaves and destroying an estimated £1,603,880 worth of property. The British Government made a donation of £50,000, and as a mark of goodwill temporarily lifted the customary and controversial $4\frac{1}{2}$ per cent custom duty.

In spite of the 1831 catastrophe, the colony experienced bumper harvests in 1832 and 1833, and talk of economic recovery was not uncommon. Sugar production levels continued to rise through the 1830s (Table 12), but planters were aware, none the less, that as their returns on capital increased, the traditional structures of their economy were being torn down. In 1832 the colony exported 13,325 tons of sugar, and its total export values were £408,363, while in 1838 it exported 23,679 tons of sugar, and had total export values of £960,368. Though a rapidly increasing import bill during the 1830s reduced the value of benefits derived from rising exports, planters in Barbados, unlike most of their colleagues in the other islands, were

Table 12. *Volume changes in sugar production in British West Indies,*
1831–34, 1835–38

Colony	Percentage of increase or decrease	Colony	Percentage of increase or decrease
Barbados	+24	Jamaica	−15
British Guiana	+ 9	Grenada	−20
St Vincent	− 5	Dominica	−33
Trinidad	− 7	Tobago	−36
St Lucia	−12	Nevis	−40
St Kitts	−13	Montserrat	−50

Source: C. Levy, *Emancipation, Sugar and Federalism,* p. 59

satisfied that emancipation had not adversely affected their economies and, if anything, it had brought some degree of prosperity. After 1838, sugar producers prepared to strengthen their colonial position, and contemporary observers, far from suggesting the ruin of this class, made reference to its socio-economic revitalisation.

CHAPTER SIX

Crisis of the free order, 1838–1897

CONSTRAINTS TO SOCIAL REFORM

If emancipation represented a major battle won by blacks and the British anti-slavery movement, then it would not be unreasonable to suggest that in Barbados slave owners might have benefited from their defeat. During the period after 1816, the year that slaves had attempted to free themselves by armed rebellion, the imperial government made some effort to loosen, even if slightly, the firm grip which the slave-owning community held over the black population. On 16th May 1838, the Assembly's Act for the abolition of the Apprenticeship System meant that slave owners had no choice in removing the traditional legal forms of socio-political control. However, neither the blacks nor the Colonial Office were surprised when they immediately began the task of reconstructing a new machinery of labour domination and the formulation of policies for the control of the new social order. These measures were designed to ensure that the plantations survived by having access to a reliable supply of cheap and subordinate labour.

The spirit of emancipation, as perceived by the Colonial Office, was resisted by planters in the years after 1838 as tenaciously as in the years before. Both blacks and the British abolitionist movement had hoped for an emancipation that would result in 'humane and amicable labour relations'; instead they were confronted with the stubborn determination on the part of planters to retain effective control over the labour market in a manner which was reminiscent of slavery. In addition to a failure to relate to the freed blacks in an equalitarian manner, sugar planters, who still dominated government at all levels, refused to place the kind of importance on the pro-worker rehabilitation social policies, such as education, health, poor relief and housing, that the imperial government had wished for. Rather, the planter legislature concentrated upon the task of strengthening social control over blacks since it feared that the abolition of the slave laws opened up avenues along which blacks might wish to travel to the detriment of the white community.

The power of the planter class and hence the socio-economic domination of white elite community, was undoubtedly based upon its ownership and control of economic resources and the administrative structures of government. The sugar interest remained predominant and therefore the legislature was mobilised into action in order to protect that interest as perceived by sugar planters. The first and major consideration was the question of retaining an adequate supply of disciplined labour; around this objective all other matters revolved. Indeed, it was the determination of the legislature to defend the sugar interests that defined the limits and nature of government policies in the years after emancipation, rather than considerations of restructuring the new order along lines of reasonable representation for all sections of the society. Not surprisingly, historians have made much of the fact that two months after the abolition of the Apprenticeship the legislature sent for approval at the Colonial Office, Acts designed to

(a) authorise the appointment of rural constables;
(b) prevent the increase of vagrancy;
(c) prevent the occurrence of tumults and riotous assemblies.

Robert Bowcher Clarke, Solicitor-General, and owner of several plantations, who had shown noteworthy liberalism in his judgements during the Apprenticeship, became a principal defender of the planters' vision of the role of blacks in the new order. In his portfolio as a law and order man, he was respected by whites for his allegedly skilful judicial mind. In commenting on the above-mentioned pieces of legislation, Clarke spoke of the need for 'preserving peace in the negro villages', and checking 'the spirit of litigation with which the negro character is strongly imbued'. Indeed, he was instrumental in giving legislative form to the repressive attitudes and opinions of former slave-owners, and therefore was a leading architect in the abortion of the hopes which emancipation offered for substantive change.[1]

In August 1838, then, some 83,000 blacks, 12,000 coloureds and 15,000 whites, embarked on a social course which the ruling elite hoped to charter. Sugar planters remained in a monopolistic position as far as the economy was concerned and assumed that their political authority should not be questioned. In 1838 only one of the 297 major sugar plantations was owned by a non-white, namely Ellis Castle (480 acres). This number had increased to six by 1860, but fell away to no more than two by 1900. In Bridgetown, the capital, whites owned 75 per cent of properties of an annual value of £30 or over; of the remaining 25 per cent, coloureds held an overwhelming share. Whites did not intend to undergo any reduction in their wealth or power, and considered it necessary to intensify the use of the ideology of racism in order to further distance themselves from coloureds and blacks. Neither did they intend to loosen their grip upon decision making within public institutions. In 1838, Codrington College and Harrisons School, two leading educational institutions, were still refusing coloureds and blacks, and the Anglican clergy showed no serious signs of de-segregating churches.

The limitations which planter government imposed upon reforms in education for freed blacks, were illustrative of those found in other areas. First, planters did not accept the imperial ruling that basic secular education for blacks should be a prerequisite for freedom. Rather, they held to the traditional concept that education would create among blacks certain unrealistic expectations and therefore reduce their willingness to be productive workers. Second, they argued that educational instruction would make it more difficult for blacks to accept their subordinate social status. That the leaders of the 1816 rebellion were described as literate, seems to have hardened this view among the planters.

Emancipation, none the less, opened up possibilities for blacks to pursue educational development. There developed a 'cult' of education among the older generation who insisted upon their childrens' acquisition of literate skills. The 1838 report of an education commission stated that 'on the part of the labourers themselves there appears to be generally a greater wish to secure for their children the blessings of education'. But as blacks' demand for education was expanding, the financial base of educational programmes was contracting owing to imperial reduction in interest and planter–government indifference. Church of England financial contributions diminished considerably in the 1840s, and the imperial education grant issued in 1834 was terminated in 1845.

While the Governor and the radical coloured activist, Samuel Prescod, called upon planters to vote moneys for educational development, the Assembly failed to respond enthusiastically. The £750 reluctantly voted for the education of the 'poor' in 1846 for three years was considered meagre, if not insulting to educational interest. Planters remained more concerned with religious instruction for blacks as part of their renewed campaign to 'improve their morality and character, and to create a docile labour force'. When Governor Grey suggested in 1845 that the education of blacks should be of a secular nature, he immediately incurred the wrath of the Assembly, as well as that of prominent Anglican clergymen. Black children, they insisted, should be taught how to labour honestly and 'fear God', while schools for white children were maintained from vestry funds, in addition to receiving money votes from the Assembly.

This state of affairs remained largely unaltered when Bishop Mitchinson submitted his report on education in 1875. His opposition to the status quo led to the perhaps misguided opinion that he was anti-planter in terms of his social visions and attitudes. This report, none the less, led to the 1878 Education Act which represented the basis of a modernising approach to working-class education. It provided for the removal of responsibility for education from vestries to central government, established the basis for compulsory elementary education, removed financial aid for schools that were exclusively white, and established a Board of Education to manage and develop educational facilities and instruments. It took government, therefore, some forty years after emancipation to accept legislative responsibility for the education of the black working class within the framework of a comprehensive, structured policy.

The development of government policy on social welfare was also hampered by the presence of planter opposition and an application of extreme conservative attitudes towards ex-slaves. The official committee on poor relief reported in 1844 that poverty among a major section of the ex-slaves was increasing and manifested in rising infant mortality rates. The report illustrated that vestry poor-relief facilities were undoubtedly inadequate for the new era, as plantations had relinquished their respons-ibility for their sick, infirm and aged persons at emancipation; only a central government policy could cope with the care of these and other such socially disadvantaged persons. Since the vestry had no legal obligation to provide poor relief, and these bodies were managed by planters, many persons were refused assistance on the basis of their having a labour record which was considered to be unexemplary.

The legislature moved slowly and reluctantly in the piecemeal establish-ment of public welfare facilities. In 1844 it provided £4,079 for the construction of a lunatic asylum for the mentally ill, but still holding to the opinion that the poverty of the unemployed poor was self-imposed, continued to pay less attention to poor relief. In addition, the matter of public health facilities was not given governmental priority. The expansion of slums around Bridgetown after 1838 and the unplanned growth of plantation-based villages contributed greatly to already known insanitary conditions about the island. Minor epidemics of dysentery, yellow fever, whooping cough, smallpox and measles during the 1840s did not jerk the legislature into action, even though the mortality rate was recorded as high – especially among black youths. There had been a Board of Health operative since 1833, but it was assigned the task of using the quarantine technique to prevent the spread of contagious disease; preventive medicine, increasingly popular in England, did not figure prominently in government policy.

It was fear of cholera, already widespread in some parts of the Caribbean, notably Jamaica, which during the mid-century forced government to look more closely at a public health policy. This disease, noted for striking down not only poor blacks but whites of all classes, was perhaps the catalyst which government seems to have required. The Public Health Act of 1851 addressed matters of sanitation, and gave health commissioners extensive powers to search and investigate communities throughout the island. The Act was amended in 1853, extending the powers of commissioners in their preventative measures, but in 1854, the disease struck, killing more than 20,000 people. Because of high urban mortality levels, Bridgetown was reported to be the most insanitary town in the West Indies – its water supply was polluted, open cesspools and canals were being used to remove sewage from households, gutters were clogged and stinking, and filth lay about even major thoroughfares.[2]

After the epidemic, Governor Colebrooke dismissed the Board of Health and appointed a new Board. This action was followed by the 1856 Public Health Act which illustrates clearly, for the first time, the planters' recognition that a centralised public health machinery was not only necessary, but vital. Bridgetown was divided into seven districts for health purposes with two medical officers appointed to each; the General Hospital came under greater administration control by the central government, and for the first time, the basics of health studies were included in school curricula.

While social welfare measures always seem to have been taken too late by central government, in contrast, law and order provisions were hastily put in place. Indeed, the legislature was at its most productive during the decade after emancipation as civic order bills dominated the proceedings of the Assembly. The abolition of the slave codes, and the removal of planters' personal policing powers, meant that government became the central law-enforcing agency. In 1834, a police force was legislatively constituted, and the island was divided into seven districts for police administration; the Bridgetown district, as well as the six rural districts, each had its own police force, in addition to a prison. Between 1838 and 1850, law and order expenditures represented between 50 and 60 per cent of all government expenditures, while education, health and poor relief amounted to no more than 10 per cent.

In addition, police magistrates were given extensive powers over the ex-slave population, which they generally exercised in favour of the white community. Vagrancy laws were worded so as to give police the right to arrest blacks in transit at any time and confine them to prison. Laws against 'riotious assemblies' were used by legal officers to break up even civic or ceremonial gatherings by blacks. These provisions constituted a successful frontal legislative assault upon the rights which blacks had gained in 1838. Though Governor Smith had insisted that the legislature would never act 'except for themselves', his successor did little to prevent the erosion of black civil rights. It was left to the blacks, and their coloured allies, to mount effective protest against this development.

LABOURERS AND PEASANTS

Labour arrangements

In one respect the imperial government assisted in perpetrating the tendency among planters to perceive ex-slaves as servile individuals when it offered to supply them after emancipation with juvenile labour from English prisons or Africans from captured slave vessels. Robert Clarke, replying to the imperial offer on the Assembly's behalf, stated that colonists would not wish to be accused, once again, of enslaving whites, nor would they wish to have African 'savages' in their midst, especially after they had removed the dependency of their economy on the slave trade. The offer, moreover, even if a gesture, was reflective of the imperial government's determination to ensure that emancipation did not undermine the plantation system by placing its labour supply in jeopardy.

In 1838, both workers and their employers were unaccustomed to the spirit and practice of free collective bargaining over the terms and conditions of employment. Blacks wanted what they considered to be a fair wage for their labour, and un-slavelike conditions of work. Planters believed that blacks tended to over-value the worth of their labour and that some measure of coercion was necessary in order to maintain a reliable supply. Conflict of interest was therefore inevitable, and both groups showed signs of digging in their heels for a struggle over the labour culture that was to evolve. Furthermore, it was clear to all parties concerned that the labour market would also be influenced by non-economic forces, as employers found difficulty in coming to terms with the fact that they were required to sit down and negotiate with their former slaves.

In 1838, the Barbados legislature declared the planters' intentions towards labour in the passing of the Masters and Servant Act, which became known as the notorious Contract Law. Other colonies had resorted to contract laws in order to maintain legal control over the freed blacks, and the Barbados law was worded from the Antiguan law which had been passed in 1834. According to the Barbados legislation, any worker who provided five days of continuous labour to a planter was deemed as being hired for one year. The worker could reside on the plantation, and occupy cottages provided by the planter. The law also made provision for a legal dissolution of the contract by either party by giving one month's notice. It was the consequences of contract-breaking which showed the extent to which workers were placed at a substantial disadvantage. If a worker terminated his contract he was required to remove himself and his belongings from the plantation premises. If he was dismissed by the planter, then he was entitled only to the value of crops planted by himself on plantation lands allotted him for use – the value of which was determined by a Justice of the Peace from the parish in which the estate was located.

The 1838 law also provided for the socio-political control of the hired worker during working hours. It is here that the legislation transcended mere labour supply considerations and touched upon issues of public order. If a worker behaved in a manner considered by the planter as insubordinate he could be evicted from his cottage, and the plantation, without wage compensation, and imprisoned. In addition, workers could be imprisoned for foul language, gambling or forming illegal combinations. These provisions, in a very real way, returned to the planter some rights of social control which government had fully assumed responsibility for under the emancipation laws. Planters implemented this last provision under a clause within the Contract Law which gave them the right to employ private policemen for their estates.

Governor MacGregor was not satisfied with the Contract Law; he considered it unfair to workers, and believed that it was implemented within the spirit of the old slave codes. That five days' continuous labour should be considered the basis of a year's hiring was, in his opinion, grossly unreasonable to workers, and the hiring of special policemen no more than an attempt to bully and intimidate them into submission. He succeeded in persuading the Colonial Office to disallow the law, as well as the vagrancy law, which planters were already using rather indiscriminately. On the other hand, he supported the planters' call for the removal of special (stipendiary) magistrates on the grounds that they rarely knew enough of local circumstances to adjudicate fairly in master–worker conflicts.

Conflicts over wage levels and terms of labour, however, created the context for the passing of a mildly modified contract law in 1840. Workers believed that the 10d. per day offered by estates for field work was too low and planters seemed unwilling to negotiate. In nearby Trinidad and Guiana, wages fluctuated between 20 and 25 pence per day, and knowledge of this fact confirmed the impression among workers in Barbados that their employers were determined to pay 'slave' wages. In addition, many were prepared to work no more than a few days a week so as to undermine the contract law, even in cases where employers were prepared to offer higher wages for a week's work.

Under pressure from employers, and unaware that the imperial government had disallowed the law, Governor MacGregor informed workers that five days of continuous labour constituted a verbal contract for one year, and that only a month's notice was required to terminate the agreement. Once again workers would forfeit their right to estate housing and use of its lands if they did not contract on the estate on which they lived. Correspondence reached the Governor in October 1838 that the law had been rejected, and estate life was once again brought to crisis levels. MacGregor accepted the imperial ruling, and suggested to workers that they should meanwhile make verbal but unofficial agreements with employers and continue to negotiate for better conditions. This call had some positive results and by November, most estates were reported to be in a productive and satisfactory state.

The modified Contract Law of 1840 provided for contracts of one month instead of one year. In addition, the worker was now required to pay his employer a rent for plantation buildings and land he used which amounted to one-sixth of his wages. This law, therefore, transformed the free wage worker into a 'located' plantation tenant. Of course, if the worker was not a tenant on the plantation for which he worked no deductions were made from his wages. For most of 1840, wage levels for resident fieldhands fluctuated between 9 and 11 pence per day, and for non-residents one shilling. The tenant was required to provide labour exclusively for the estate on which he resided, and in return, employers reduced the rent on cottages and ground provisions. Irregular labour could lead to the tenant's eviction with one month's notice from the estate manager.

Blacks seeking to make the best of these limited conditions would attempt to move from estate to estate in search of lighter work and better wages, but even this strategy encountered opposition from planters, government and imperial officials. When the 1840 law was finally accepted by the British Parliament, there was no doubt that it allowed for planters to coerce blacks on a labour market that already favoured the plantation. But the Colonial Office, perhaps idealistically, believed that within it, none the less, resided elements for the future establishment of mutually acceptable labour relations.

The emergence of the tenantry system as the main institution for adjusting labour relations was the logical outgrowth of two circumstances:

(a) during slavery, slaves were never able to own their own homes or accumulate property of much worth;
(b) the planter community had a virtual monopoly of farming land.

These two circumstances combined to create a situation whereby after emancipation a workforce which did not own homes, or have access to land, was created with an inbuilt dependency on the plantation and, by extension, on the white community for survival. Furthermore, the tenantry system was considered ideal and natural by most planters given the 'total plantation' structure of their economy. The system provided planters with an adequate supply of labour, and afforded them considerable control over that labour.

But the requirements of adequate supply and effective legal control of labour were not all that planters wanted; they also wanted socio-political control over labourers. In order to attain these ends, planters made adjustments to the located labour system by penalising tenants who did not provide regular work to the estate. Any tenant who absented himself from work between Monday and Friday was liable to have 5 pence or 10 pence deducted from his wages for every day absent. This development represented a major increase in the degree of coercion applied to workers. In 1841 a police magistrate summed up the tenantry rent system as follows:

The conditions of tenancy, as they exist at present, are, I conceive, inconsistent, in a great measure, with the free agency of the labourer; his action is circumscribed. The labourer received a house from his employer, of which he is to be tenant without rent as long as he gives his continuous service to the employer; but if he be absent without reasonable cause from his work, a rent is charged for that day, and in most cases an exhorbitant rent, so as to compel his constant service.

Workers had little room in which to manoeuvre; they were given the choice of starving, working under unsatisfactory conditions, or migrating. Rapid population growth over the century increased labour supply to the estates. In spite of this level of coercion, production hours did not diminish since, as Governor Colebrooke stated, there 'exists little diversity of employment' for labourers. Rural unemployment was a structural feature of the economy, and the already severe competition for limited tenantries increased rather than decreased. The located labourers system, and rent exactions for absent days, continued until June 1937, when the Contract Law was repealed.[3]

Emigration

During the slavery period, Barbados was one base from which the colonisation and settlement of Trinidad, Guiana and the Windward Islands was launched. Blacks, both slave and free, were part of this process, and assisted the slave community in developing a considerable knowledge of regional affairs. In addition, Barbadian runaway slaves regularly fled to these neighbouring colonies, and together with those blacks who worked on the schooners that plied between the colonies, contributed to the store of information available to plantation hands on economic conditions in the region. Over time, these groups formed contacts and established a regional perspective for survival strategies. This information represented the basis on which blacks built their emigration movement after 1838.

Information received by Barbadian workers suggested that wages in Trinidad and Guiana were much higher than at home, and that in those colonies there was relatively unrestricted access to farming land, and at lower prices. Such factors alone were sufficient to entice Barbadians to migrate to these colonies once the tenantry system had taken on the image of a new form of slavery. From the days of the Apprenticeship, Guianese planters had expressed an interest in attracting Barbadian workers; from this time they had also incurred the disapproval of Barbadian governors and sugar planters. Governors feared that able-bodied migrants would abandon their families and other dependants who would then add to the list of poor-law recipients. Planters feared a drain upon their prime labour stock, and subsequent increases in wage levels. Not surprisingly, the legislature passed a law to prevent persons enticing inhabitants to 'desert their homes and families and helpless infants'. This law provided that the would-be migrant had first to obtain a ticket of leave from the vestry of the parish in which he resided, which was empowered to refuse the issue of such a pass if it believed that the applicant would leave any dependants unprovided for.

But the Guianese planters saw in the Barbadian worker, a seasoned, hardworking colonist who was prepared to tackle frontier conditions. As such, in 1838, their legislature voted £400,000 local currency for the sponsoring of an immigration programme to attract Barbadian and other

West Indian workers. Barbadian planters went on the offensive and launched a propaganda campaign to the effect that the Dutch and English planters in Guiana were preparing to re-enslave blacks, and that the majority of migrants would die of yellow fever, malaria or cholera within one year. In addition, the Barbados legislature provided that a fine of £50 would be imposed upon any person who attempted to encourage workers into emigration.

Workers responded by accusing the legislature of tampering with their rights as free persons to travel and work where they so desired. Governor MacGregor denied that this was the intention, and set about to ensure that emigration schemes were bona fide and that facilities on ships were adequate. By 1840, hundreds of predominantly male workers had departed for Trinidad and Guiana. In that year, the Barbados legislature, defending the interest of the plantation sector, passed a law which made it illegal for emigration agents to function in Barbados, which was not disallowed by the Colonial Office, though pro-emigration lobbies in Barbados argued that it infringed upon workers' rights to move about the region in search of betterment. By January 1841, however, over 2,500 workers had departed for Guiana, and by 1870 at least 16,000 had emigrated to various colonies.

Not all migrants, though, turned their backs totally upon the land of their 'nativity'. For most, migration was one way of socio-economic betterment and not an anti-Barbados action. The evidence on the Guiana migration shows, for example, that Barbadians rarely committed themselves to any estate for a length of time, but attempted to use the variation in seasons between the two countries to their advantage. The Guiana immigration report for 1883 stated:

They seldom labour for more than limited periods on sugar estates. A large proportion of them arrive in the colony after the end of June when work becomes scarce in Barbados, and return to the island to spend Christmas and crop-time, while large numbers of them remain in Georgetown to swell the ranks of the unemployed.

This pattern of seasonal migration, then, reflected both workers' regional perceptions of the labour market as well as an attachment to their island. Though some workers went as far as Cuba, Curaçao and Brazil, migration was not an attractive option for most, and the 110,000 blacks recorded in the 1871 census attest to this. Most workers settled in to make the best of the limited opportunities offered in the colony, and this assisted in ensuring that the plantation system survived as the predominant socio-economic unit.[4]

Peasants

The ability of ex-slaves to cement their freedom with the ownership of land was limited by four major factors, all beyond their control. First, the plantation sector had a monopoly over land ownership and land use patterns: 441 of the 508 estates in 1842 were in control of 81 per cent of the 106,000 acres of land which comprised the colony. Second, the planters refused to provide land for sale to workers as policy; there were no Crown lands, as in Jamaica, which could be squatted on by workers. Third, the price of arable land was prohibitively high, which meant that the accumulated wages of workers could hardly allow them to enter the land market (see Table 13). Fourth, governments – both local and imperial – were committed to a policy of creating from the slave population a landless proletariat rather than a peasantry.

The plantation sector in Barbados was clearly victorious in confining peasant activity and formation to levels tolerable to sugar production and the white community's conception of the role of blacks within the economy. In 1845, 30,000 people provided regular labour to the estates. These workers, who were offered the lowest wage in the region by a major sugar economy, could not be expected to make cash down-payments on land. Some did manage, however, to obtain freehold ownership of small amounts of land, and functioned socio-economically as peasants. They were few in number, and posed no problem, political or economic, for the planter class. In 1842, the police magistrate of the St Michael parish gave the following account on the factors limiting peasant development:

Little progress has been made by the labourers in establishing themselves as freeholders, not from any disinclination on their part to become so, but,

Table 13. *Land values in the West Indies in the late 1840s*

Colony	Average price range per acre (£)
Dominica	1–3
Trinidad	1–13
Guiana	1–30
Jamaica	4–20
Antigua	40–80
Barbados	60–125

circumstanced as our island is, there is little probability of any great number being able to obtain freeholds. The reason is obvious; there is not in the whole island a spot of waste land fit for cultivation; and as the land is principally divided into plantations, the proprietors are not likely to sell off small plots for that purpose; and there being no public lands available; it is plain that freeholders to any extent cannot be established in this country.

The tenantry system did allow ex-slaves some access to land, and plantation owners were, in general, keen to allocate marginal lands for their use in return for a resident labour supply. But the insecurity of land use under this arrangement, plus the fact that land was rented in return for regular labour, meant that ex-slaves could hardly have perceived this form of access to plantation land as an effective way of entrenching their socio-economic freedom, and insulating themselves from the coercive powers of planters. At best, the tenantry system was an extension of what had gone before during slavery – where planters in order to reduce their food bills and allocate good arable land to sugar, allowed slaves to cultivate small plots around their homes. The tenantry system did allow some ex-slaves to become, over time, leasehold users of land without offering their labour to estates, but this development should be distinguished from the socio-economic implications of owning land by freehold. None the less, it has been estimated that by 1897 about 8,500 of these small proprietors had legally acquired about 10,000 acres of land, while another 4,580 acres were rented by labourers from plantations.

Occasionally, acts of planter philanthropy allowed some ex-slaves to obtain freehold ownership of land. For example, the death of Reynold Alleyne Elcock in 1821, owner of the 620-acre Mount Wilton estate in the St Thomas parish, afforded his slaves the opportunity of buying land through his bequest. His will of 1821 provided for the establishment of an annuity for all his labouring adult slaves:

. . . In consideration of the uniform good conduct of my negroes, and more particularly in the Insurrection [1816] I am determined that they shall enjoy a fair portion of my wealth, and therefore *I direct that the sum of £5 be paid annually on the 1st day of June to each labouring adult, besides their usual allowances of food and cloathing,* and I also direct that out of the crop, every Saturday afternoon be given them, and every other Saturday during the crop, unless their misconduct shd render it necessary for the trustees to deprive them of it pro tempore as a punishment – which may be done, as I wish a very rigid discipline observed – well knowing that good order tends more to Happiness than any thing else.

According to Professor W. K. Marshall, Elcock's will was proved in

October 1821, but Mount Wilton labourers did not receive their annuities until 1841. When they did, in June of that year, they received lump sums in the form of cheques drawn on the West India Bank for £85 currency. Elcock's heirs, Marshall states, 'claimed that the indebtedness of the estate was the reason for the delay in executing Elcock's wishes'.[5] With these sums of money, some of the Mount Wilton labourers purchased land within the parish, including a significant proportion of the neighbouring Rock Hall estate which was subdivided for sale. As a result, the village of Rock Hall was established by labourers, though the estate bearing that name disappeared. Similar circumstances surrounded the formation of Workman's village in the St George parish. In this case, Peter Chapman, owner of Workman's estate, divided up 102 acres of the estate in 1856 into one- to two-acre lots which labourers purchased by instalments.

Ex-slaves who were artisans, or in possession of well-remunerated skills, who could accumulate savings, constituted the majority of those who held freeholds on land. In 1860 the number of freeholders was officially stated as 2,674 and in 1878, 4,982. Some of these freeholders were poor-whites; others were coloureds and blacks who were probably not ex-slaves in 1838. Most, however, used their access to land in order to accumulate cash by producing and marketing foodstuff; this meant the consolidation of the traditional occupation of huckstering which was the main way in which slaves had participated in the economy as autonomous agents. Some planted sugar cane which was milled by plantation factories and received annually relatively large sums of capital. In such cases, their dependancy upon the plantation sector meant that they could not articulate opinions considered hostile to the white community. In general, then, some ex-slaves were able to use land ownership as an instrument to strengthen their position within the plantation-dominated order. But very few were able to emerge as substantial landowners with social and political influence.[6]

PRESCOD AND SOCIAL PROTEST

Sugar planters were not convinced that they had eliminated the radical leadership of the slave community during and immediately after the 1816 Bussa Rebellion. In the 1820s anti-slavery protest continued, though no one individual emerged as a popular leader. By the mid-1830s, however, Samuel Jackman Prescod, a free-coloured man, became associated with anti-slavery opinions that emanated from the slave yards. By 1838, he had emerged as the most popular and astute spokesman for the emancipated people and represented a major figure around which criticisms of planter policy were rallied.

Samuel Prescod, from a painting of anti-slavery leaders.

Prescod was in many respects an outstanding individual. He was born in 1806, the illegitimate son of a free-coloured woman and a white planter. Though he had broken socio-politically from the pro-slavery ideological thrust of his social group, during the latter part of the Apprenticeship period he became editor of *The Liberal*, a radical newspaper which expressed the grievances of the disadvantaged propertied coloured community. Under his editorship, *The Liberal* gave expression to many of the grievances of the black working class. On 6th June 1843, black, coloured and white voters in Bridgetown elected him to the Assembly as their representative – the first man of known black ancestry to sit in the House. Prescod and Henry Sharpe, the Attorney-General, elected under the double member system, were therefore the first representatives for the newly created Bridgetown constituency. By the time of his death on 26th September 1871, Prescod had agitated on behalf of the less privileged classes on a wide range of issues. The nature of his political role suggests that he was undoubtedly the greatest leader of popular opinions in the colony during the post-slavery era.

On Wednesday, 1st August 1838, Prescod wasted no time in congratulating the apprentices on the attainment of full legal freedom. In the editorial of *The Liberal* for that day, he wrote: 'Fellow men and Friends! I have lived to see you declared Freemen, and I hope . . . to live and see you made free. . . .' This statement illustrated the perceptions of Prescod on the meaning of emancipation and his intention to agitate on the freedmen's behalf for the gaining of the civil rights which would give acceptable meaning to the term 'freedom'. Neither did he procrastinate in informing slave masters that there would be no tolerance of the socio-political disabilities which still shaped the lives of these unpropertied people. On 11th August 1838, a commentary in *The Liberal* which echoed Prescod's sentiments, stated: 'Gentlemen, you cannot require me to inform you, that it is, not by declaring people free, that they are made free in reality – but that it is by conferring on them such privileges as put some proportion of the power which you now exclusively enjoy into their hands.' It was the objective of winning some measure of political power for the freed people, by strictly constitutional means, that shaped the political activities of Prescod over the next twenty years,

The social forces behind Prescod's agitation emerged from the protest actions of ex-slaves in relation to the provision of the Contract Law. Articulate ex-slaves were known to be expressing their grievances at the community level, though it is doubtful that their opinions ever did reach directly the ears of the governor or members of the legislature. Prescod's contribution, therefore, was not in the initiation of protest or formulation of radical thought, but in the expression and leadership of such opinions at the highest levels of society. Ex-slaves, for example, were first to recognise the extent to which the Contract Law attempted to perpetuate some slavery aspects of labour control, though it was Prescod who was identified with the articulation of this theme within official circles. In a memorial written on behalf of the Central Negro Emancipation Committee, addressed to Lord Glenelg, Secretary of State for the Colonies, which was also published in *The Liberal* of Wednesday, 27th October 1838, Prescod stated:

That the majority of the colonies have abolished the apprenticeship system, and thus destroyed the last vestige of legalised slavery is a matter for unfeigned thankfulness; that they have clogged the infant liberties of the negroes with unjust and illegal restrictions and thus destroyed the grace of this act, is a matter for deep regret. The Committee will not stop to inquire into the motives which induced the local legislature to terminate the existence of slavery – whether they arose from a sense of justice or whether from the manifest impolicy and danger of its continuance; but they cannot fail to remark in the legislative acts which preceded it, and which had in view its termination as well as in those measures which accompanied and succeeded it a fixed determination to coerce labour under the new system and as much as possible to bring the negro freeman under the tyranny of his old master.

Governor MacGregor was also accused by Prescod of plotting with planters to reduce the civil rights of blacks by means of repressive legislation, and Prescod suggested that workers should withdraw their labour until Lord Glenelg at the Colonial Office offered a clear opinion on matters concerning labour laws. Several black leaders were arrested for the expression of these and similar opinions, but Prescod remained free on this occasion, to write his critiques of the Contract Law in *The Liberal*.

It has been suggested that Prescod was probably at his most effective in assisting blacks to resist the imposition of the emigration laws which were designed to prevent their movements into other colonies. He had accepted the role as sub-agent for Thomas Day, the Chief Emigration Agent for British Guiana, who arrived in Barbados to encourage black emigration to that colony. He charged the legislative council with attempting to control the movements of blacks in the manner that slave owners had done. In a hard-hitting statement he warned the Council: 'One of the rights of freemen . . . is that of going wheresoever they please . . . Now that the people are free, some of them . . . to escape the evils of their condition here

. . . are leaving the island of their own free will . . .' [but there is nothing you can do, for] 'the people will go!' When Prescod and other prominent non-whites attempted to form a Barbados chapter of the Anti-Slavery Society, Governor MacGregor referred to them as 'unhappy imitators' seeking 'outlets in the Colonies for the diffusion of their revolutionary poison'.

Prescod was also accused by officials within the Colonial Office of attempting to orchestrate the triumph of coloureds and blacks over whites in Barbados. But he rarely referred to racial struggle within his campaign but spoke endlessly of the privileges of the propertied classes, and the misery of the landless, within the context of Christian theological precepts. As leader of the 'Popular Party' (or 'Liberal Party') he had also attempted to win over the support of middle-class whites, especially the more liberal urban mercantile community. This group was also in need of an effective political lobby, and Prescod hoped to provide it by also carrying the mass support. One prominent white to join Prescod was F. B. Goodridge, a Speightstown property holder, who was also a powerful speaker in his own right. The manifesto of the Party called for the protection of blacks' civil rights, reduction of race/colour prejudice within institutions of governments and elsewhere, and the extension of the franchise.

Determined to ensure that the 'labouring classes' be given 'all the civil rights and immunities of free men', Prescod agitated for the extension of the franchise. On 6th June 1840 the legislature finally agreed to a Franchise Bill which Robert Bowcher Clarke, Speaker of the House, considered 'as liberal a measure as will ever be obtained from the representatives of the present constituency'. The new constituency of Bridgetown was created, but the juggling of reduced property qualifications made minimal difference in terms of the extension of the franchise to blacks. Prescod referred to it in this regard as only the 'postponement of the question'. The Colonial Office agreed with Prescod and disallowed the law, though this ruling was later reversed by Lord Stanley who took over at the Colonial Office. In effect, there was no meaningful increase in the number of voters. Before the Act in 1840 there were 1,153 voters, and in 1849 there were 1,322 – less than 5 per cent of the population. At his death in 1871, the franchise qualifications still rigidly excluded the vast majority of blacks.

THE CONFEDERATION REBELLION

A major achievement of Prescod was his education of the working class by illustrating how the planter oligarchy was concerned primarily with using the legislature to protect the sugar interest at the expense of all other interests within the society. Working people had no doubts that the objective of this elite was to confine them to the role of producing cheap labour. This was being done by excluding them from political involvement and by refusing to implement even the basis of a comprehensive social welfare programme in order to assist the development of the free order. The imperial government had given Prescod some respectability for his anti-oligarchy stance, and as the planters sought to intensify their political grip on the colony by eroding the power of the executive, the Colonial Office became more determined to impose executive rule as the necessary basis of cohesive social development.

Since emancipation the Colonial Office had sought to replace the old Representative System with executive authority throughout the West Indies; Jamaica resisted this policy adamantly during 1839, and Parliament backed off to reconsider strategy. By 1875, the Colonial Office's political policy for Barbados was twofold: (a) a confederation with the Windward Islands (b) a Crown Colony government. The Barbados Assembly prepared to resist this policy, by suggesting that the loss of the Representative System would be the denial of ancient rights, and a triumph of imperial interests. Trinidad was already a Crown Colony, and the Jamaica planters, in order to prevent blacks and coloureds taking over the Assembly under franchise reforms and undermining white authority, did not resist the imposition of the Executive System. The Barbados planter class had no such fear, and considered that there was no political crisis within the colony to warrant Crown government.

The precedents for confederation were ample. Barbados had been involved in such a structure during the late seventeenth century with the Leewards, and after 1834 with the Windwards. In 1871, also, the administrations of the Leewards were successfully centralised. For these, and related reasons, the Colonial Office believed that Barbadian confederation, coupled with Crown Colony rule, would not lead to any major political crisis. At the end of 1875 John Pope Hennessey was appointed Governor with the duty of implementing these aspects of Colonial Office policy. Hennessey failed. In the process the colony was torn by rebellion and bloodshed – the only extensive surge of islandwide violence since the 1816 slave rebellion.

The Colonial Office sought to legitimise its policy on the grounds that a confederated executive system would be efficient, economical, and the only way to achieve political representation for the wide cross-section of free society. On these points the Barbadian ruling elite was divided, and for

View of the Parliament Buildings, Bridgetown, from the south, c.1890. The careenage is at the fore.

the first time since emancipation, sections within it were pitted against each other. In March 1876, Governor Hennessey had received reports, which he passed on to the Colonial Office, that the anti-confederate defenders of the status quo had begun to organise themselves to resist, even if violently, his political programme. The vanguard organisation of this group was the Barbados Defence Association (BDA) which pledged to defend the 'constitution' and protect the social order. Some of the more prominent members of this group, according to Hennessey's report, were S. Yearwood, J. Smith, J. A. Lynch, Thomas Sealy, Sir John Sealy, J. H. Shannon, J. Spencer, S. H. Collymore, J. Innis, B. Innis, T. Gill and D. C. DaCosta.

The BDA also drew up a list of prominent persons whom they considered confederates and supportive of the Governor in the 'destruction of the colony's ancient constitution'. This list of more than twenty names was published in the The Agricultural Reporter, and was headed by Bishop Mitchinson, Lord Bishop of Barbados, and Sir Thomas Graham Briggs, member of the Legislative Council (owner of Farley Hill). With the 'enemy' identified, the BDA mounted an islandwide political campaign to strengthen opposition to Governor Hennessey. It held mass rallies and used the oratorical skills of Thomas Gill, a former Speaker of the Assembly, and Joseph Connell, owner of Oughterson's plantation, to attract the attention of blacks and whites alike. At a mass meeting held at the Promenade Gardens in Bridgetown, speakers accused the confederates, among other things, of plotting to restore slavery, removing the political rights of inhabitants, imposing heavy taxes on property owners for the financing of government in the Windward Islands, and seeking to gain their ends by orchestrating disruption and violence within the society. Variations of these themes were published in The Agricultural Reporter and The Times – newspapers of the planter class and the middle-class coloureds respectively.

The confederates also attempted to mount a mass campaign, both to defend themselves against the BDA, and to propagate the merits of their case to the populace. To assist in the attainment of these ends, they established The Barbados People and Windward Islands Gazette, a newspaper designed to reach those sections of the community which, for various reasons, stayed away from political meetings, as well as to present political information clearly and simply for the labouring classes.

It was the first time that blacks found themselves at the centre of ruling-class conflict. The West Indian, a conservative newspaper, particularly in the early part of April 1876, suggested that Governor Hennessey had sought to lodge his case at the lowest social level with the result that a class war had been unleashed within the society. Such conflict, the paper argued, would lead to mob politics, mob violence, and a cult of destruction. In addition, the confederates were accused of misleading ill-informed working people with communistic doctrines about equalitarian distribution of land, and the Utopian uplifting of the poor to the material and social standard of their employers.

Though the confederates did not openly suggest that Crown Colony rule would lead to any major distribution of wealth and power in favour of the poor, labourers had already adopted the policy that any movement which sought to break the perceived tyrannical power of oligarchical government could only assist them in the attainment of greater civil rights. As such, working-class spokesmen sought to win mass support for Hennessy, while large sections of the black and coloured middle class rallied behind the Barbados Defence Association. By the middle of April, working-class leaders, ahead of their small armies, attempted to resolve the impasse with a strategy of open rebellion aimed at toppling the recalcitrant planter class. The accumulation of grievances by workers since the dreaded Contract Law of 1840, had convinced them that the planter class stood in the way of their attainment of socio-economic betterment. As such, the constitutional debate provided the political context in which they saw the possibility of expressing their disapproval of post-slavery developments, and for offering the imperial government the perfect opportunity to implement policies for genuine socio-economic reconstruction.

The rebellion was short-lived – though it lasted much longer than the revolt of 1816. It began on the night of 17th April and lasted until the morning of the 26th. Black workers mobilised in units of hundreds, some carrying flags and professing to be agents of Governor Hennessey, moved through the town and country confronting police with an assortment of agricultural weapons and stones. Plantation properties were destroyed and foodstuffs removed from ships and stores, while many whites fled to safety aboard ships anchored in Carlisle Bay. It was on the night of the 20th, when the Governor received reports that several prominent whites were threatened with execution by blacks, that he called out the troops to assist the battered police force which had failed to impress. Within five days the rebellion had more or less been suppressed.[7]

Unlike the rebellion of 1816, the mortality among blacks did not run into hundreds. Seven or eight blacks were reported to have lost their lives, and no whites. Hundreds of blacks, however, and eight policemen, were wounded. The rebellion was defeated, partly because the mass participation was not effectively led, and also because of confusion arising from perceptions of the Governor's true position in the matter. A letter which is alleged to have been written by a worker, addressed to the Governor, illustrates, perhaps, the fact that blacks saw themselves as the final catalyst in the conflict between Parliament and Assembly, and that they alone could remove oligarchical government in the colony. It is also interesting to note that, like the 1816 revolt, blacks believed that they could defeat the planters' militia and police, and that the imperial troops, who on both occasions they believed would assist them, represented the victorious force. Summing up the situation in the colony, one Colonel Sarjeant, Commander of the British Troops, reported to the Colonial Office:

. . . There can be no doubt that since the commencement of those riots, a great amount of wanton destruction of property of planters and others has been perpetrated throughout the country . . . from the 21st instance and during the 22nd and 23rd instance . . ., sufficient in itself to create the greatest and most intense alarm in the minds of landed proprietors . . . There can be no doubt whatever that after the experience gained by the present transaction that Barbados can never be left without the presence of European troops. I am fully convinced that if we had not sufficient force to stem the spirit of riot and disorder openly and unreservedly shown by the evil disposed on this occasion, that the white population, and I have no doubt, would have met with consequences of the most grave and painful character.

Governor Hennessey was praised by the Colonial Office for doing a good job in suppressing the blacks, though officials were not prepared to dismiss the Assembly's view that he was not to be far removed from the source which had caused the insurrection. Parliament, however, decided to reconsider their confederation policy, though many members were of the opinion that some planters had deliberately sponsored and stimulated the violent upheaval as part of their campaign against the imposition of Crown Colony rule. It is also true that there were suspicions within the BDA that confederates had engineered the riots so as to provide Parliament with the context for firmly imposing executive authority. As part of Parliament's retreat, Governor Hennessey was 'promoted' to the post of Governor of Hong Kong in November, and members of the disbanded BDA celebrated their victory.

Hennessey was replaced as Governor by Captain George Strahan. Under his administration Parliament entertained the possibility of imposing Crown Colony rule, though without the confederation. But the Colonial Office, receiving reports that Barbadians would continue their resistance, proposed a new line of action which represented an attempt at conciliation.

Lord Carnarvon at the Colonial Office offered Barbadians the option of keeping their representative system, on condition that they allow two members appointed by the Crown to sit in the Assembly. The legislature convened to discuss the offer, and rejected it outright.

With the assistance of the able Conrad Reeves, a prominent mulatto lawyer, the solution to the constitutional problem was found in 1881. A new executive committee was established by an Act of the legislature which was chaired by the Governor and its members appointed by him from his Council and from the Assembly. This committee, therefore, represented in principle the marriage of the powers of the executive with those of the Assembly. In effect, it represented a partial victory for the representative system. The executive committee was given exclusive powers in the initiation of money votes and in budgetary preparations. This system stayed in place until the 1950s when it was replaced by cabinet and ministerial government.

In order to consolidate this triumph of the representative system, Conrad Reeves began his agitation for franchise reforms – picking up where Prescod had left off – so as to increase the size of black political participation. Unlike Prescod, Reeves was not a radical. He shared the conservative ideology of the more liberal minded among the elite. For this reason, he was able to assert more influence on the legislative process. In 1884 he succeeded in persuading the legislature to pass a Franchise Act which reduced the property qualification. The Act provided for a reduction in freehold qualification from £12. 16s. 4d. to £5, and the £32. 1s. occupation qualification, which was formerly imposed upon urban inhabitants, was reduced to £15 for town and country alike. The qualification for rate payers was also reduced; this was cut from £3. 4s. to £2 for Bridgetown, and to £1 for rural inhabitants. In addition, it enfranchised all workers in town or country whose annual income was £50 or more. The number of voters was only slightly increased, and in 1900 there were still less than 2,000 registered. In this regard, the legislature had succeeded in defeating Reeves as it had done Prescod earlier, by allowing only marginal increases in the number of blacks who could exercise the franchise.

SURVIVAL OF THE SUGAR INDUSTRY

Immediately following the termination of the Apprenticeship System in 1838, the colony experienced a sudden drop in levels of sugar production and reduced production of food crops. The toll of black lives occasioned by

Conrad Reeves, coloured lawyer and Chief Justice of Barbados, 1882–1901.

these developments was noticeable to most observers. Some planters attributed the cause of declining economic activity to the anti-plantation stance of labourers. Reflecting planter opinion on this question, Robert Schomburgk in his 1848 *The History of Barbados* stated that though the prolonged drought was a significant factor, 'the chief cause of the deficiency was the relaxed labour of the peasantry, and the great injury which the cultivation and manufacture of sugar suffers by want of continuous and regular labour'. One clergyman suggested that in the summer of 1841, for instance, 541 working-class children died of malnutrition and nutritional-related illnesses, compared with an average of 185 for the previous three years.

The decline, however, was shortlived; so too were fears among the plantocracy that the sugar industry was, in their own words, 'fast dying a sort of natural death'. From 1844, the statistics show that sugar production and exports had picked up and were rapidly increasing to new record levels (Table 14). Production in 1847 amounted to 33,111 hogsheads, in 1850 to 35,302, and in 1858 to 50,778. The explanation for this remarkable recovery has to do with planters' assertion of effective control over the labour force, increased acreage placed under sugar, and increased yields resulting from improved cultivation techniques. Widespread use of chemical fertilisers and more efficient factory techniques also contributed to greater yields.

Sugar planters, therefore, despite the 1846 Sugar Duties Act, which provided for the gradual removal of all protection for West Indian sugar on the London market, and the collapse in the same year of the Bridgetown-based West Indian Bank which was a major supplier of credit to the

Table 14. *Exports from Barbados,*
1848–58

Year	Total value of all exports (£)
1848	659,073
1850	831,534
1852	951,726
1854	945,849
1856	971,028
1858	1,468,449

Source: Barbados Blue Books,
1848–58, CO 33/58–68

plantation sector, were able to expand production and maintain their market share. The collapse of London sugar prices in 1848 to a mere 23s. 8d., the lowest level since 1832, did not produce panic among planters; they responded by temporarily shifting greater acreage into food crops and cutting their import bill by over £90,000 in 1849. More importantly, they were able to transfer the pressures of falling sugar prices onto the shoulders of workers by means of wage reductions during the 1850s. By slashing the size of their labour bill, planters were able to withstand the sharp edge of competition from slave-owning sugar producers, especially after 1854 when the Free Trade Act of 1846 was put into fuller effect (Table 15).

Reduction in wages, without violent rebellious responses from workers, also gave planters the room and confidence to implement certain technological adjustments within their industry. During the late 1840s, Governor William Reid had urged planters to modernise their production, and on one occasion insulted them by making references to the 'bad state' of their working cattle, the dilapidated condition of their windmills, and the disgust experienced on seeing their 'weak oxen drawing a waggon'. Whereas in 1841 there was only one steam factory on the island, in 1859 there were at least twelve, and ninety-five in 1890. Steam factories were estimated to produce between 12 and 18 per cent more sugar than the traditional windmills, and this development greatly assisted those few planters who were able to raise the capital for modernisation. On the whole, though, technological backwardness remained a feature of the post-slavery sugar industry.

The period between 1854 and the mid-1880s was one of uncertainty. Though sugar prices remained stagnant, output increased slowly. Planters' confidence in the industry was not undermined by market trends, and

Table 15. *Wages in the West Indies, 1846–50*

Colony	Average wage per day (pence)
Trinidad	24
British Guiana	20
St Lucia	16
Jamaica	15
St Vincent	10
Grenada	9
Antigua	8
Barbados	6

Bridgetown street scene, c.1890. Note the tramlines running along the centre of the street.

between 1860 and 1887 few estates were sold, and the average price of these remained above the satisfactory rate of £50 per acre. In those years when sugar prices declined, profit levels were maintained by the increase in volume of sales (Table 16). It was during this period, also, that Barbadians were able to take advantage of openings within the North American market. Since the 1840s the balance of trade with the United States had been negative; exports to the United States in 1845 were valued at £1,750 while imports were valued at £188,686. The increase in sales of sugar to this market was slow and inconsistent until the mid-1850s, since Barbadians sold their sugar mainly to English merchants to whom they were indebted. Available data show that between 1855 and 1858 the value of Barbadian sugar exports to the United States jumped from £8,865 to £60,000. Since lower-cost Cuban and Puerto Rican sugar producers had captured a sizeable portion of this market, British West Indians did not consider themselves competitive, and in 1893, the value of Barbados sugar and molasses exports there amounted to only £755,465.

The deep end of the sugar crisis was reached in 1884 and continued until the turn of the century. For the first time since emancipation, planters sincerely expressed their inability to cope with market trends, and confidence in the industry declined rapidly. The root cause was the sudden drop in European sugar prices – the result of rapidly increasing subsidised

Table 16. *Sugar exports from Barbados, 1883–97*

Year	Tons	Price per cwt £. s. d.
1883	46,242	19.0
1884	54,263	13.3
1885	52,649	13.6
1886	40,047	11.9
1887	60,263	11.9
1888	63,882	13.0
1889	57,106	16.0
1890	74,606	13.6
1891	44,226	13.6
1892	51,849	14.3
1893	58,765	11.3
1894	57,967	10.0
1895	33,331	10.9
1896	45,170	9.3
1897	51,257	9.6

domestic sugar beet production. Between 1884 and 1897 planters reported the disappearance of their small profit margins. Production levels fell marginally and even then most major producers were operating at cost levels above what was required to make a profit. The volume of exports did not show any appreciable decline, though with collapsing prices, returns fell off sharply. In 1886, for example, the values of exports were about 40 per cent below the 1884 level. The crisis within the industry was reflected in the collapse of sugar estate values; estates sold in 1884 at between £65 and £70 per acre while in 1887 sales were recorded at £25–£30 per acre.

The worst years of the crisis were the mid-1890s. Though property values fell sharply, few, if any, estates were abandoned, unlike Jamaica for example. In 1896, a Royal Commission was appointed to investigate the sugar crisis. The Agricultural Aids Act of 1887, which was passed to allow government to provide short-term financing for sugar planters, had some positive effects, but the economic crisis was seen to be leading to social unrest among the increasing impoverished labouring poor. As usual, planters slashed wages in response to falling prices, and evidence of rising mortality and general malnutrition caused much concern to law-enforcing agents. Finally, in a desperate attempt to shoulder up the industry and ease, indirectly, the social crisis within the colony, government assisted by the establishment in 1902 of the Sugar Industry Agricultural Bank – the result of a grant of £400,000 from the British Government. It was not until during the First World War (1914–18) that profits returned to the sugar industry, as many of the beet sugar zones of Europe were destroyed. These years, and the period shortly after, were times of great prosperity, and for a while memories of the crisis of the last part of the nineteenth century were pushed into the background.

RISE OF THE MERCHANT ELITE

The economic depression of the 1880s and 1890s not only eroded the minimal material gains which workers had slowly attained in previous years, but also produced significant changes in the ownership of arable land and hence the social composition of the elite. The most important development of this period was the rise of the local merchant class as a new force within the social elite – merging with, and to a large extent pushing aside, sections of the traditional plantocracy.

The ascendancy of the local merchant capitalists was characterised by their forceful entry into the plantocracy by means of financial arrangements and marital links. This development had to do with two important features of the post-slavery order, the first of which was the ability of planters to retain the old representative system, and hence their control over the legislature. This meant that planters were able, by means of manipulating the organs of government, to ensure that estate ownership, even in the most difficult of times, stayed in local hands and was not transferred to English merchant houses to which they were indebted. Second was the development of local financial institutions and merchant companies that were able to rescue, and purchase, many estates before absentee interests were able to do so.

Unlike the Jamaicans, for example, the Barbados legislature had refused to accept the imperial Encumbered Estates Act of 1854 through which bankrupt plantations were put up for sale on the London market. Generally, such estates did fall into the hands of English merchant consignees who held liens on them, a process made legal by the English Chancery Court. The Barbadians resisted this solution to plantation indebtedness, and implemented, with the reluctant acceptance of the Colonial Office, their own Chancery Court system which was designed to ensure that indebted estates were resold to locals. Between 1854 and 1870 the majority of estates sold in Chancery in Barbados, unlike other colonies, went to local buyers.[8]

Many of these estates fell into the hands of the local urban merchant class, who hitherto had been slighted by the planter elite as an under-group, in spite of their obvious substantial financial worth and capacity. Bridgetown merchants had long been consolidating their economic base with an eye to buying into the plantocracy which was still considered, in spite of its economic decay, as the social elite. This of course had to do with planters' firm grip over the political machinery. In 1840, for example, the Barbados Mutual Life Assurance Society (BMLA) was formed by a planter-merchant group, and by the 1860s this institution had become a major supplier of finance capital to sugar planters. The general policy of the BMLA was to allow planters to use their crop as security for short-term loans and to obtain a lien on estates for long-term loans.

The development of a local capital market resulted in the planter class having to lean heavily upon merchant finance, with the result that by the early twentieth century, Bridgetown merchants were taking over and buying a considerable number of sugar estates. Indeed, most reputable Bridgetown merchant houses by this time had either controlling interests in sugar estates or owned sugar estates. For example, by the end of the nineteenth century the BMLA appeared in the Chancery Court as plaintiff for more than thirty cases. By 1905, Bridgetown merchants were clearly the leading force in sugar plantation modernisation. After this date the number of estates falling into their hands increased as they suspended loans to planters unable to resolve their financial difficulties.

By 1905, most prominent Bridgetown merchant families were considered an integral part of the plantocracy. Families such as the Cavans, Austins, Camerons, Brydens, Wilkinsons and DaCostas had already consolidated their financial links with the plantation sector, and had also established marital ties with traditional planter families such as the Chandlers, Piles, Sealys and Haynes. While the merchant class rose 'phoenix-like out of the ashes of the depression', the urban-based poor-whites were also enjoying some socio-economic mobility. Indeed, it seems as if the circumstances of the late nineteenth century provided the context for losing the rigidities which had formerly kept static the white community. Some poor-white families, such as the Goddards, Dowdings, Seales and Emtages, emerged also as substantial Bridgetown merchants – joining the more traditional merchant families, who assisted them with contracts, loans and information.

Traditional planter families, none the less, continued to dominate both the Assembly and the legislative councils, though the most prominent of them were now linked financially and maritally to the new merchant elite. G. Laurie Pile was undoubtedly the largest planter within the Assembly during the late nineteenth century. Representing St George between 1884 and 1905, he owned the following estates: Windsor (250 acres), Valley (250 acres), Jordans (235 acres), Carmichael (257 acres), Boarded Hall (318 acres), Bulkeley (390 acres), Brighton (393 acres) and Buttals (209 acres). He was also attorney for the three estates of the Earl of Harewood. He was financially involved in several merchant companies and was an influential member of the Chambers of Commerce and Vice-President of the Agricultural Society. His agro-commercial interests, therefore, represented the trend which the traditional planter elite was forced to follow in order to survive the economic challenges of the time.

The political challenge of the Bridgetown merchants, however, was not as successful during the late nineteenth century. Merchants tended to represent Bridgetown and St Michael, while planters held on to their rural seats. Although James A. Lynch was a coloured man, his career as a merchant-politician probably represented the ideal sought by his white commercial associates. He represented Bridgetown during the early 1880s and sat on the Legislative Council. His elevation has to do with his role as founder of the firm James Alsop Lynch and Company and ownership of the 164-acre Friendship estate. His son James Challenor Lynch built upon this foundation, and as a planter, merchant and lawyer also won a Bridgetown seat in 1888.

Other merchants such as John Gardiner Austin, senior partner of Michael Cavan and Company, whose son founded Gardiner Austin and Company after his death in 1902, also represented Bridgetown from 1895 to 1911. Arthur Sydney Bryden, an English-born commission agent, and founder of A. S. Bryden and Sons in the 1890s, represented St Michael from 1894 to 1899. He was also a director of the BMLA and of the Barbados Fire Insurance Company of which G. L. Pile was a Chairman.

Some merchants also succeeded in winning rural seats that were traditionally held by resident planters. For example, J. O. Wright of the firm Collymore and Wright, later Plantations Limited, represented St Andrew between 1899 and 1904. On the whole these merchants were white, though a few Jews and coloured merchants were able to rise to prominence in the political community; for example, E. I. Baeza, a Jew, represented Bridgetown in 1908, and H. W. Lofty, a coloured man, represented St Michael between 1899 and 1905, and Bridgetown in 1910.[9]

In general, then, merchants used their economic power in order to infiltrate the political institutions of the colony, and had become a powerful lobby by 1900. They sat on vestries and statutory boards, as well as in the Assemblies, legislative councils and the executive committees. Commercial Hall, the Bridgetown Chamber of Commerce, was never unrepresented in the making of important political decisions. In fact, it was generally stated that the merchants at Commercial Hall had easier access to governors than members of the Agricultural Society, and that their political power exceeded their physical representation within the polity.

The overall result was a strengthening of the plantocracy as merchant families generally aspired to the socio-ideological standards and values that had been established by planters since the seventeenth century. This meant that though the economic depression led to structural change in the social composition of the plantocracy, it certainly entered the twentieth century as a financially reinforced elite confident in its ability to rule even during the difficult times ahead.

CHAPTER SEVEN

Depression, reform and revolt, 1897–1937

1897 ROYAL COMMISSION

The appointment by the Colonial Office of a Royal Commission to investigate conditions in the depressed West Indian sugar industry reflects imperial concern that the economic crisis was structural and long term, and that the social and economic implications for all classes would be severe. It was the first comprehensive investigation of the sugar industry in some fifty years, and the appointment of commissioners familiar with West Indian conditions also suggests the seriousness with which its report would be received.

When the findings were submitted later that year there were few surprises for Barbadians. The conclusion that the sugar industry would continue to decline and that alternative export crops would have to be found, did not comfort plantation owners, but the idea was not original. That bounty beet sugar was the principal factor in the market dislocation of cane sugar was also not new, though Barbadians were less than pleased with the recommendation that no discriminatory taxes or duties should be imposed on beet sugar since the British consumer was benefiting from cheaper sugar.

It was, none the less, pleasing to black Barbadians that the Commissioners recognised that the imperial government had some social responsibility towards the working classes who were absorbing a disproportionate share of the economic crisis. More significant were the recommendations that peasant expansion be encouraged so as to allow a greater number of blacks to establish their own patterns of subsistence since sugar could not support them; that new crops and new markets be found; and more importantly, for Barbadians, that the imperial exchequer should offer a loan to the colony for the establishment of modern central factory equipment and facilities.[1]

Sir Henry Norman, Chairman of the Commission, a former governor of Jamaica, was determined that the recommendations should be quickly implemented. In 1902, Parliament approved a grant of £80,000 for the modernisation of the Barbados sugar industry. In addition, because of the hurricane of 10th September 1898, which killed 112 people and destroyed the homes of over 10,000 black workers, a grant of £40,000 was allocated for working-class assistance and £50,000 for sugar plantation repairs.

Planters considered the grant to the sugar sector modest, given the backwardness of the industry, but were not prepared to bargain on this matter. They were, however, not prepared to consider the question of black peasant development as a strategy for socio-economic rationalisation. In fact, during the commission hearings in Bridgetown, a resident watchmaker, Walter Marston, had given evidence which suggested that W. K. Chandler, Master of Chancery since 1882, with planter support was engaged in a system of over-appraising estate values so as to exclude blacks and coloureds from purchasing land.

When, in 1903, the £80,000 was made available to the Government of Barbados, disputes arose as to the manner in which it should be disposed. The resolution of the debate came with the establishment of the Barbados Sugar Industry Agricultural Bank, which granted loans from the fund to individual planters. A series of Plantation Aid Acts assisted the management of the funds, and in 1904 at least 107 of the colony's 411 estates had borrowed under these provisions. It was not until the 1910s that central factories began to appear, though planters remained concerned that the implications for the traditional-style family operation would not be all positive.

The Commissioners had no difficulty in illustrating to planters the relationship between economic decline and social unrest. The report stated that the British Government had 'placed the labouring population where it is, and created for it the conditions, moral and material, under which it exists and cannot divest [itself] of responsibility for its future'. Planters interpreted this concern to mean that workers had to be encouraged, by means of education, to respect and appreciate plantation labour, rather than pursue peasant development. The Agricultural Conference which was held in Barbados in January 1900, had given support to the idea that working-class boys should be discouraged from seeking clerical work and should be 'trained in an atmosphere favourable to agriculture', and that they 'should learn that tilling the soil and caring for crops is . . . worthy of being studied by intelligent minds'.

Planters, furthermore, considered that the context for such a development was already established, especially as J. E. Reece, the Barbadian Inspector of Schools, had reported in 1899 that the children of most agricultural labourers tended to continue in that occupation. This was in spite of the fact that the 1878 Education Act, and the recommendations of the Bree Commission Report of 1896, had called for compulsory education for working-class children under the age of 12. Typical of planter opinion on this question was a report entitled 'Are the masses responsible?' published in the planters' newspaper, the *Barbados Agricultural Report*, 26th October 1905:

It is admitted that the Negro, if properly handled, is an excellent labourer. The question then is one of proper handling. Handle the negro properly, and there would be no lack of workers. Such handling would involve, amongst other things, the giving of a sound practical education. Some book learning is of course essential, but the mistake of conveying to the child the idea that such education as he acquires at school is calculated to make him eligible for the highest honours in life must be avoided.

At the village level, planters had ready social allies in the Anglican clergymen. The official clergy had long merged with the plantocracy and had also made their inputs into the evidence collected by the Royal Commissioners. Planters saw them as providing assistance in shaping the consciousness of villagers in such a manner as to be conducive for agricultural labour. The parish minister was certainly a very powerful figure in the villages and could determine the fate of families by severing or creating bridges to plantation resources. The 1891 census shows that of a total population of 182,867, some 147,000 were Anglicans, and the respect which black Anglicans conferred upon the church, and its minister, they were also required to confer upon plantation owners and managers.[2] Though Methodists, Moravians and other denominations accounted for some 19,000 Barbadians, their presence in the rural villages did not counter the alliance between the Anglican church and the plantation.

The Royal Commission had heard countless statements from witnesses that the 'ambition' of every working-class person was 'to own a piece of land'. It also heard that very few had succeeded in obtaining freehold, and that the vast majority of those who had access to land were plantation tenants – whose material subsistence had been much reduced by the depression in the sugar industry. Poverty on the tenantries was expressed in the 1895 'potato raid' on several plantations, a form of praedial larceny in which workers expressed the ideological notion of 'justified appropriation'.

On 1st July 1898, for example, shortly after planters had vocally rejected the call of the Royal Commissioners for an extension of the peasantry, a

Street hawker selling yams, c. 1900.

group of some 400 men and women raided the potato fields of Bowmanston plantation in the St John parish, and took provisions for several days' sustenance. Nineteen of these persons were convicted and sentenced. Such events were not uncommon in the 1890s, and reports of starvation in the countryside were numerous. The Commissioners also heard evidence from labourers who stated that starvation on the tenantries was leading to the widespread criminalisation of workers, since food scavenging was the order of the day. But planters were able to deflect such discussions by focusing the attention of the Commission upon the problem of sugar marketing and the industrial modernisation of the plantation.

For sugar planters, the existence of rural poverty constituted an effective hold over the labour of villagers. Indeed, the 1878 Commission on Poor Relief had indicated, in response to a suggestion that wages be increased to alleviate poverty, that 'more money per day would, in by far the majority of cases, probably mean more idleness per week'. Wages had remained inadequate since then, and the Royal Commission, when informed by planters that the daily wage for estate mechanics was 2s., for men field hands 10d.–1s., women field hands 7½d., and children under the age of 16, 5d., knew that these levels were exaggerated. Certainly, the Colonial Blue Books for the period 1901 to 1911 quote 8d. per day as the norm for male field hands.

The high death rate among impoverished workers immediately after the 1898 hurricane was due in part to outbreaks of typhoid and dysentery. Adding to their plight was the smallpox epidemic which began in February 1902 and which lasted until April 1903 and claimed 118 lives. On this latter occasion the island was quarantined by neighbouring colonies. Then there was the yellow fever epidemic of 1908, the first since 1881, all of which contributed to the economic depression in the colony by reducing trade levels and government revenues. In 1910, a medical officer noted that 'chronic pauperism . . . like a chronic disease is . . . undermining the population of this island'.

Meanwhile, planters' hopes of economic recovery were pinned upon Joseph Chamberlain's campaign to abolish the sugar beet bounties. When Chamberlain became Secretary of State for the Colonies in 1895, he expressed great concern for the plight of West Indians and was hailed in Barbados among planters as a hero. At the 1902 Brussels Convention he managed to persuade the Europeans to remove the bounties on beet sugar, but his assistance was insufficient to generate renewed enthusiasm among planters, who at this critical stage found that they were losing ground on the American market.

Since the 1880s, sugar planters had been looking more to the United States for markets, and the indices of exports illustrate the changing pattern of the colony's trade (Table 17). By 1902, when the bounties on beet sugar were removed, Barbados was exporting more in value to the United States and Canada than to the United Kingdom. In that year the value of exports to the United States of America was $1,359,888, to the United Kingdom $109,420 and to Canada $586,355 – 63.5 per cent, 5.1 per cent and 27.4 per cent of the total value of exports respectively. The expansion of the sugar industry in Cuba and Puerto Rico, however, which were structurally and financially linked to the United States, represented the basis of Barbadian displacement. The slump in Barbadian trade with the United States was sudden and substantial, and though this was partly compensated for by expanding trade in syrup and molasses to the United Kingdom and Canada, the overall level of exports showed a down trend until the First World War.

In 1903 molasses exports were valued at £136,548 and rose to £232,920 by 1907. This export item brought measurable relief to sugar planters whose spirits were also lifted by good crops in 1910, 1911 and 1914. Peasants and tenants, however, continued to experience severe hardship. There was prolonged drought between 1910 and 1912 which took a heavy toll of food crops. Rising sugar output, then, was associated with diminishing food production and inflationary prices for scarce foodstuffs.

Table 17. *Value of Barbados exports to the USA and Canada, 1902–14*

Year	Value ($)	US % of total exports	Value ($)	Canada % of total exports
1902	1,359,888	63.5	586,355	27.4
1903	1,211,107	60.0	649,622	32.2
1904	1,369,017	45.4	1,195,195	39.6
1905	1,180,752	35.3	1,322,337	39.5
1906	718,012	23.7	1,387,012	45.9
1907	240,513	8.1	1,774,910	60.2
1908	888,041	30.2	1,395,676	47.8
1909	178,646	6.4	2,019,403	72.9
1910	372,715	9.9	2,323,713	61.8
1911	383,462	11.0	2,360,395	68.0
1912	321,388	8.7	2,781,038	75.6
1913	332,160	13.1	1,718,481	67.8
1914	357,507	11.2	2,420,721	76.2

Source: Barbados Blue Books, 1902–14

The rising sugar output, in spite of the drought, had to do with the new variety of cane that had recently been introduced (B.6450) which proved resistant to drought conditions.

It is during this period also that the modern tourist industry has its origins. Hotel development was a noticeable economic feature, catering to winter visitors from North America and the United Kingdom, and also from Latin America – especially Brazil. In 1912, the Colonial Secretary remarked that 'the colony owes much of its increasing prosperity to the visitors who stay in the island', thereby recognising the importance of the tourist trade to economic expansion. This industry remained subordinated to the sugar sector for another half-century, though growing in relative importance, until it surpassed sugar as the main foreign exchange earner during the 1970s.

The responses of the impoverished blacks to the economic depression were not uniform. There were food riots, social restlessness and political turmoil – and these caused some concern to legal and political officials. But on the whole, the nature of the responses of most was summed up by Dr J. F. Clarke's testimony before the 1897 Royal Commission:

Through all the hardships the labourer endures he assumes a pleasant demeanour, and which is mistaken by his employer for comfort and happiness . . . . He is often taken to the magistrate of his parish and punished for breach of contract, or for taking a few points of sugar cane from the plantation . . . and yet he returns to the very plantation and resumes his work peaceful and quiet.

Such was the consolidated power of the planter-merchant elite and their control of economic resources which ensured social order even when living standards of workers around them were falling.

PANAMA MONEY AND MIGRANTS

Emigration had long been conceived by the worker as a major strategy for socio-economic betterment. The economic depression of the late nineteenth century, however, had the effect of expanding significantly that pool of potential migrants. But the emigration outlet that irrevocably changed Barbados and widened the horizons for the black Barbadian working class appeared in 1904. In that year, the United States renewed the construction of a canal across the Isthmus of Panama. Labour was required, and Barbadian male workers having never experienced employment on a large scale in a non-agricultural sector, saw the opportunity to reject sugar planters and plantations, and pursue an autonomous path. When, in 1905, the Panama Canal Agency established a labour recruitment office in Bridgetown, it was obvious that persuasion was not necessary.[3]

The initial reaction of sugar planters was that the surplus unemployed labour was being siphoned off the economy which could only lead to better labour relations. By the end of 1906, however, their vision had changed as the flow of migrants was unexpectedly large and eroding their labour supply. The steamers which sailed between Bridgetown and Colon had taken over 10,000 by the beginning of 1908, and by 1914, at least 20,000 men had been contracted and had departed for the canal. It was the largest wave of black migration in the colony's history, and the impact upon economy and society was considerable. It has been estimated that the total number of non-contracted and contracted migrants amounted to 45,000, in spite of the legislative attempts to contain it in 1904 and 1907. The censuses show that between 1911 and 1921 the island's population fell from 171,983 to 156,312, a decrease of some 15,671. Though many factors contributed to this net reduction, there can be no doubt that the Panama emigration was the chief cause.

The migration opportunity was undoubtedly seen by blacks as a chance finally to cast off the yoke of plantation domination. J. Challenor Lynch, for instance, reported to the Legislative Council that before boarding, blacks would abuse whites and aggressively denounce them. It was also considered, by those who wanted to stay behind, as an instrument to strengthen their hand on the labour market in bargaining for better wages. Bonham Richardson has recalled that labourers would chant the following song during industrial disputes:

> We want more wages, we want it now,
> And if we don't get it, we going to Panama
> Yankees say they want we down there,
> We want more wages, we want it now.

Whereas the drastic reduction of male labourers on the estates should have led to wage increases, planters were able to prevent this by employing women to do what had become 'men's work' at wages below what men generally obtained. As a result, wage levels in the plantation sector did not increase. Black women, who took opportunities to remove themselves from some of the more physically arduous tasks on estates after the abolition of slavery, found that they were unable to refuse the wages which field labour offered and continued to be the dominant sex in field gangs, as well as in the factory.

But it was the remittances of money to Barbados from Panama, and the

Female plantation labour during the period of male migration to the Panama Canal.

Women in a cotton factory.

capital brought back by returnees, which were to have a profound impact upon the island (Table 18). While in 1910, for example, the merchant community had advanced £80,000 to planters to assist their sugar industry, in the same year official sources show that black Barbadians brought and sent back £83,000. Though many migrants died in the canal zone (one respected estimate is 15.5 per cent), some of those who returned with capital were able to achieve considerable social and economic mobility. In 1906, 3,501 returnees declared £18,000, and the following year 3,525 declared £26,291. Between 1906 and 1915, some 20,326 returnees declared a total of £171,641. These ex-field hands had hopes of buying land, opening shops, learning a craft or obtaining an education for clerical and business professions. There certainly was a startling appearance of village shops and corner stores in the suburbs that can be attributed to 'Panama' money.[4]

Many planters, by sheer necessity, sold off their properties to 'Panama men' in small lots, and by 1930 the pattern of landownership had changed significantly. In 1897, for example, the Royal Commission was informed

Table 18. *Postal remittances sent from the Panama Canal Zone to Barbados, 1906–20*

	No. of postal orders	£
1906	3,613	7,509
1907	19,092	46,160
1908	26,360	63,210
1909	31,179	66,272
1910	31,059	62,280
1911	24,968	51,009
1912	28,394	56,042
1913	31,851	63,816
1914	22,619	39,586
1915	14,210	22,874
1916	11,241	17,539
1917	10,430	15,194
1918	8,777	12,680
1919	7,747	12,591
1920	5,782	9,173
Total		545,935

Source: B. Richardson, *Panama Money in Barbados, 1900–1920*, p. 157

Barbados windmill, used for crushing canes.

that there were only 8,500 small proprietors who owned only 10,000 acres, while in 1929 the number of small proprietors had increased to 17,731. At least one estate was bought whole by Panama money, though this practice was not approved of by the dominant white community. In 1910, for example, Dr E. G. Pilgrim, Assemblyman for St James, sold a large proportion of his estates at Carlton, Sion Hill, Reids Bay and West-moreland in small lots to 'Panama men'. For the first time, blacks were making significant inroads upon the land-ownership pattern of the island.

Under the influence of the sudden supply of money, land prices rose dramatically, and even in the outlying parishes the price of £125 per acre in 1925 was normal. At these prices only successful returnees could purchase land, and many struggling planters took timely opportunities to speculate on the land market by putting their marginal lands up for sale. By all criteria, most returnees had been able to attain a better quality of life, though for the majority of the labouring poor, conditions worsened during the 1920s, as the wartime boom in the sugar economy had collapsed by late 1920. Renewed outbreaks of 'potato raids' were reported and social tensions rose. On 13th May 1921, for example, fourteen men raided the fields of Porters estate in St James and shot at the watchmen, injuring one. Violent armed attacks on plantation food supplies were reported as commonplace, as the desperately poor workers sought to feed themselves and their families. Assemblyman for St Lucy, H. W. Reece, distinguished himself for suggesting that the House should not consider persons who confiscated provisions to 'appease hunger' the same as robbers who sold stolen items on the markets. Violent clashes between police and workers occurred in most parts of the countryside, as planters, refusing to push up wages, marketed their provisions at prices considered by labourers as unreasonable. Panama money, then, had an effect of heightening dif-ferences in the material and social standing of black workers; those who struggled to make a living saw the Panama men as symbols of success, and seemed prepared to confront the established order in ways they knew best, for the attainment of a more secure livelihood.

CENTRAL MILLS

If it was the recommendations of the 1897 Royal Commission report, and the provisions made thereafter, that focused the attention of sugar planters upon the need to modernise their industry technologically and organis-ationally, it was the shortage of prime male labour resulting from the Panama migration which prompted them into action. Between 1907 and

1911, the central factory concept was widely debated among planters. Most agreed that such a departure was in itself a good one, but many feared that the consequences would be damaging to planters as a social group. For instance, it was feared that since capital was scarce, central factories would be owned and managed by merchants or new-style industrialists who might not be sympathetic to the planters' concerns. The notion of having their cane milled in operations beyond their control disturbed many planters, yet they recognised the economic need of modern-style factories. The abandonment of the old, small windmills for large-scale steam mills was rational, and planters knew they had to do this if they wanted to stay in business. Also, since the old-style family estate was giving way to the corporate plantation, this operational change was inevitable.

The 1911 Central Milling Act illustrated the planters' desire to do what was necessary to survive in a depressed industry. Central mills were the norm in places like Cuba and Puerto Rico where the sugar industry was considered efficient and profitable, and where the corporate ownership of mills was considered organisationally effective. Between 1911 and 1923 the number of sugar factories in Barbados diminished from 329 to 263. The number of steam mills fell from 109 to 85, and windmills from 220 to 178. Throughout the countryside the small, inefficient windmills were being replaced by large, central factories whose higher-quality produce and increased capacity attracted canes from surrounding estates. The central factory at Locust Hall, for example, though located in the parish of St George, milled canes from plantations in St Thomas and St Michael parishes. Foursquare and Carrington, the two largest sugar estates on the

Table 19. *Barbados sugar tonnage, 1913–19*

Year	Sugar yield (tons)
1913	11,327
1914	29,404
1915	29,847
1916	73,581
1917	69,367
1918	57,191
1919	69,628

Source N. Deerr, *The History of Sugar*, vol. 1, p. 194

island, both obtained the latest technology in vacuum-pan refining and steam milling. The advent of the central mills led to rising sugar yields, which contributed significantly to the large output that allowed Barbadians to take advantage of wartime sugar price increases (Table 19).

CRICKET AND SOCIAL ELITISM

If the establishment of central factories constitutes proof of the survivalist economic attitudes of the transformed sugar plantocracy, then organised cricket was symbolic of its need for a sophisticated social instrument of cultural domination and distinction. From the 1870s, the game was not seen by the planter elite as simply a form of recreation; there were visions of its role as a force in social cohesion, as well as an index by which social classes could be clearly distinguished during this time of unprecedented restructuring of the social order. While merchants were rapidly becoming planters, and some coloured and black men emerging as merchants and politicians, the still dominant traditional planting families sought to maintain their class distinctions within the area of social culture.

The establishment of cricket clubs and competitions during the late nineteenth century gave rise to the use of sport as a mirror-image of the old order. According to Brian Stoddart, 'plantation owners, merchants, bankers, clerks, and civil servants came to competition matches categorised by their place in the hierarchy of sugar production; and from its organised outset cricket was a powerful agency in the preservation and promotion of that hierarchy'. Certainly in 1892 when the Barbados Challenge Cup competition was established, the sugar elite was the cricket elite and clubs were ranked by the class of their membership.[5]

In 1877 Wanderers Cricket Club was formed, and for the remainder of the century its membership was drawn exclusively from the white merchant-planter elite. The leading players and administrators of this club were the most prominent politicians and businessmen of the day; one long-serving president was J. O. Wright, a leading planter, merchant and politician. D. C. DaCosta, J. Gardiner Austin and A. S. Bryden, symbolic of the new merchant-planter elite, were also members of this club; so too was R. S. Challenor, whose son, George Challenor, became a leading West Indian batsman. The merchant-planter elite, then, saw the Wanderers Cricket Club as a social institution through which they asserted the cultural authority of their class at a time of rapid social change. Most of the club's prominent members had been supporters and activitists of the Barbados Defence Association during the confederation crisis in the year prior to its formation, a fact which enhanced the image of the club as representative of traditional elite conservatism.

Other cricket clubs which were formed later, such as Spartan and Pickwick, were the preserve of the professional upper and middle classes. Spartan, the propertied coloured man's club, boasted the fact that Sir Conrad Reeves, the coloured Chief Justice and respected lawyer, was its first president, while Pickwick, a whites-only club, had as a player and president G. A. Goodman, the colony's Solicitor-General. These clubs took pride in their support for the English standard of sport ethics, and considered offenders of regulations and values as traitors to country and empire. In general, the members believed that the principles of the cricketing culture were admirable guidelines for social behaviour and held these up as standards to be emulated by an oppressed and mostly landless working class. In the schools the children of the white upper classes and black and coloured middle classes were inculcated with these concepts. Harrison College and The Lodge, schools for the white elite, exposed students to cricket as a social institution of great magnitude. Combermere, the school of the black middle classes, did not question these values, but mimicked them in a manner which suggested profound acceptance.

Meanwhile, the impoverished children on the tenantries and in the urban ghettos played their adopted version of the game in a robust spirit which signified some measure of cultural resistance and autonomy. They transformed the spirit and structures of the game, reduced its degree of formality, and hammered it into a shape best suited to urban alley and plantation tracks. While all social classes played the game as popular recreation, it also served to enhance the rigid structure of social distinctions. At the organised level, the game emerged as a social institution which was shaped by race, colour and class forces, while its advocates consistently described it as an agency of social cohesion.

The white and coloured propertied classes, however, denigrated the matches played by black labourers on the tenantries. For many elite gentlemen the aggressive and sometimes violent nature of the game played by the lower orders was an affront to their sensibilities. They were none the less impressed with the way in which the labouring classes had developed a great enthusiasm for the game, though the remark was frequently made that, as was the case with Christianity in the slavery period, blacks did not grasp its finer conceptual points.

Blacks, on the other hand, turned out in their thousands to watch the upper classes compete among themselves, and with other regional elites in the inter-colonial games. By 1930, cricket in Barbados was a mass game, though whites continued to dominate its financial and organisation structures. No such status, however, was enjoyed by whites in the department of technical skills on the fields; this aspect of the game went increasingly to the blacks, as represented by the great player Herman Griffith, and the formation of the black middle-class club, Empire.

BLACK SELF-HELP ORGANISATIONS

Friendly societies

The injection of 'Panama money' into working-class communities allowed them, for the first time, to develop islandwide financial institutions, designed and managed by themselves. The friendly society movement was revived, transformed and popularised as the leading force within the financial culture of the labouring classes during the early twentieth century. Societies allowed workers, on the weekly payment of about ten to twelve pence, to insure for sick and death benefits. Located in rural villages and in the towns, their accounts were managed by treasurers who were bound by law to deposit all funds at the National Savings Banks.

Between 1907 and 1910 at least 110 societies were established, a remarkable increase over previous years. There were few black families on the tenantries and in the urban areas who did not participate in the movement, and the 1921 census showed that some 156,312 persons were covered by over 260 societies. These black organisations attracted the attention of the legislature for the principal reason that the large sum of capital they collected could be used against the interests of the white community if properly mobilised. For example, societies could purchase land on behalf of members and influence the pattern of land distribution. The 1905 Friendly Societies Act made it illegal for individual societies to hold 'land exceeding one acre in extent'. This legislation immediately undermined the potential of societies to become agents of social change.

Restricted by the 1905 legislation, societies became attractive primarily for the Christmas money 'bonuses' they paid to members. That is, members who paid their weekly subscriptions were entitled to a lump-sum repayment in December, in which case societies functioned more like savings banks than insurance institutions. The important fact was, however, that this way, funds were kept within the hands of blacks rather than falling into the hands of land speculators who were seen to be capitalising on the 'thirst' for land among Panama returnees. In 1946, there was a total of 161 friendly societies on the island, representing 97,639 due-paying members. In that year the societies' members contributed £130,217, and the societies paid out Christmas bonuses of £93,913.

It was undoubtedly an institutional innovation from the black community which reflected the general trend of economic rationality during the depressed years after the mid-1880s. Societies were vital to the survival strategies of communities even after, as in 1905, their wings were clipped by planter legislation. It showed the determination of blacks to keep their hard-earned and scarce capital within institutions that they managed, and in this sense the proliferation of societies constituted a level of economic resistance to planter-merchant domination of the monetary and financial structures of the colony.

Landships and lodges

The social security functions which the early friendly societies had provided for the working class were supplemented by the development and expansion of the 'landship' movement, especially during the depressed years of the 1920s. Described as 'voluntary neighbourhood associations', landships provided the working class with a social organisational structure which at once satisfied the need for cultural expression and socio-economic assistance for workers at times of severe need. Rather than merely subscribing to friendly societies, workers created 'landships' which were associations whose members were ranked and defined according to the status hierarchy used by the British Navy. Their meetings and parades also took on the naval-style display of drill, uniforms and discipline. Members were referred to as 'crews'. The meeting house, invariably a chattel house on a tenantry or in Bridgetown, was the 'ship'. Male youths who joined the ranks were known as 'blues' while the females, who provided medical assistance, were known as 'stars'. The flag of the association was affixed upon the house, or 'ship', as a mask, and within, meetings were conducted in the strictest manner by observations of rank, station and naval protocol. All ships were given names, and 'docked' at frequent intervals. For example, the Rosetta, with its crew from the Bay Street area in Bridgetown, 'docked' every Monday, Wednesday and Friday between 7.30 and 9.30 p.m.

Many communities developed their own 'landships' during the 1920s and 1930s, and these competed in displays of discipline, uniform, drill, and other naval rituals. It has been estimated that during the 1920s more than sixty ships were established throughout Barbados, with over 3,800 male and female crew. Also, it has been argued that the landship was a 'powerful social factor' in the lives of its members.

The movement was essentially unique to Barbados within the Caribbean context and is said to have fulfilled the need of the unemployed poor for order, discipline, respectability and mutual assistance during the depression. 'Crews' paid their weekly fees, and these constituted premiums for insurance against sickness, unemployment and death, while at the same time forcing workers to be frugal with their very limited finance. Members were generally buried in grand military style, with long processions and community attendance.

Like fraternal lodges and friendly societies, the landship movement represented a commitment to self-help and survival within the working classes. It reached its highest organisational level in 1933 when most 'ships' were brought together as a 'fleet' in the Barbados Landship Association, which created the naval rank of admiral for veteran officers. At this stage, the movement displayed its potential for political activity and influence, although on the whole it was not fulfilled. The movement illustrated the organisational capacity of the working class, and pointed towards the development of its political consciousness; at best it indicated that workers were prepared for the rigour of organised mass politics.

Revivalist churches

Like friendly societies and the landship movements, the revivalist church made its impact upon black communities during the 1920s, and emerged as an important social institution. During the 1880s and 1890s, when economic conditions adversely affected the material lives of the working classes, religion became another area in which they asserted their cultural independence and self-leadership. During this time, the revivalist church emerged as expressive of their general rejection of the established Anglican church and other 'white-controlled' denominations. It also symbolised the denial by villagers that social respectability could only be gained by conformity to the dominant Anglicanism, and confirmed that some workers saw social legitimacy in terms of their own autonomous expressions.

A principal origin of the dynamic revivalist church was the United States where Pentecostal and Baptist missionaries, having made substantial inroads within the black communities of the southern states, launched into the Caribbean to serve the spiritual needs not met by the elitist Anglican clergymen. The most prominent among the evangelicals were the Christian Mission, Church of God, Pilgrim Holiness, and the Salvation Army. The Christian Mission began their proselytizing in 1891, and led the way for the other groups to establish what became known as the 'people's ministries'. By the 1920s, these groups had captured the imagination of the black poor who, throughout the island, built their own churches, threw up their own preachers, and managed their own affairs. This self-leadership was in direct contradiction to the traditional practice of blacks congregating under the white clergymen on Sunday mornings. By 1930, most villages and towns were affected by this fundamentalist Christian proliferation; everywhere could be found the tiny wooden churches of Pentecostalists, Plymouth Brethren, Spiritual Baptists, other Baptists and Brethren which fitted congruously with surrounding chattel houses. Meanwhile, the working-class congregations of the Anglican, Wesleyan, Moravian and Methodist churches showed no significant increase, and in some cases declined.

Black Pentecostal preachers, male and female, expounding the gospel in the lively musical and theatrical form of Afro-Barbadian traditions, became a central feature of social life, and represented village autonomy at its most dynamic. The preacher was more than a translator of the scriptures; he or she was the embodiment of respectability, social morality and community leadership. Conflict and tension between the official church and these groups was common. White Anglican clergymen frequently denounced the revivalists from their pulpits and attempted to use their Afrocentric forms of worship as a basis of denigration.

The 1920s, then, was a major watershed in the development of the black community. Certainly, the depression enhanced the spirit of self-help and organisational independence which was expressed in the proliferation of landships, friendly societies and the revivalist churches. A limited conception of these organisations might suggest that they were apolitical in form, but they certainly represented the basis upon which the black community was able to build for its mass entry into the wider political arena, and with their own organisations. In this sense, then, they played a positive role in the development of community cohesion and political confidence.

BLACK POLITICAL MOBILISATION, 1919–37

The proliferation of black socio-economic organisations after the turn of the century, especially the friendly societies, lodges and the Barbados Labour Union (formed in 1919), provided many of the prerequisites for the development of a radical political movement. Indeed, these apparently non-political organisations had been the incubators of the spirit of political agitation and the schools in which working people learnt the skills of political mobilisation. At the end of the nineteenth century, the respected black educationalist, Rawle Parkinson, head teacher of the Wesley Hall School, had impressed upon black workers the importance of recognising the relationships between political activity, economic survival, and the acquisition of formal educational training. By the early 1920s, these developments had coalesced against the background of Marcus Garvey's pan-Caribbean and international 'black power' movement. Garvey's politics, more than any other single factor, rooted within the consciousness of Barbadian workers the fact that only organised mass political action could deliver in a general way those social and economic objectives which they had pursued through their friendly societies.

It was Clennell Wickham who, after the war, did most to provide the working classes with a theoretical framework for political agitation. He did this by articulating working-class interest and frustrations within the context of an aggressive and incisive criticism of planter-merchant elitism. Wickham was a veteran of the First World War, during which his experiences as a black man contributed to the development of his anti-imperialist consciousness. It was difficult for him to reconcile the facts that as the British sought to impose a firm colonial grip on Africa, the landed elite in Barbados was attempting also to strengthen its control over the labouring poor by means of monopoly corporate organisation.

In 1919, Clement Innis established the *Barbados Herald*, a weekly newspaper which has been described as providing, for the first time in the colony's history, 'biting, acerbic, working-class views'. Wickham soon became editor of this newspaper, and used its pages to provide working people with information and analyses relevant to their political condition (Table 20). In the process of debating the crisis of social and economic

Table 20. *Population of Barbados by age groups, 1921*

Age group	Number in group	Number of females in excess of males
Under 10	35,229	363
10–19	36,523	1,953
20–29	24,925	8,167
30–39	16,944	7,542
40–49	16,617	5,253
50–59	12,786	3,120
60–69	8,397	2,123
70–79	3,774	1,288
80–89	976	468
Over 90	132	76

Source: H. Lofty, *Report on the Census of Barbados, 1921*, p. 17

relations in Barbados, he developed a socialist agenda for action, and came close to being the country's first Marxist theoretician and activist. In Wickham, the emergence of a working-class radical intellectual was something new; the politics of the country would henceforth be conditioned by this force from below.

But the man who brought formal political organisation to the working classes for the first time was Charles Duncan O'Neale. As a medical student in Edinburgh during the first decade of the twentieth century, O'Neale had established connections with the British Fabian Socialist Movement which appeared supportive of black radicals committed to the decolonisation process in their colonies. He was a St Lucy man, born in 1879, from a petty-bourgeois family. On his final return to Barbados in 1924, after short periods of medical practice in Newcastle, England, and then Trinidad, O'Neale decided to organise a socialist forum to give representation to working-class interests as articulated by Wickham. As a medical man, he was particularly disturbed by the colony's high and rising infant mortality rates and the generally poor health standards within the black communities. In his estimation little had changed for the better in terms of working-class health and sanitary facilities since his departure from the island as a student in 1899.

In Trinidad, O'Neale had been impressed by the organisational style of Captain Cipriani, the champion of the 'barefoot men' in their struggle for civil rights. He had also been influenced by the black nationalism of Marcus Garvey, in both its organisational and its ideological forms. Under these political influences, O'Neale, undoubtedly a middle-class socialist, projected himself into the leadership of working people. He considered the time right for radical action, since working-class consciousness had been stirred by the 'black power' ideologies of Garvey, as well as the trade unionism which sprang from Cipriani's agitation. According to George Belle, he began to do for the black working class in Barbados what Garvey had been doing for them in Jamaica and the United States – organised them with a clear and viable political agenda.

Within weeks of returning to Barbados, O'Neale had been consulting with Wickham on the political situation with the intention of formulating strategies. In May 1924, he had organised along with Wickham, and other labour supporters such as J. T. C. Ramsay, John Beckles the Garveyite, and J. A. Martineau, a delegation that petitioned the Governor requesting him to use his executive powers to obtain legislation for the termination of the most backward aspect of plantation culture – child labour. This move was designed primarily to attract public attention to their presence and intentions, rather than obtain results, though this demand was made frequently for another ten years. Out of this and other forms of initially limited political actions, emerged in October 1924 the Democratic League – the first political party in Barbados. Though it was initially considered a black middle party with working-class pretensions and a socialist mani-festo, O'Neale's leadership was consistently reflective of the wide range of demands put forward by the disfranchised working class.

The support base for O'Neale's Democratic League was wide and varied. It was supported by black and coloured middle-class professionals as well as the labouring poor. There was a branch of Marcus Garvey's Universal Negro Improvement Association (UNIA) in Barbados from 1920, and the hundreds of active Garveyites threw their support behind the League. The strategy of the League was to contest as many elections as possible and use their base within the Assembly in order to influence the Legislative Council. But the restricted nature of the franchise during the 1920s meant that only a small percentage of the working people possessed the vote. The 1901 Representation of the People Act had placed an income qualification on the franchise of £50 per annum and a freehold qualifi-cation in respect to land and properties of rent £5 or more annually. The small but growing black lower middle class could vote and so could some artisans, but these were insufficient in most parishes to give comfortable majorities to League candidates.

In December 1924, Chrissie Brathwaite won a St Michael seat in a by-election on the League's ticket, and paved the entry of the movement into Parliament. Brathwaite demanded compulsory education for black youths and the banning of child labour. Both O'Neale and other prominent League leaders were branded by the planter press as 'racist', and 'bolsheviks'. In response, O'Neale went to great lengths to illustrate the Christian nature of his socialist philosophy and the moderate quality of his party's agenda. He would frequently state, as did Wickham, that only the most inhumane and unchristian members of the ruling class would seek to oppose measures designed to reduce infant mortality, remove child labour from plantations, and protect working people from the scourge of malnutrition. But the moral appeal of the League was hardly effective within a polity that was dominated by an elite which saw its interests in narrow terms, and had not yet developed a socially holistic vision of its leadership.

Other members of the League were to win seats over the next decade, but defeats came more frequently than successes. Brathwaite was a favourite with the electorate, and in 1930 he finally got some support in the

House when Erskine Ward won the City seat for the League. O'Neale was to eventually win a Bridgetown seat in the 1932 general elections – defeating the prominent merchant H. B. G. Austin by one vote. Until his death in November 1936 he retained this seat, though the strained financial circumstances of the 1930s depression proved not to be a suitable context for the implementation of his social reforms.

O'Neale had also recognised the need for an organisation to further the economic aims of the working class, to represent them on the labour market, and to assist workers to invest their accumulated savings for their collective good. In 1926 he was instrumental in the establishment of the Workingmen's Association which functioned also as the 'industrial and business arm' of the League. Modelled to a certain extent on the Trinidad Workingmen's Association and the British Guiana Labour Union, the Barbados Workingmen's Association was the parent body for two other working-class economic organisations – the Barbados Workers' Union Cooperative Company, and the Workingmen's Loan and Friendly Investment Society. These two organisations had done a great deal to open up avenues in the commercial sector to blacks – the Cooperative Company ran a store on Baxter's Road, while the Investment Society mobilised workers' savings as a friendly society.

The Barbados Workingmen's Association worked in close association with John Beckles of the UNIA. Both organisations were under constant police surveillance on Governor O'Brien's instructions. Uniformed police corporals attended their meetings, took notes, and kept the Governor informed on their activities and ideas. To counter this situation, meetings generally carried some religious and pro-British overtones. As a result, O'Brien was able to report to the Colonial Office that as meetings began with the National Anthem and much singing and praying, they could not be described as being of a revolutionary nature.

But the political militancy of these groups was well cloaked for strategic purposes, and there was no doubt that workers understood the difference between form and content. For example, Moses Small, a radical spokesman for the Workingmen's Association, after singing hymns at the beginning of a meeting on Passage Road, Bridgetown, on 8th December 1927, launched an attack upon the Anglican clergy in the island. He described them as racist and anti-worker, and pleaded with members to reject their 'hypocritical treasures in heaven' theology, but instead to vigorously pursue wealth, property, and general material advance. This was the only way, he argued, that the black race would gain respect and power.

It was during the dockworkers' strike of April 1927 that the

Workingmen's Association made its most incisive impact as a workers' organisation. Trade union activities were still outlawed in Barbados, and employers and government readily unleashed reprisals on protesting workers. O'Neale was unperturbed by the aura of criminality which surrounded his decision to support the workers' strike. Less committed leaders of the Democratic League, and the Workingmen's Association which represented the striking workers, dissociated themselves from O'Neale's actions in fear of employers' and official reprisals. Grantley Adams, the young lawyer, was perhaps most acerbic in his critique of O'Neale's defence of the workers.

Just back from Oxford studies in 1925, Adams had been politicised in England as a 'Liberal Party' associate as opposed to a Labour Party socialist. The Barbados elite recognised his legal skills and moved to absorb him as a supporter of the status quo. He was made editor of the *Agricultural Reporter*, the planters' paper that had taken an aggressive anti-worker stance since the mid-nineteenth century. It was in this capacity that he attacked O'Neale and other working-class leaders during the strike. He described them as hotheads speaking claptrap on political platforms. The strike action was effectively suppressed and the legislature produced the Better Securities Act which provided additional legal machinery for the prosecution of strike leaders and their supporters.

Adams' entry into the political culture of Barbados as the formulator of conservative opinions in the leading planter journal enhanced his image within the workers' movement as a planter-merchant supporter. Wickham used his editorials in *The Herald* to attack Adams, and to illustrate the anti-worker stance which his alliance with the elite represented at this critical stage in the struggle for civil rights. Adams, however, with the might of the establishment behind him, was to become instrumental in the final undoing of Wickham, and *The Herald*. Representing the libel suit of a client, W. D. Bailey, a Bridgetown merchant, against Wickham for statements made in *The Herald*, Adams used his legal skills and official support to the full in gaining what Professor Gordon Lewis described as the 'vindictive judgement of the Barbados Grand Jury' in 1930. Damages to £1,450 plus costs were awarded. This judgement was to ruin Wickham financially and led to the change of ownership of the newspaper.

The taming of *The Herald* and the silencing of Wickham represented a major blow for the Democratic League and the workers' movement, though in 1934 Wynter Crawford started the *Barbados Observer*, an equally radical newspaper dedicated to decolonisation and socialist advancement. Adams continued to criticise the policies of O'Neale and to suggest that the workers' movement needed to come to terms with the realism of planter-merchant power, and to recognise that only gradualist non-confrontation policies could gain important concessions from employers. Refusing to accept the centrality of race prejudice and domination within the political culture, Adams advocated a brand of liberal pragmatism which seemed out of touch with the social forces that had been represented by the Garveyites, O'Neale and Wickham. At the same time, many sections of the workers' movement saw in Adams an outstanding ability which they recognised as misplaced and a sharp intellect only in need of decolonisation.

Adams' criticisms of the Democratic League did much to undermine its potential as a parliamentary force. By the early 1930s it seemed that the conservative and liberal elements in the country had won out against the assault of the Garveyites and socialists. At this stage a measure of frustration crept into the affairs of the League. Measures introduced into the House by its representatives, such as franchise extension, workmen's compensation, compulsory education, and the abolition of child labour, were suppressed or thrown out. For example, between 1930 and 1936, its members in the House sought to reduce the income qualification on the franchise from £50 to £30 per year, and the freehold qualification from £5 to £3, and failed to gain the support of the legislature. Reform efforts were frustrated by select committees and the Legislative Council which were still dominated by conservative members of the merchant-planter elite, one of whose chief spokesmen was Douglas Pile.

Against the background of Wickham's diminished capacity to agitate for the working classes, O'Neale's absorption with Assembly politics, and frustration within the Democratic League, Grantley Adams made his entry into the House. The year was 1934, and his debut represented a triumph for the liberal black middle classes who were now confident that they had found a leader who could withstand the pressures of Garvey's black nationalism and O'Neale's socialism on the one hand, and white racism and conservatism on the other.

Both O'Neale and Chrissie Brathwaite extended a welcome to Adams when he entered the House. They assumed that if he remained true to his liberal principles, these would soon be transformed into radicalism on encountering the rigid conservatism of the planter interest. The events of the next two years showed that there was some truth in their assumptions. In defence of middle-class interest, and in protecting the rights of the 'respectable' working class, which were threatened by the corrosive forces of the 1930s economic depression, Adams became increasingly supportive of measures which were designed to assist the working-class. For example, in the debate over the 1936 Franchise Bill, he emerged as the leading critic of Douglas Pile who had consistently resisted the extension of the franchise. Adams argued that the qualifications had to be reduced, otherwise the economic depression would disenfranchise many persons who hitherto had only marginally qualified, by reducing their income levels. He also declared himself supportive of many of the items that had been on the League's agenda since its inception – such as compulsory education for black children, abolition of child labour, and workers' rights to combine in trade unions.

O'Neale's death in November 1936, therefore, did not result in the crushing of the ideas he had advocated for the establishment of a workers' movement. Wickham had also noted that Adams had become increasingly concerned with defending and extending workers' rights by constitutional reform, and welcomed him as a critic and opposer of planter chauvinism and oligarchy. The Democratic League did not survive O'Neale, and with Wickham's political exile, Adams was well positioned at the parliamentary level to subordinate what was in fact a socialist workers' movement under the wider umbrella of a radical civil rights movement. Wickham had long recognised and argued that the representation of workers, and the general pursuit of civil rights, were two distinct processes, but realised that with the presence of Adams a 'marriage of convenience' was perhaps necessary.

The disintegration of the Democratic League did not result in the disappearance of grass-root political organisations and debates. In fact, workers continued to place great emphasis upon the role of friendly societies and lodges as places of community politicisation. The UNIA branches continued to be active and political meetings became a feature of village life during the 1930s. While Adams was consolidating his position within the Assembly, radical workers, some of whom remained sceptical and hostile to his liberal political style and ideas, saw the need for autonomous organisations to further the process of agitation. It was this development which embraced the radical Clement Payne on his arrival in Barbados, and which constitutes an important part of the background to the 1937 workers' rebellion.

CORPORATE CONSOLIDATION

In order to take advantage of the wartime boom in the sugar industry, and to withstand the pressures resulting from the growing domination of plantation ownership by the mercantile elite, the remaining elements of the traditional plantocracy were forced to adopt strategies for survival. In 1917, they established a large corporation, Plantations Company Limited, with the intention of increasing the size of capital funds available to the industry, and to enable them to purchase and retain plantations, thus minimising the land engrossment tendency of the Bridgetown merchant houses. In addition, the company was designed to pilot the planters' entry into the commercial sector, thereby taking competition to the merchant class, and to capitalise on investment funds being accumulated in the non-sugar sectors.

Since the 1880s, planters had been complaining that the market manipulations of wholesalers and retailers were critical factors in their inability to share the economic benefits accruing to businesses that revolved around the supply of goods and services to their plantations. Commission agents in particular, who controlled price levels, credit lines and the pattern of commodity supply, were identified as their main aggressors. These agents dominated the Commission Merchants Association, as well as the Barbados Mutual Life Assurance Company – a major credit supplier. Plantations Company Limited, therefore, was designed as an instrument of planter defence and counter-aggression within the 'cut-throat' competitive market of the depression years.

In 1920, the merchant sector, realising the effectiveness of the planters' corporate innovation, responded by forming their own large-scale firm – Barbados Shipping and Trading Company Limited. This company became known as the 'Big Six' since it resulted from the amalgamation of the six largest commercial companies operative in the island at that time: Manning, Gardiner Austin, DaCosta, Musson, R. and G. Challenor, and Wilkinson and Haynes. The formation of this company was both a response to planter consolidation, and the inevitable response to the threat of accumulation posed by the depression. The presence of these two corporations – Plantations Company Limited, and Barbados Shipping and Trading Company Limited – signalled the origins of monopoly capitalism in Barbados, and the final stage in the successful economic domination of the colony by the merchant class.

During the 1920s, these two companies competed for trade, arable land and control of government policy. But the threat of black political agitation, which emerged after the mid-1920s, forced their directorates to consider strategies for the consolidation of their power within the polity. The development of organised radicalism in the workplace following the defeated dockworkers' action in 1927, presented the context for the abandonment of outright competition between the two companies. In 1934, they established between themselves the Barbados Produce Exporters Association (BPEA) which, at least symbolically, represented the consummation of the planter-merchant economic alliance, and the triumph of corporate organisation within the economy.[6]

It was against this economic background that the workers' movement had risen during the 1920s and early 1930s. It was this level of organised power which had drawn the boundaries of politics in which Adams was prepared to struggle for a more liberal order; it was this corporate organisational force that socialists like O'Neale and Wickham, and the Garveyites, wanted to confront fully and defeat with worker militancy. The death of O'Neale, then, and the demise of the Democratic League, left the black community without an effective political organisation with which to agitate or mobilise against the agro-commercial elite.

THE 1937 REBELLION

In 1934, when the merchant-planter elite formed the BPEA, the price of sugar collapsed to 5s. per cwt from a level of 26s. in 1923. It stayed at the 5s. level for another three years. Employers reduced wages, cut back on the number of employees, and passed on much of the financial grief to the already impoverished labour force. Workers demanded employment and better wages but were confronted with legislation to prevent combinations. With the closing of large-scale emigration outlets and increasing pressure upon their organisations and leaders by the State and its supporters, workers were driven on the defensive. The 1929 sugar commission which investigated the effects of low sugar prices on workers spelled out gloom and offered no positive suggestions. The daily wage of most labourers remained below the 1s. mark, hardly an improvement since the mid-nineteenth century. With rising levels of inflation after the 1870s, the real income of agricultural workers was slowly eroded. By the mid-1930s, living standards were no higher than at the end of the nineteenth century (see Table 21). At the same time, workers complained that the prevalence of anti-black sentiments had increased since the era of Panama migration, and that on the whole the quality of race relations, already bad, had deteriorated.

By January 1937, therefore, workers were on the receiving end of increasing material pressures and severe social discrimination. They also found themselves lacking effective leadership, at either the organisational or the intellectual level. Wickham was now marginalised, and O'Neale had died. Adams, still oscillating between the defence of a misguided colonial liberalism and the parliamentary representation of the limited civil rights of

Table 21. *Death rates and infantile death rates in Barbados, British Guiana and Trinidad, 1924–29*

Year	Death rate per 1,000 inhabitants			Death rate under 1 year per 1,000 living births		
	Barbados	British Guiana	Trinidad	Barbados	British Guiana	Trinidad
1924	29.5	25.6	—	298	165	—
1925	29.5	24.2	29.5	312	155	134
1926	29.6	25.5	28.8	314	159	143
1927	20.2	26.0	17.8	201	158	130
1928	30.1	27.9	18.7	331	185	129
1929	23.7	23.5	18.5	239	146	128

Source: Report of the Acting Chief Medical Officer, 1929, p. 4

the black middle class and the more secure workers, added to, rather than removed, the bewilderment among the labouring poor. The man who brought sudden dynamic and potentially revolutionary leadership to the workers was Clement Payne, a young man in his early 30s, of Barbadian parentage, though born in Trinidad. He arrived in Barbados on 26th March 1937, and with the assistance of Fitzgerald Chase, and Israel Lovell the militant Garveyite, he rapidly established a large following in the Bridgetown area during his four months' residence.

A major part of Payne's activities concerned the organisation of workers into a strong trade union force in order to counter the power of the corporate merchant-planter elite. Collective bargaining was still outlawed, but Payne sought to impress upon workers the critical importance of confronting 'capitalism' with 'strong trade unions'. He argued that this was the only way to deal with depressed wages, price inflation, and the victimisation of workers in the workplace. His rhetoric attracted workers in their thousands, especially in the Bridgetown area, who had already benefited from the politicisation of the Democratic League and the Workingmen's Association.

Payne succeeded in combining the incisive socio-political analysis of Wickham with the organisational drive of O'Neale, and in a short period of time captured the imagination of radicals, and the younger generation. He did not confine his fiery speeches to the labour question, but spoke of race relations, black cultural suppression, the pan-American nature of Garveyism, and Italian aggression towards Ethiopia. Ernest Mottley, the black real-estate agent and supporter of the planter-merchant elite, stated that Payne's politics were of the black versus white nature, and thought that his ideological position was, unlike O'Neale's communistic.

Mottley, like many among the upper middle-class blacks, considered political references by black radicals to African liberation and black cultural nationalism, as racist attacks upon the dominant Euro-cultural element within the colony. As such, he considered Garveyites racist, and Payne's criticisms of the liberal black middle class communistic. Payne also incurred the wrath of respectable black professionals because he placed the issue of racial and cultural domination at the fore of the old debate about economic exploitation.

In addition, Payne's political agitation centred around the need to defend strike actions that had been proliferating throughout the West Indies. In St Kitts, for example, workers on a sugar estate had rioted in January 1935 over wage levels and money bonuses. The riot was put down by armed police who shot dead three workers and wounded another eight. Payne brought such information to the attention of Barbadian workers, and also informed them that riots were taking place throughout the West Indies as a result of similar circumstances. Coal workers in St Lucia and oil workers in Trinidad quickly followed those in St Kitts, and Payne held forth these events as evidence of the rising consciousness of black West Indians.

Government officials and police authorities had been closely monitoring Payne from his first public meeting in Bridgetown. They had recognised in him a new quality of leadership, one that was aggressive, intellectually forceful, and attractive to the younger generation. He was considered dangerous to the social order, and had to be removed. The Government decided to act by putting Payne on trial for declaring falsely to the immigration authorities on arrival from Trinidad that he was born in Barbados. The objective was to gain a conviction for his deportation. His conviction on 22nd July was reversed by the Court of Appeal, but on the evening of 26th July 1937, Payne was clandestinely spirited out of the island by Barbadian police acting in association with their Trinidadian counterparts.

The trial of Payne was a major public event; workers assembled outside the court in their thousands to keep abreast of proceedings. In the trial Payne appeared in court without a lawyer and pleaded not guilty. His counsel in the appeal trial was Grantley Adams, who though not still committed to worker radicalism, and who did not believe in Payne's authenticity as a labour leader, considered that the government was exerting pressure unconstitutionally on the judiciary in order to gain a political victory over workers. On being convicted, Payne led a force of several hundred workers to publicly appeal the decision before the Governor. The police refused to let him see the Governor, and when he persisted he and a number of his followers were arrested. An order was then issued for his deportation.

On the 26th, the Court of Appeal quashed his conviction on the grounds that since he had spent a number of years as an infant in Barbados, he might not have known that he was born in Trinidad. During the course of the day workers prepared to act on the court's decision by rescuing Payne from police custody, but discovered during the evening that he had already been deported. Angered by the actions of government, workers converted Bridgetown into a riot zone, clashing with police in Golden Square, destroying private and public property. Cars were smashed, and public lighting utilities along River Road and Jemmott's Lane were damaged. Armed police managed to control the situation that evening, but the following morning, 27th July, riot flared up once again in Bridgetown and spread into the countryside.

The violent assault by workers on officialdom and its immediate representatives, the police constables, on the morning of 27th July, was not expected. Government had assumed that workers' grievances had been expressed and quelled the previous day and was therefore not politically prepared. Workers had not revolted in this violent manner since the 1876 confederation affair, and the ruling classes saw no reason to believe that it would occur then. Armed with stones, bottles, sticks and similar instruments, workers began their attack upon the heart of ruling-class power – the commercial district of the city. They smashed office fronts and store windows and overturned cars on Broad Street; they attacked the 'marooned' employees in the Barbados Mutual Office, and threatened to burn the building. Before doing so, they were attacked by a police detachment who fired blank volleys from their rifles. Properties were also damaged in Bay Street and Probyn Street, most of these before the rebels had crossed Chamberlain Bridge from the Golden Square area and moved across Trafalgar Square into Broad Street.

By midday the police had been instructed to use all possible means to restrain and subdue the rebels. The police reported being informed that some of the rebels had been in possession of firearms and were prepared to use them. With bayonets fixed to their rifles which were loaded with live rounds of ammunition, police detachments confronted blacks in Bridgetown and killed several. This display of naked power threw unarmed rebels on the defensive; groups broke up, as individuals fled in fear of their lives.

Meanwhile, news of the morning affair had spread to the countryside, and hungry workers there responded by looting potato fields and plantation stocks, and threatening white plantation personnel. In St Lucy and St Andrew, workers were most determined to appropriate as much food from the plantations as possible. In these parishes planters enlisted specially armed constables to restrain workers, who also added to the list of fatalities by shooting persons suspected of looting. By the morning of 30th July, the revolt was crushed by these various armed forces, and calm was restored to both town and country. No whites were killed, while 14 blacks were reported to have lost their lives and 47 injured. Over 500 were arrested and approximately 260 tried and convicted after receiving, in many cases, severe beatings from the police and special constables.

With the removal of Payne from the colony, the working classes were not left leaderless. Indeed, Payne had been particularly effective within the short space of time precisely because he worked in conjunction with other working-class leaders, especially Israel Lovell, Darnley Alleyne, Mortimer Skeete, F. G. (Menzies) Chase and Ulric Grant and used existing organisational structures. In his absence, Israel Lovell, who had been critical to the development of the Garveyite movement, came to the foreground. In fact, it was Lovell who led the agitation against the Government during the Payne trial, while Ulric Grant has been immortalised for making the statement that 'there was no justice in Coleridge Street' (location of the court), for which the judge, in sentencing him for sedition, was excessively harsh.

In an attempt to keep the Payne movement alive, Lovell often told workers assembled in Golden Square that he could not be deported, that he was not afraid of the police or the courts, and that he was prepared to die in the process of building a workers' movement. He also told workers that the successful criminalisation of Payne by the government was the result of workers' organisational deficiency. In response to one statement about workers and praedial larceny, he stated: 'We cannot steal from the whiteman because, if we take anything, it would be only some of what they have stolen from our fore-parents for the past two hundred and fifty years.'

The political speeches of Lovell were steeped in the history of economic and social relations between workers and employers in the colony. He was aware of the need to bring historical awareness to workers so as to mobilise them into conscious, determined action. In one speech he stated: 'We make the wealth of this country and get nothing in return. Our slave fathers were in a better condition than we are today. The world is against us, so let us unite in mass formation and stand up like men.' These utterances reflected clearly the Garveyite nature of his ideology, and illustrated the fact that with Payne's removal during the trial, the UNIA had assumed temporarily the leadership of the workers' movement.

Events which followed immediately after the rebellion established the nature of the reformist leadership which dominated the labour movement for the next two decades or so. The Deane Commission of Enquiry was established by the Governor to investigate and report on the origins, causes and nature of the rebellion. For several sittings after the rebellion, the Assembly did not discuss the matter, and many middle-class black politicians distanced themselves from it altogether. As the defence counsel for Payne, Adams was concerned that government officials would attempt to link him in some way to the event, and sought a meeting of clarification with the Governor, along with Chrissie Brathwaite, W. W. Reece, J. E. T. Brancker and Hilton Vaughan. When the Deane Commission began to hear evidence for the first time on Friday, 13th August 1937, Adams was the first witness. There, he espoused the view that the 'riot' was the result of rapidly deteriorating social and economic conditions among workers, and that liberal reforms could restore healthier social relations.

For Adams, such statements to the Deane Commission were insufficient to protect his image as the most forceful black parliamentary reformer, and so in September he sought council with Governor Young to inform him that he was going to England on personal business and that he was not 'running away' from the situation. He was given some assurance by the Governor that there was no official suspicion of his involvement in the rebellion, and that he was still held in some confidence by the Executive. While in England, Adams sought, with much persistence and cunning, an audience with the Colonial Secretary so as to strengthen his leadership position in Barbados. Governor Young informed the Colonial Secretary that such a meeting would be of service to Adams 'politically', which might explain the two months that Adams was kept waiting by the Colonial Secretary.

Adams believed that his professional political career as a social reformer could be enhanced only by close association with the Colonial Office which was already committed to a loosely articulated reform policy. As such, he did not depart from England until he had won the confidence and support of most high-ranking colonial officials. This factor is of critical importance in understanding the remaining years of Adams' career. Colonial Secretary

Ormsby-Gore wrote after his first meeting with Adams: 'I saw Mr Adams and liked him.' He was considered the kind of man the Colonial Office wanted to lead the ethos of reform to colonial politics in order to undermine radical black nationalists and socialists alike.

Adams enjoyed the status of a Colonial Office favourite from then into the 1950s. While in England, he had also cemented a supportive relation with the Fabian Movement, Labour Party officials, and the well-known and respected colonial reformer, Arthur Creech-Jones, who became the Secretary of State for the Colonies in Atlee's post-war Labour government. Adams returned to Barbados fortified with imperial support, which he used aggressively over the next decade in order to suppress radicals within the labour movement and dominate its leadership.

CHAPTER EIGHT

From colony to state,
1937–1966

The report of the Deane Commission of Enquiry into the 1937 workers' rebellion charged that 'the audiences which Payne attracted at his open air meetings were composed largely of the young and irresponsible members of the community of Bridgetown . . . whose enthusiasm was easily fired by the prospect held out to them of getting more money and the vapid language of his speeches'. This perception of the generality of Payne's followers was shared, in part, by sections of the more privileged black community which had supported the defunct but respectable Democratic League.

Conservative blacks, of whom Adams was clearly the primary spokesman, also condemned workers' resort to violence and armed confrontation. Adams, none the less, was aware of the need to mobilise and direct the upsurge of political enthusiasm and energy released as a result of the disturbances, and some of his ardent followers set about the task of forming an organisation to lead and represent working-class opinion. The body which was launched in October 1938 to achieve this end was the Barbados Labour Party – a political organisation designed to 'provide political expression for the island's law-abiding inhabitants', as distinct from the so-called 'lawless' poor among whom Payne was alleged to have found extensive support. This organisation soon changed its name to the Barbados Progressive League.

The Progressive League was, in a general way, within the tradition of the Democratic League; it was essentially a middle-class-led organisation vying for a mass base in order to confront and eventually reduce the oligarchical political power of the consolidated merchant-planter elite. Logically, therefore, it was composed partly of former Democratic League Assemblymen and followers, and some new radical activists and liberal professionals. Of the former group, C. A. (Chrissie) Brathwaite and J. A. Martineau were most prominent. Brathwaite was a black, small entrepreneur, who had made some headway in the real-estate business, and also owned a store in Bridgetown; Martineau was a beverage producer with a secure financial standing. The League's ranks were also strengthened by Wynter Crawford, an anti-colonial activist with an interest in the publishing business whose political views, though to the left of Adams, were not as radical as those of Payne or Garvey. There was also Edwy Talma, like Adams a self-defined liberal, and the radical Garveyite, Herbert Seale. Brathwaite was selected President, Talma, General-Secretary (after Crawford's refusal), Martineau, Treasurer, and Adams, Vice-President. Seale, who was appointed Assistant to Talma, was soon made General Secretary in order to exploit his organising skills.

Within its first year, the League was torn by ideological conflict over the question of working-class representation and leadership. The main division which surfaced involved Adams on the right, Seale and his supporters on the left. Both men had substantial support within the League; Adams, unlike Seale, had support within officialdom, and fresh from his English political tour where he had solicited much influence within the Colonial Office, the cards seemed stacked against Seale even though he was closer to the grass roots. Seale had already identified with the political ideas which Payne had sought to bring to the Barbadian worker: firm, aggressive trade unionism within the black consciousness programme as outlined by Garvey.

Adams was the 'gradualist' liberal reformer, the colonial moderate, who believed that the workers' main grievances were economic in nature. Adams, then, became publicly critical of Seale's worker radicalism, as he had been critical of Wickham and O'Neale during the 1927 dockworkers' strike. He accused Seale of confrontationalist politics, though he accepted that Seale had been the most active campaigner in terms of taking the League's programme to the working classes, and mobilising large crowds for public meetings. For Seale, the liberal element within the League was retarding the struggle for workers' rights; Adams believed that Seale was making 'things move too fast, without at the same time securing a foundation'.

Adams' strategy for social reform was to tap the minuscule liberal element within the empowered merchant-planter class, to force them to see that making legislative concessions to workers was in their long-term interest. Seale wanted workers' power consolidated in strong trade unions so as to be able to dictate terms of employment which workers could accept. Within the labour movement, Seale's followers accused Adams of betraying worker agitation, while Adams argued that Seale was creating a

Clement Payne, political activist, civil rights campaigner, and central figure in the 1937 workers' rebellion.

Grantley Adams talking to sugar-workers. He was the leader of the organised labour movement during the 1940s and early 1950s, the first (and only) premier of the West Indies Federation, and first premier of Barbados.

climate of hostility that could only have adverse effects on the workers themselves. These debates of 1939 took place within the context of a large number of cane fires, unauthorised strikes and widespread militancy among workers.

Seale was instrumental in the organisation of the 21st February 1939 general strike which sought to increase wage levels in the sugar and urban-based industries. Adams was accused by some workers of plotting to compromise their rights, and for using his high-level political influence to that end. It has been suggested that Seale and Cox were concerned principally with creating the context for toppling the President and Vice-President of the League, and to bring firmer leadership to the labour movement. Workers in the sugar industry, on the docks and in the omnibus company were most militant. Adams' response was to win support within government, the merchant community, and the planter press for a condemnation of the strike, including Seale's participation and leadership. In a speech on 1st March 1939, in Queen's Park, Adams outlined his approach as follows:

. . . we have the government willing to assist us, we have an influential body of merchants willing to go thoroughly into the facts and figures connected with workers in Bridgetown. We give them the assurance that we as your officers of the Progressive League will keep the workers in check, and will tell them how stupid apart from being criminal it is to strike when negotiations are the correct way to improve conditions.

Adams' supporters outside the League also pressed for Seale's removal from the executive of the League. He succeeded also in obtaining effective support within the executive in order to isolate Seale by condemning the strike action. The *Barbados Advocate* reported:

The Progressive League has done a service to labour and to the community by resolutely condemning the unauthorised strikes that occurred in the city on Monday . . . The Executive Officers of the League, Mr. G. H. Adams, Mr. C. A. Brathwaite, and Dr. H. G. Cummins acted in a manner that is in the best traditions of Trade Union Leadership . . . It is gratifying therefore to find its leaders emphasizing that the unauthorised strikes were calculated to harm the cause of the Progressive League and of Trade Unionism in Barbados. The 'Advocate' is prepared to lend its wholehearted support to all those who are resolved to give labour such responsible guidance.

On 4th March it was reported that Seale had been forced to resign from the League's executive committee. But Adams was not satisfied with this

*Charles Duncan O'Neale, socialist
agitator and reformer, and co-founder
and leader of the Barbados Democratic
League.*

*Clennell Wickham, journalist, socialist
and political activist of the 1920s. He
was the leading critic of the
merchant–planter conservative elite,
and founder of the democratic
movement.*

victory. He was determined to overturn a decision the executive had made to offer Seale a $50 honorarium for his outstanding services. He went to the League's membership and accused the executive of plotting to squander their money on Seale, the adventurist; this time he won his biggest victory – the resignation of the executive committee.

When the committee was reconstituted by elections in July, Adams was the new President, Talma, his loyalist, was Treasurer. The new members, Barry Springer (Vice-President) and C. A. Nurse (General Secretary) were also Adams loyalists. Both Brathwaite and Martineau were removed. It was a major triumph for Adams. He was now at the helm of the organised labour movement. Seale was pushed into the background, along with the radical workers he had worked with. The surviving veteran element of the Democratic League was purged, and Adams' power within the organisation seemed unlimited. A significant section of the working classes, however, continued to oppose Adams' accommodationist politics, and many also suspected the sincerity of his concern for workers' rights. These elements continued, none the less, to support the League, but sought to identify alternative spokesmen to counter Adams' leadership.

POLITICS OF LABOURISM

The ability of the Progressive League to mobilise a mass following within a year of its formation had to do with Herbert Seale's promotion of it as an organisation committed to labour solidarity, political agitation, and social welfare considerations. The tripartite nature of its programme attempted to cover most aspects of working-class demands. The slogan of the League, 'Three units, one arm: raising the living standards for the working classes', reflected these distinct but related dimensions of its programme.

Almost from its inception, the executive of the League vigorously lobbied governmental officials for the right to represent working-class interests before the Royal Commission appointed 'to investigate social and economic conditions in the West Indies'. In this objective it succeeded, and Adams became its principal spokesman before the Commission which arrived in Barbados on Saturday, 14th January 1939. Lord Moyne, the chairman of the Commission, arrived in Barbados the following week, and the exchange between himself and Adams not only influenced considerably the conclusions of the Commission, but illustrated clearly the political interests of Adams and his leadership of the League.

Adams went to great lengths to convince the Commission that neither he nor his colleagues were communists or supporters of such organisations, but socialists committed to an equitable distribution of economic resources and the liberalisation of social institutions. In full awareness of the fact that the sugar plantation system represented the basis of merchant-planter oligarchical conservatism and illiberalism, Adams focused upon the need to reconstitute the ownership of the sugar industry as the key to socio-political transformation. He argued for the partial nationalisation of the industry as a prerequisite for social reform, but Lord Moyne, recognising the political difficulties implicit within the proposal, moved quickly for a fuller explanation. The exchange was as follows:

ADAMS: I suggest that the plantation system is basically the cause of our trouble, and I think that the system which has survived in Barbados for three hundred years, of having a small narrow, wealthy class and a mass of cheap labour on the other side, should be abolished . . . As I have pointed out My Lord, even such social legislation as we have had in the last ten years or so has been rather the result of fear, than of a real sense of social justice . . .

LORD MOYNE: Well then, you recommend the nationalisation of the sugar industry. Do you really think you could get a greater efficiency in that way?

ADAMS: When we use the term nationalisation perhaps it connotes more than we intended, that is to say – not in the English sense a complete nationalisation; we are really suggesting government ownership of sugar factories, cooperative production, and marketing.

LORD MOYNE: Provided that your scheme remains in the realms of practical politics and that you're content with making the best of the present system and seeing that there is a fair distribution of the resources of the industry, I think you're on rather safe ground.

Adams was soon to reverse his ideas about containing planter-merchant oligarchical power by undermining their monopolistic ownership of the sugar industry. In accounting for Adams backing away from structural change within the industry, Professor Gordon Lewis wrote:

The Adams leadership apparently accepted the widespread Barbadian belief that a radical stance on the sugar question destroys a political career; it apparently also accepted the belief, sedulously spread by the plantocracy, that a nationalisation policy would lead to economic disaster and social chaos.

By 1940, the League was no longer seriously concerned with the question of nationalisation. The West Indies Labour Congress of 1938 promoted nationalisation as a manifesto issue of most labour organisations. But

Adams had sensed that the Moyne Commission, and the British Government, were not supportive of such a strategy for socio-economic reform. Since he had decided that it would be possible to push meaningful labour reforms through the House only if he stayed close to executive power, Adams opted instead for a strategy of 'responsible' dialogue with the landed elite in the hope of gaining concessions for labour.

By the end of 1940 the economic lobby within the League was placed in the forefront of its reform strategy; the friendly society unit and the political wing, which were designed to mobilise the limited electorate (3.5 per cent of the population in 1940) in order to win seats in the House, receded temporarily into the background. The Trade Disputes Act of 12th June 1939, and the Trade Union Act of 1st August 1940, both recommended by the Moyne Commission, created the legislative context within which trade unionism could function constitutionally. On 4th October 1941, the Barbados Workers' Union was formed, the outgrowth of a number of committees within the League that had dealt with the question of workmen's compensation, and had agitated for a Wage Board to assist the process of legalising wage agreements.

Adams' dominance of the labour movement during this period was reflected in his appointment as President of the Union, as well as his appointment by the Governor to the Executive Council as the workers' representative for the 1942–44 session. During the 1940s, when the legislative foundations for effective trade unionism were established, his style of leadership and political ideas were stamped on most important proceedings. That the Trade Union Act had not given workers the right to picket as an important instrument in bargaining, illustrated the compromising nature of his leadership – one which emphasised the need to extract concessions from employers without irritating or confronting them as a class.

The Workmen's Compensation Act of 1943 was an important victory for the League, though like the Trade Union Act, workers found themselves entrapped in a web of conditions, provisions and limitations. Meanwhile, the employers were also making great strides towards the establishment of protective organisations in order to combat labour combination. On 11th May 1945 the Shipping and Mercantile Association was formed. This was followed by the Sugar Producers' Federation, the Bus Owners' Association, and the Barbados Hackney and Livery Car Owners' Association, on 8th December 1945, 16th April 1947 and 9th October 1948 respectively.

Despite the limited franchise, the political wing of the League succeeded in mobilising sufficient votes to win seats in the Assembly for five of the six candidates proposed in 1940. Adams and Crawford had already parted company, and Crawford contested the election as an independent after leaving the League. He won the St Philip seat with a handsome majority. In 1941, Adams, Hugh Springer and Dr H. G. Cummins were sitting in the legislature on behalf of the League, and J. T. C. Ramsay, a known grassroots politician, had won a by-election and was sitting in the House. It was this group which pioneered the legislative labour reforms of the early 1940s, which were consistent with many of the suggestions of the Moyne Commission.

The League's biggest challenge, however, came in April and May 1943 when the House debated the Representation of the People Bill, a measure designed to extend the franchise to a larger section of the labouring population – also recommended by the Moyne Commission. The ruling elite showed its opposition to the measure from the outset. Indeed, Wynter Crawford, a former League member, and now the leading radical labour leader on the left of Adams, stated that the government's bill was brought to the House with much imperial support, which weighed against the real preference of the elite for a reduction rather than an increase of the franchise. Adams and Crawford demanded adult suffrage instead of the government's proposed reduction of the income qualification to £30.

In spite of Adams' radical rhetoric on the franchise question, it was Crawford who carried the debate for the workers by illustrating the rigid conservatism of the governing merchant-planter elite. Crawford, none the less, was not successful in obtaining adult suffrage; the motion was defeated and the bill amended to reduce the income qualification to £25 was passed on 4th May; it became law as the Representation of the People Act, 1943. The number of persons now able to vote increased by some 510 per cent, and women, for the first time in the colony's history, got the franchise. These were important, though limited, developments in the rise of democratic rights within the colony, and represented triumphs for organised labour.

The franchise extension of 1943 meant that the 1944 general election would take place within larger political dimensions. By this time, the political leadership of the labour movement was divided, with Adams and Crawford representing the two main contending factions. Contesting the elections were Adams' Progressive League, the newly formed militant West Indian National Congress Party of Crawford, and the planters' political party, the Electors' Association. It was an aggressively fought election; never before had the ideological divisions within the island's

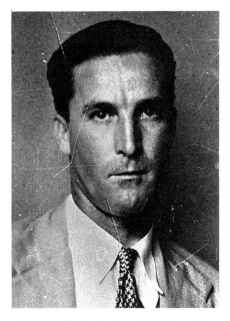

Ermie Bourne, the first woman to win a seat in the House of Assembly, as the Barbados Labour Party representative for the St Andrew constituency in the 1951 general election.

A.E.S. 'T.T.' Lewis, the radical labour leader and trade unionist who used his political skills to support the black nationalist movement. He was known to the workers in Bridgetown in the 1940s and early 1950s as 'the white man with the black heart'.

Errol Barrow, premier and first Prime Minister of Barbados.

Wynter Crawford, the founder leader of the Barbados Congress Party and leading civil rights agitator of the 1940s. He was a staunch defender of the working classes from the 1930s to the 1960s.

politics so clearly articulated and exposed for public discourse. The conservative and right-wing policies of the Electors' Association reflected the determined stance of the planter-elite to hold on to political power, while the Congress Party, rooted within radical elements of the working class, sought to break planter-merchant political leadership and advance towards socialist government. The Progressive League, critical of both these right and left parties, pledged itself to labour reforms, social welfare policies, and a gradualist approach in the search for liberal political democracy.

The election was fought over many of the issues that had surfaced during the 1937 workers' rebellion and the investigation thereafter. The Congress Party was most incisive in its evaluation of those events, and its campaign revived memories of Clement Payne's movement. It made no compromises in its self-assertion as the radical wing of the labour movement, and Crawford in particular suggested that both Adams and the Electors' Association were involved in plots to undermine the workers' search for power and to deflect the movement from socialism. Throughout the country, the Congress Party called for adult suffrage, a government nationalisation programme, compulsory education, free books and hot lunches for school children, a national health and unemployment scheme, state ownership of important parts of the agricultural sector, and the disestablishment of the still influential Anglican Church. This party emerged during the campaign as the radical vanguard of the labour movement, imposing a major psychological blow to Adams and the Progressive League. Its manifesto called upon workers to 'vote for a new Barbados', and the *Barbados Observer*, the Party newspaper edited by Crawford, carried the messages: 'Forward to a People's Victory' and 'Bring Socialism to Barbados'.

The *Barbados Advocate* carried the programme of the Electors' Association, while the *Barbados Observer* was particularly venomous in its attack upon the planters' party. The *Barbados Observer* of Saturday, 4th November 1944 carried an article which illustrated what the radicals thought of the Electors' Association:

. . . Throughout the history of this island, it has been dominated by a small and selfish clique and it is indeed remarkable that now, this clan senses that it has reached a crisis, it has actually had the shamelessness and the temerity to publicly appeal to the people of this island and ask them to help them consolidate their weakening position . . . for sheer presumptuous impudence it is unparalleled. It is an absolute insult to the intelligence of the people. Only the congenital idiots among the masses will vote for the candidates of the Electors Association on November 27th.

Two weeks later the *Observer*, by way of deepening its political critique of the ruling class, carried a column which stated:

Barbados is in revolt against the status quo. Throughout the country thousands of middle and working class men and women are voicing the most determined protests against poverty and unemployment. These thousands are resolved to put more of the wealth in the colony at the service of the people; these thousands are in deadly earnest, this spirit may well be called NEW DEMOCRACY . . . No longer are the people of this island prepared to entrust their destinies to the representatives of big business.

When the votes were counted on 27th November, the Congress Party had won eight seats, the League seven seats, and the Electors' Association eight seats. These results represented, at least in theory, a resounding victory for the labour movement over the traditional planter-merchant political forces. Crawford spoke of the end of the planter-government and the triumph of the progressive democratic forces, while the leadership of the Electors' Association began to prepare a strategy for the protection of its members' economic and social interests.

THE BUSHE EXPERIMENT AND THE RISE OF THE BARBADOS LABOUR PARTY

The development of party politics and the ideological nature of the 1944 general election exposed fully the undemocratic nature of the govern-mental structure. With a considerably enlarged electorate sending rep-resentatives to the Assembly, the system of government in which an executive governor was held fully responsible for political administration seemed contrary to the principle of democratic representation. If power was to reside in the Assembly, it seemed clear that responsibility for government should likewise be found there.

In 1946, Governor Bushe emerged as the agent who sought to attach responsibility for government to the Assembly's determination to hold political power. He proposed a system of government whereby member-ship of the executive committee would reflect the distributions of seats held by political parties within the Assembly. Such a system of power sharing had already been suggested by radicals within the labour movement as a democratic solution. The Congress Party had never been comfortable with the system whereby the Governor arbitrarily selected the members of the powerful Executive Committee. In this sense, then, the Bushe reform represented a partial victory for the labour movement.

The basis of this constitutional reform was that the officer in charge of governmental administration would approach the parliamentary leader of the political party which held a majority in the House and request that such a person recommend parliamentary members to sit on the Executive Committee. Constituted in this manner the Executive Committee would then be held responsible for government programmes. Individual members would be placed in charge of sections of government business, with responsibility for policies. In effect, this was the beginning of what became known as 'semi-ministerial' government. Bushe also proposed that since the Attorney-General, E. K. Walcott, was an active member of the Electors' Association, he should not be considered the government's spokesman in the House, and suggested that this role should be performed by the majority leader. This system of government eventually led to the establishment of cabinet government in 1954.

The Congress Party, in particular, stood to benefit from the new system of government. But since the 1944 election victory, Governor Bushe had decided that the Congress leadership was too radical and therefore not fit to be represented on the Executive Committee; as a result, he gave preference to the Progressive League in the persons of the pro-British Adams and his loyalist Hugh Springer. Not surprisingly, when the Assembly debated that year a motion for the increase of the Governor's salary, Crawford voted against it while Adams and Springer voted in favour. Governor Bushe expressed his preference for Adams as a labour leader, and made no secret of his disapproval of Crawford and the socialist anti-imperialist Congress Party. At the same time he reported to the Colonial Office on the disunity within the leadership of the labour movement, and the implications this had for the constitutional reform he proposed. The whites, he stated, were generally opposed to any measure that would strengthen the political hand of the blacks, while the latter, he added, 'are divided among themselves, suspicious of one another, and apparently incapable of any concerted or constructive action'.

The experiment in semi-responsible government, Bushe reported to Whitehall, could be effective as long as 'the progressive leaders', whom he did not 'trust', could be persuaded to be 'moderate'. While he was being assured by Adams that moderation would prevail, the labour scene was increasingly being characterised by unofficial strikes, and an almost unending series of cane fires; these developments, according to the Governor, reflected the growing militancy of grass-root political activists. The full details of Bushe's plan for governmental reform were finally presented to the legislature on 1st October 1946. It represented the beginning of the end of traditional executive government, and the first part of the victory for the principle of popular representative government. In political terms it meant the seizing of legislative power from the planter-oligarchy, and a major triumph for the labour movement.

The general election of 1946 presented the first opportunity to witness the functioning of the Bushe reforms. This election was contested by the same political parties as that of 1944 – but the League had now been reconstituted and renamed the Barbados Labour Party. It was also an aggressively fought election, with ideological differences held out to the electorate, and bitter attacks levelled at opposition leaders and parties. The departing Governor Bushe was also caught within the electioneering cross-fire. The Barbados Labour Party, through its organ the *Beacon*, praised him as the kind of progressive governor the island had always needed. He was described as an historic figure committed to the development of the island's national interests.

The Congress Party, on the other hand, held an opposing view of Governor Bushe. Crawford, in particular, had observed how Bushe had favoured the anti-socialist Adams faction, a reflection of the Colonial Office's preference for the brand of politics they espoused. The *Observer* accused Bushe of blocking the progressive policies of the Congress, and declared that he had conspired with Adams to keep Congress members off the Executive Committee. Furthermore, the Congress Party accused Bushe of fostering the development of an accommodationist labour movement with the assistance of Adams and the Electors' Association, as part of a strategy to suppress worker radicalism, slow down the pace of decolonisation, and derail the movement toward socialism.

The basis of Crawford's charge was the fact that during the 1945 Congress-led sugar-workers' struggle for wage increases, the Progressive League, led by Adams and Springer, moved into a reactionary alliance with the Electors' Association in order to break Congress' unionisation of the sugar workers – and all with the full support of the Governor's Executive. The Congress Party, then, though with the most seats in the House, was under-represented on the Executive Committee since, in the words of Bushe, there was no member of that party whom he could 'consider' for selection.

The election results reflected in part the nature of the organised pressure exerted upon the Congress Party. The Barbados Labour Party won nine seats, Congress seven, and the Electors' Association eight, and one independent candidate was returned. According to the rules of the Bushe reform, Adams, as leader of the Barbados Labour Party, was called upon to lead the government in the House, and to nominate four candidates for the

Executive Committee. The names submitted by Adams, in addition to his own, were Hugh Springer from the Barbados Labour Party, and Crawford and H. D. Blackman from the Congress Party.

The Barbados Labour Party, however, had no working majority in the House, and was forced into a coalition with the Congress Party in order to push through reform legislation. It was an uncomfortable coalition from the beginning. Crawford was not impressed by Adams' alleged subservience to the Colonial Office, nor his accommodationist attitudes towards the conservative Electors' Association. He wanted rapid socioeconomic changes, but Adams, as in the late 1930s, wanted moderate reforms to proceed slowly and without political acrimony. Some members on the Congress backbenches were also not fully committed to the alliance with Adams' Labour Party, and took the opportunity to vote against measures agreed upon in the Executive Committee by Crawford and Blackman.

Meanwhile, as the coalition showed all signs of disintegration, Adams initiated a number of political measures designed to split the Congress Party. By October 1947, Crawford had resigned from the Executive Committee, but Adams succeeded in countering this move by enticing three of Congress' prominent leaders to cross the floor and join the Barbados Labour Party; these were C. E. Talma, A. E. Lewis and H. D. Blackman. The Barbados Labour Party now had a total of twelve seats in the House, though this was soon reduced to eleven when Hugh Springer removed himself from politics to become the first Registrar of the University of the West Indies, which was established in Jamaica in 1948. In this year, the Barbados Labour Party won the general election, taking twelve of the twenty-four seats.

Adams' dominance of the parliamentary labour movement was now consolidated. Meanwhile, his reputation in the Colonial Office as a man to be trusted to protect British colonial interest had been illustrated by his inclusion in the British delegation to the United Nations to debate the question of decolonisation. There, he emerged as a staunch defender of Empire, and incurred the wrath of African and Asian delegates. Adams' status was also enhanced regionally by his 1947 election to the Presidency of the Caribbean Labour congress, much to the distress of socialist activists such as Richard Hart from Jamaica, C. L. R. James from Trinidad, and Dr Cheddi Jagan from British Guiana.

Within the House, Adams resolved the problem of not having, once again, a working majority by enticing another Congress member, D. D. Garner, to cross the floor and join the Barbados Labour Party. He also engineered the appointment of a Barbados Labour Party member, K. N. Husbands, to the Speakership. But legislative reforms were still being frustrated by the power of the executive, which remained intact under the Bushe experiment, and the non-cooperation of the Legislative Council, which was still dominated by the conservative members of the planter-oligarchy. In 1949, the Barbados Labour Party won the debate on a motion within the House which called for the restriction of the power of the Legislative Council, and the House voted in accordance. The next major hurdle for the Barbados Labour Party was the attainment of universal adult suffrage, and the abolition of property requirements for membership of the House of Assembly.

ADULT SUFFRAGE AND THE 1951 GENERAL ELECTION

During the 1940s, the Congress Party had been calling aggressively for adult suffrage while the Labour Party, especially immediately after the 1946 election, seemed less persistent on the question. However, by early 1950, Adams – now with a majority in the House, and realising that the parliamentary Congress Party was experiencing internal problems – took the opportune initiative of introducing a bill to amend the Representation of the People Act 1901. For Adams, this was the beginning of the final phase in the rise of liberal democracy, and the basis of the undoing of the planter-elite's political control over the legislature. The measure was also timed to take advantage of problems within the Congress Party and win for the Labour Party, and himself, the recognition of delivering the vote to the masses, an achievement with which they would possess a distinct advantage over other parties in the forthcoming general election.

The unpredictable nature of Adams' political tactics, and the forcefulness of his intellect, proved difficult to counter by both the Electors' Association and the Congress Party. He introduced the bill merely as a measure designed to expand and deepen the process of democratisation, an objective which had the general support of the British Government and even some conservative members of the Electors' Association. In his opening remarks he stated:

Mr. Speaker, – This is a Bill which one might say is a Bill of very great importance. I think that all honourable members and members of the general public who are not still labouring under the delusion that you can have a democracy and at the same time have limited powers of the expression of will by the people who form that democracy, will agree with a Bill of this sort the chief object of which is to give the right to every adult member of the population to vote for members of the General Assembly.

Recognising that Adams had succeeded in seizing the full support of the House for adult suffrage reform, Crawford stated:

Mr. Speaker, – I think it is unnecessary in a Chamber constituted as this is at present and at this time in our history to labour the desirability of granting adult suffrage. It is now more or less generally conceded by the people in this island who are in line with general democratic thought that every single taxpayer whether he or she pays direct or indirect taxation is entitled to some say in the election of people to control the affairs of the colony.

J. H. Wilkinson, the veteran leader of the Electors' Association replied:

Mr. Speaker, – I am very glad to hear the honourable senior member for St. Joseph [Adams] say in respect of this bill that there is no Party question . . . We believe that there should be adult Suffrage.

The bill was passed, and in April 1950, property or income requirements for both voting and House membership were removed. The electorate, which had stood at near 30,000 in 1948, was now near 100,000. Three political parties immediately began their campaigns to woo the enlarged electorate for the general election the following year. Open-air meetings, loud music and rallies became the order of the day. Food and money were also being offered to potential electors in return for their vote. Adams advised workers not to corrupt their newly won franchise by accepting the bribes of money and rum from the Electors' Association, while Crawford urged them:

On Election Day, vote right. If money is offered to you for your vote, TAKE IT. You need it. They owe it to you!! But don't let that prevent you from VOTING RIGHT. Remember the Ballot is secret. No one can know how you vote except yourself and God!

During the election campaign, the Electors' Association failed to shake off its image as a white elitist organisation committed to maintenance of planter-merchant power. Ernest Mottley, the coloured conservative Bridgetown businessman, was presented by the party as an example of its commitment to multiracialism. Mottley, however, was already known for his practice of securing the vote of working-class city dwellers by generous donations of food, money, and other forms of welfare. Indeed, his 'charity for votes' political style became symbolic of the last refuge of the Electors' Association to maintain some working-class support within the city. In

Elombe Mottley, a leader in the Afro-Barbadian cultural renaissance of the 1960s and '70s.

George Challenor, the outstanding Barbados and West Indies cricketer of the 1920s.

Sir Garfield Sobers, considered one of the greatest ever all-round cricketers. Captain of Barbados, the West Indies, and Nottinghamshire.

order to counter the move made by the Barbados Workers Union to mobilise votes for the Barbados Labour Party, the Electors' Association formed their own union – The Caribbean Workers Union – under Mottley's leadership. The transparent intention of this union to round up working-class votes was forcefully resisted by workers, and the Union collapsed under the weight of its own unconvincing programme.

The manifesto campaign of the Barbados Labour Party reflected more the increasing political conservatism of Adams' leadership than an interest in socialism which had been the vision of the party's rank and file. By his 1948 defence of British colonisation before the United Nations, he had convinced the Colonial Office that his vision of political change and development in the island was in line with imperial policy; now he sought, at the height of electoral fever, to convince a cross-section of the planter-merchant community that the Barbados Labour Party was the party to protect their long-term interests. This offer was made in conjunction with reassurances to the working classes that the labour reforms and civil rights achievements of late would be expanded and consolidated. By now, Adams' commitment even to the rhetoric of socialism was abandoned, and references to nationalisation, common to the Party's manifesto since its beginnings, were also abandoned. In addition, the promises to provide industrial investment inducement legislation, to build a deepwater harbour, and to establish boards to regulate public utilities, were designed to attract votes away from the Electors' Association and win support within the white business community.

The results of the election reflected the growing stature of Adams' leadership, the rejection of planter politics by the new electorate, and the diminishing appeal of the Congress Party. The Barbados Labour Party won sixteen seats with 60 per cent of the popular vote, the Electors' Association won four seats with 30 per cent of the popular vote, while the Congress Party was rocked and shattered with only two seats, both from the St Philip parish where Crawford remained strong. The Congress Party which in 1944 had risen to the status of major party in the House fell into insignificance within less than a decade, while the Barbados Labour Party grew steadily in strength. Ermie Bourne became the island's first female parliamentary representative, winning the St Andrew seat for the Barbados Labour Party.

Adams succeeded in effectively manipulating workers' concerns about so-called left-wing adventurism as well as their fears of right-wing planter authoritarianism. He had succeeded also in wiping out effective opposition within the House. The young radical element within the Labour Party had also been stirred and mobilised by the more progressive politics of some newcomers – namely Errol Barrow and Lorenzo Williams. It was this faction within the Labour Party, inspired by Barrow, that emerged as the real parliamentary opposition to Adams.

Adams, however, completed the task of pushing for full ministerial government, and on 1st February 1954, a semi-cabinet system was put into operation. Five ministers were given portfolios: Adams, R. G. Mapp, C. E. Talma, Dr Cummins and M. E. Cox. Their duties were to formulate and manage the implementation of government policies, and to use the Executive Committee and the House to debate and win support for such policies. Adams also ensured that constitutional changes provided that the Cabinet was the main source of parliamentary power. Members of the House who were nominated to the Executive Council could no longer sit on the Executive Committee, and the Governor was bound to accept policy decisions made by ministers. As far as Adams was concerned, the island was now enjoying a practical degree of internal self-government, and it was his leadership of the Barbados Labour Party that had attained that ultimate goal.

THE BARBADOS LABOUR PARTY: DISUNITY AND DECLINE

The victory of the Barbados Labour Party in the 1951 election, which established the almost authoritarian power of Adams over the organised labour movement, also carried within it the seeds of internal opposition to his leadership which were soon to grow into a formidable force. Once again, Adams found himself having to perform the role of critic and suppressor of political radicalism, both within the Barbados Workers Union and the Barbados Labour Party. This time, his chief assistant would not be Hugh Springer, now at the University of the West Indies, but Frank Walcott, the General Secretary of the Barbados Workers Union of which he was President General. While Walcott took orders from Adams to remove radicals, the so-called 'iron curtain group', from the Union, Adams considered ways to purge the Labour Party of its progressive element. Errol Barrow was undoubtedly the most forceful opposer of Adams' liberal leadership within the Party, and not surprisingly, Walcott on more than one occasion attacked him in the House for his dissension. Crawford, meanwhile, used his editorship of the *Observer* to exploit such clashes, and to urge Barrow to leave the Party.

Adams' response to radical elements within the party and the Workers Union was to urge rank and file members not to embrace communists and extremists, and to reject their attempts to create internal strife within the labour movement. At a public meeting held by the Barbados Labour Party and the Barbados Workers Union in Queen's Park on the evening of 24th July 1952, at which Jamaica's Norman Manley and Grenada's T. A. Marryshow were guest speakers, Adams reminded workers that Trinidad was once in the vanguard to the Caribbean Labour Movement, but now they were at the 'bottom of the ladder' because 'its lieutenants began fighting each other'. Manley's speech was reported as being strongly anti-imperialistic while Adams called for moderation and loyalty, a division which the *Observer* described as being akin to 'the forefront of the jackass going up the hill while the hind part persists in going back down'. Adams also expressed his dissatisfaction that two labour radicals, Farrell, President of the Electric Company Workers Division of the Union, and Layne of the Rediffusion Company, were both elected to the Executive Council. He warned that as he had purged the Progressive League of such radicals over a decade ago, it was his intention to do likewise with the Barbados Workers Union and the Barbados Labour Party.

Such utterances added to the flames of opposition within the party. During the year, Barrow was reported as making frequent critical comments on Adams' conservatism and illustrating that he had the intellectual capacity and stamina to cope with Adams' assaults. The debate over a motion to nationalise Barbados Rediffusion Limited in August 1952 was the first major occasion that the party's division surfaced at a vote. The press wasted no time in popularising the political divisions within the Government, and suggested that Barrow had piloted the action in order to embarrass Mr Adams and impress the electorate.

Talk of political crisis and an early general election was commonplace by the end of the year, and Barrow was seen as the most able, though not the most obvious, leader of the anti-Adams faction. Even F. S. 'Sleepy' Smith, a young barrister, popular with the working classes, who had showed a fondness for worker agitation, and whom it was reputed Adams was grooming to replace Walcott as General Secretary of the Workers Union, now began to identify more closely with Barrow. During August, while the Workers Union was tied up with the organisation of parish beauty shows prior to the election of 'Miss Barbados', some workers broke away and organised themselves into a new political party, the Barbados United Party. This organisation was led by Grafton Clarke, a builder, and in its own words was dedicated to the protection of workers' interests while the Barbados Labour Party's reform mandate was being crippled by internal personality and ideological crises.

Adams, however, persisted with his strategy of seeking membership support for the removal of radicals from the Workers Union, and to silence dissenters within the Labour Party. On Labour Day, 6th October 1952, he based his speech at the Workers Union headquarters on a warning to workers that 'it was not all roses in the garden' and that they should be prepared to pluck out 'undesirable weeds'. He referred to the radical faction within the party as 'rebels' on the verge of committing 'suicide', and concluded his speech by reminding them that 'every lion in the forest which seemed to be sleeping, might not be sleeping, but only peeping'. While chastising the dockworkers for their go-slow at the harbour, which in his opinion was damaging to the island's commercial interests, he interjected news of a report which reached him that R. Mapp, L. Williams, A. E. S. Lewis, E. Barrow and C. Tudor had held a private meeting which resolved to impress upon him that if the same Lewis and Barrow were not placed on the Executive Committee they would secede from the Labour Party and set up their own party.

Adams' response, not surprisingly, was that the radicals were unrealistic as to the political possibilities in Barbados, and that their adoption of a rigid anti-colonial stance was not carefully thought out. For the radicals, Adams' acceptance of the official honour of a CMG, according to Government House officials, was only symbolic of the fact that he was 'an imperial stooge'. Adams countered by declaring at a meeting of the party caucus on 19th October 1952, that he offered Mr Barrow a place on the Executive Committee but he declined to accept owing to his commitments at the Bar. He then concluded by stating, according to an official report, that 'the malcontents could resign whenever they wanted to do so', and that he intended, in the event of the Five Year Plan being defeated in the House of Assembly, to call a general election to obtain electoral support to purge them from the party.

Government House officials in Barbados recognised that there were some ideological differences between Adams and the radicals of the party, but admitted that these differences were inflamed by two aspects of Adams' political style. First, his strategy of frequently leaving the island so as to slow down the pace of social reform and keeping 'the backbenchers of his Party at arms' length'. Second, that 'he shares the knack of Sir Robert Walpole for driving young men into opposition'. As Adams expected, however, it was the debate over the Five Year Plan in late October which provided the context for the departure of the radical wing of the Party.

Adams introduced the Five Year Plan on 28th October 1952, in a speech of four hours' duration. Lewis, Vaughan, Crawford and Allder attacked its provisions and omissions, especially the absence of a provision for a deepwater harbour. Taxation provisions were attacked by the right and the left; the former described the plan as 'Russian', designed 'to soak the rich' while the latter said it was designed to 'drown the poor'. One important outcome of the debate was the resignation of C. Tudor. In his letter of resignation Tudor is said to have stated that he disagreed so profoundly with the leadership of the Government on general policy, and particularly on financial policy, that it would be intolerant for him to loyally abide by its decisions. He is also reported to have stated that 'he was in no way interested in organising or being a member of any third party or group'.

Meanwhile, Adams' politics continued to be concerned with attacks upon the left in both Union and Party. He also sought to dissociate his leadership of the Workers Union from the Marxist element within the Caribbean Labour Council – particularly Richard Hart in Jamaica and Dr Jagan in British Guiana. On 14th November 1952, he held a meeting in Queen's Park in order to attack the critics of his Five Year Plan as well as Jagan and Hart who had been in Barbados on Caribbean Labour Council business. He began by stating that he was running out of tolerance with these radicals and that he would not 'allow the labour movement in Barbados to be wrecked by people who were in their diapers when it started'. The trade unionists, Farrell and Layne, were denounced as communist sympathisers; he stated that he regretted that F. S. 'Sleepy' Smith had joined the 'rebels and renegades', but added that he thought Smith 'did not know any better and had been misled'. Barrow and Tudor were hardly mentioned, but he was particularly bitter in his criticism of Lewis.

On Monday 17th, at a meeting of the Executive Council of the Workers Union, Adams successfully won a motion to expel Layne and Farrell, but he was forced to use his casting vote because of a three-way split. He did, however, refrain from seeking the expulsion of Lewis from the Barbados Labour Party, since he was not 'prepared to play Mr. Lewis' game and present him with a martyr's crown'. Adams, then, had succeeded in purging the Union's executive of radicals, and with Walcott's keen loyalty, consolidated his hold over the Union. By August 1953, he had taken the Union out of the Caribbean Labour Council, now described by him as 'the chief instrument of the communist front organisation in the area'.

He was, however, less successful in silencing the 'rebels' within the party. The pending implementation of the ministerial system was clearly going to accelerate the pace of the Party's fragmentation. Adams was reported to be preparing C. E. Talma as his replacement as President of the Union following his resignation on becoming Chief Minister of Barbados. In

February 1954, however, probably because he refused to offer Walcott a government ministry, or indeed any of the radicals within the party, Walcott went on the offensive. He emerged as an ardent critic of Adams, and succeeded in reducing substantially the Union's support for the government. This was a critical blow for Adams' leadership. The following month Barrow resigned from the Party and publicly disassociated himself from the government. Tudor in the same year returned to the House after winning a by-election in St Lucy as an independent anti-Adams candidate. The rift had taken place, and the party's leading agitators were now officially its opposition.

RISE OF THE DEMOCRATIC LABOUR PARTY AND THE FEDERATION CRISIS

The political leadership of Adams had been a long crusade against the radicals and anti-colonial forces within the island. The departure of Barrow from the party allowed more progressive persons and groups to rally around him as leader of the charge against the Labour Party. There had been no structural changes within the economy and society during Adams' reign as head of the organised labour movement, though he had left behind him a trail of alienated radical leaders. Barrow, Tudor and Smith were not prepared to add to this list, and now that Walcott was no longer prepared to play the role of chief servant for the party, Adams seemed more vulnerable than ever before. His had been a reign of colonial modernisation, and as Professor Lewis pointed out, his 'emphasis was laid upon constitutional advance, in willing cooperation with liberal Governors'. The rebels, it appeared, though motivated as much by personality clashes as by ideological conflicts with Adams, had more developed ideas about political decolonisation and economic modernisation.

Against the background of Barrow's enlarged political reputation, the Democratic Labour Party was formally established on 27th April 1955, as the long-awaited organisation to counter Adams' growing conservatism and softness on the colonial question. It comprised politicians already within the Assembly and many grass-root activists within the trade unions. Within the House its chartered membership included Allder, Barrow, Tudor and Lewis, and for the 1956 general election, Crawford and Brancker of the defunct Congress Party joined its ranks. Formed within one year of the forthcoming general election, the party hardly had sufficient time to develop fully its electoral image, though its leaders were experienced campaigners.

The broad front of the Democratic Labour Party campaign was socialist in theory, characterised by a demand for a reduction in the degree of social inequality, democratisation of resource ownership, socialist reforms in the areas of education, public health and social security, and diversification of the economy away from the plantation-mercantile axis. With Adams preparing for a major onslaught upon what he termed the band of 'rebels and renegades', the party at its first electoral encounter sought to hold some ground – taking the government was considered then rather unlikely. It sought to sensitise the electorate to the lack of a developmental vision for the country within the Barbados Labour Party, and to attribute this to the neo-colonial consciousness which Adams refused to eradicate from government.

The 1956 general election saw some major changes in the island's political culture. Crawford, who had led the Congress Party in defence of workers' interests since the 1940s, was now a frontline Democratic Labour Party campaigner. The Electors' Association, now renamed the Progressive Conservative Party, in the absence of the radical Congress Party, considered its chances of gaining an improved electoral position against the 'in crisis' Barbados Labour Party and the new Democratic Labour Party to be rather good. The campaign was fought with as much acrimony and bitterness as that of 1951. The results, however, were hardly surprising. The Barbados Labour Party won fifteen seats, the Democratic Labour Party won four, and the Progressive Conservative Party four. There were two surprise results, and one significant indication; of the former, Barrow lost his St George seat, though he was to re-enter the House after winning a St John by-election in 1958, and Walcott won a seat as an independent. For the latter, the Barbados Labour Party suffered an erosion of its popular support – taking only 49 per cent of the popular vote while the Democratic Labour Party emerged with 20 per cent.

While the Democratic Labour Party was making its firm impressions upon the Barbados electorate, and the political system in general, Adams had been preparing to integrate the island into the proposed Federation of the British West Indies. The idea of West Indian federation had been the subject of a major conference in Dominica in 1932 at which Barbados was represented. The leading advocates of the political union had been Grenada's Marryshow and Trinidad's Captain Cipriani, though it was not until the 1947 conference at Montego Bay in Jamaica that Barbados appears to have been a keen participant. Indeed, the Barbados Labour Party was one of the leading organisation supporters of federation, and Adams had seen in it the ultimate political development for the region. After 1947, federation discussions and negotiations were frequent. Adams had placed them as top priorities of his party during the early 1950s, alongside the movement towards ministerial government with a cabinet system. Finally, in 1956 at the London Conference, it was decided to establish the Federation as soon as technical, administrative and constitutional difficulties were resolved.

The decision made by the 1957 conference in Jamaica to locate the federal capital in Trinidad, was not well accepted in all the territories. Eric Williams, pleased with having the capital in his country, soon began to cool on the federal structure when Manley in Jamaica opposed the suggestion that the Federal Government should have extensive powers in finance, taxation and planning. Adams, however, a leading constitutional architect of the Federation, was soon embroiled in a wide range of jurisdictional disagreements which were having their impact upon the domestic politics of particular countries. While in 1958 he succeeded in implementing the cabinet system of government in Barbados, and emerged as Premier, the matter of federal elections seems to have been given higher priority on his political agenda.

The election of a Federal Government in March 1958 represented a major landmark in the development of Barbadian politics. Five seats in the Federal Assembly were allocated to Barbados, and these were contested by the three political parties. The results were favourable to Adams, and represented an indication of some degree of increased support for his brand of politics. None of the four Democratic Labour Party candidates was returned, with Barrow and Tudor suffering defeats along with Frank Walcott, the independent candidate. The Barbados Labour Party entered five candidates, and four of these – Adams, D. H. Ward, V. B. Vaughan and G. Rocheford – were returned. The re-named Progressive Conservative Party, the Barbados National Party, entered two candidates, one of whom was returned – Florence Daysch. Later in the year, Adams became Prime Minister of the Federation of the West Indies, and departed for Trinidad, the capital site. His removal from the scene of Barbados politics had massive implications for the Barbados Labour Party. Adams of course knew this, but as a professional politician he had placed greater career value upon the status of Federal Prime Minister than upon being Barbados' premier. Both of these offices, however, he was shortly to vacate, disillusioned and on the defensive amidst intense criticism of his leadership.

As division within the Federation increased on questions of internal migration, taxation, finance, planning and custom union, with Jamaica and Trinidad frequently at loggerheads, Adams' constitutional competence proved insufficient as a mediating factor. He was, in many ways, no longer in touch with the ideological pulse of the region, and his liberal political vision was considered anachronistic by both the radical nationalist Eric Williams and the Fabian socialist, Norman Manley. C. L. R. James, General Secretary of the West Indies Federal Labour Party, though more angered by Manley's refusal to aggressively politicise federalism among the Jamaican masses, considered Adams' constitutionalist approach systematic of banal political conservatism; Adams, however, explained his caution and tentative decision making in terms of his government not having a certain majority within the Federal House of Representatives.

By 1960, the federal structure was shaking at its foundations. The government was considerably weakened because the Peoples National Movement in Trinidad and the Peoples National Party in Jamaica, both firm conceptual supporters of federalism, did poorly in the 1958 federal election. Adams was frequently forced to rely upon the 'independent' vote of Florence Daysch of Barbados in order to strengthen the hand of the ruling West Indies Federal Party. Meanwhile, the Democratic Labour Party in Barbados was taking advantage of Adams' absence, and eroding the popularity of the Barbados Labour Party Government now under the leadership of Dr Cummins. The new premier and leader of the party had been chosen by Adams over the popular veteran, M. E. Cox, it is alleged, because F. E. Miller and R. G. Mapp, two party stalwarts, would not work with Cox, and because Adams considered Cox's working-class background and lack of higher formal education inappropriate for such an office. Cox's relations with the party's leadership soured, and in 1964 he was expelled from the party. As the Federation stumbled towards collapse, the Barbados Labour Party Government diminished in credibility, and the foundations of Adams' political career no longer seemed firm.

The government had emerged from the 1958 sugar crisis with a damaged image within the labour movement. In fact, it had not supported the sugar workers in their long-drawn-out wage negotiations, and the opposition Democratic Labour Party was able to get some mileage in labelling it anti-worker and representative of vested elite interests. Crawford, who since the 1940s had built up a large following within the sugar belt, and Barrow, whose radical oratory was attracting workers across the country, took the opportunity to launch a major assault upon the government at a massively attended Queen's Park meeting. Barrow's image was further improved by his election as Democratic Labour Party chairman in 1960. Dr Cummins' subsequent attempts to restore the popularity of the government failed miserably, as the ruling party showed further signs of internal division, and dissatisfaction with Adams' attempt to manipulate policy from behind. Furthermore, the Barbados Workers Union leadership had now revealed itself fundamentally opposed to the government, with Frank Walcott in particular now determined to see the end of the Adams era.

The Democratic Labour Party approached the final stage of the election build-up of 1961 in a positive and optimistic mood. It had rooted itself firmly among the working classes and elements of the black middle class, and had captured the political imagination of the urban youth. With its manifesto declaring 'operation takeover', the party was encouraged by Walcott's decision to throw the weight of the Barbados Workers Union behind it. The party's candidates vilified the moderate and limited labour reforms which the Barbados Labour Party had implemented since the 1940s, and argued that the government's lack of an effective industrialisation programme had to do with the stranglehold which the planter-merchant elite had over its policy. In addition, they argued that the high levels of unemployment, inadequate workmen's compensation and poor social security facilities resulted from the same root, and that the government was not capable of the kind of economic modernisation which was now required to get the country moving. Adams, because of his duties as Prime Minister of the Federation, could not participate in the election campaign until the very final stages, but by then it seemed that the anti-government swing had already taken place. To make matters worse for Adams, in September 1961 Jamaica's leader, Norman Manley, had been defeated by the anti-federal Alexander Bustamante in the federation referendum; Jamaica was out, and Trinidad announced its intention of following suit.

The general election of 5th December 1961 took the Barbados Labour Party out of office with a clean sweep. There were many surprises. Even the conservative Barbados National Party in constituencies where it fielded no candidates urged electors to support the Democratic Labour Party. Only five of the twenty-two Barbados Labour Party candidates were returned compared with fourteen of the Democratic Labour Party's sixteen. The Barbados National Party won four seats, and one seat was secured by an independent; five of the six incumbent government ministers, including Premier Cummins, lost their seats. On 6th December 1961, then, Errol Barrow, the 41-year-old lawyer-economist, emerged as the Premier of Barbados, replacing the 70-year-old Dr Cummins and putting an end to the local political career of Grantley Adams. Trinidad withdrew from the Federation in January 1962, and on 31st May 1962, the West Indies Federation was constitutionally dissolved.

INDEPENDENCE AND NATIONALISM

The economic aspects of the Democratic Labour Party's manifesto in the 1961 election suggested that it was a moderate party. Its policy on nationalisation was cautious and limited to minimum government ownership of public utilities; it stressed government partnership with the private sector, rather than state ownership. On the social aspects of reform policies, candidates emphasised that even though there had been significant legislation in the previous two decades, the Adams government had done little to modernise the nature of work relations, and that workers were still intimidated by employers in the workplace on a daily basis. The Democratic Labour Party, therefore, expressed a commitment to social change by placing, at least in theory, the social security of the worker at the core of its political philosophy.

Barrow's mandate for social change and economic development was not frustrated by his having to take Barbados through the final stages of the Federation's gradual demise. Pressure was put to bear on his government to encourage it to become the core of a revised federation with the Leeward and Windward Antilles – the so-called 'Little Eight'. The British Government had promised, though not as firmly as Barrow would have liked, to provide finance for the implementation of the revised federation, while pro-federation economists spoke of the economic benefits to be derived by Barbados in areas of markets for manufactures, transport and commercial development. Barrow, Vere Bird of Antigua, and other leaders held talks on various occasions and arrived at the conclusion that the federation of the remaining eight islands should be attempted. This decision was communicated to the British Colonial Office. Barrow, however, insisted on two major points: firstly that the British Government should establish an investment programme for the less economically developed islands; and secondly, that independence for the region be given immediate priority. In June 1962, the new federal structure was placed before the islands' legislatures; Barbados was to be the capital site. In February 1963, all political parties in Barbados voted unanimously to support the new federal structure, illustrating the degree of popular commitment to political integration.

During the latter part of 1963, however, difficulties with the federal structure began to emerge, most of which were linked to Britain's refusal to act quickly and with resolve in matters of investment and financial assistance. The 'mother' country, furthermore, stated categorically its refusal to commit itself to an aid package for more than five years and told the region's leaders outright that they would have to attract funds from elsewhere. The response in Barbados to this development was that the British Government since the mid-1950s had been attempting to pass down the line its economic responsibility to the lesser developed islands, first to Jamaica, then Trinidad, now Barbados.

Political differences between the region's leaders were magnified in this context of economic uncertainty and insecurity. Some disputes became personal, and Barrow showed little restraint in adjudging some leaders as careerist, 'pettifogging politicians', not fit to be managing the people's affairs. Rumours to the effect that Barrow intended to be dictatorial in relation to the federation were widespread within the other islands. Barrow meanwhile was expressing more concern for Barbadian independence, as he believed that the federal structure was doomed once Britain persisted in 'dragging its feet' on the question of financial support. One by one, countries began to dissociate themselves from the revised federation, first Grenada, then Antigua and Montserrat. Negotiations continued to make little headway into 1965, by which time Barrow publicly declared his determination to press for unilateral independence for Barbados – a decision which led to the resignation of Senator E. L. Ward, and Crawford, the Deputy Premier and longstanding federalist.

When Barrow's government approached the British government with its independence plan, it was doing so after having consolidated its position in the country and with an unprecedented level of popular political support. Little time was wasted in dissolving the traditional legislative council and replacing it in 1962 with a 21-member Senate. Since coming to office the Democratic Labour Party had done much to modernise the country's economic structure, particularly obvious in terms of its extensive infrastructural development plan. The government was attracted to the 'Puerto Rican model' of industrialisation as outlined by the eminent St Lucian economist Arthur Lewis, which emphasised the central role of foreign investment. In addition, the decision to provide free secondary education in government-assisted schools from January 1962, represented an investment in the country's youth without which industrialisation plans were considered futile. Commitment to the educational development of the population improved considerably the government's image, locally and overseas; this image was reinforced by the establishment of a Barbados campus of the University of the West Indies in October 1963. These developments were matched by strides taken in the modernisation of industrial relations. Peaceful picketing was legalised and provisions were made for workers to receive, under certain conditions, severance pay and injury compensation. These advances in socio-economic relations were predicated on the assumption that the island's economic expansion would be based upon an industrialisation model rather than a persistent plantation economy – a significant departure in the political conception of development strategy.

Government wasted no time, also, in going about the task of revising and expanding previous legislative provisions for the encouragement of tourism and agriculture. Tourism was promoted as a major industrial sector during the first four years of the regime, and government revenues earned from this sector increased at a remarkable rate. A hotel construction boom assisted in stimulating the local manufacturing sector and contributed to reduced unemployment levels. In general, the Democratic Labour Party had launched the assault upon the sugar industry's dominance of the economy, a process which earned Barrow the image of being socio-politically opposed to planter interests.

Though the tourist industry was manipulated as an employment generator for the youth, and a major foreign exchange earner, industrialisation by invitation was the policy instrument designed for economic take-off. Light manufacturing industries were encouraged, especially those with a labour-intensive bias and an import substitution potential. More liberal tax holidays and duty-free incentives on raw materials were offered to the foreign private sector in order to promote industrialisation. This policy was implemented alongside direct government action, through the Industrial Development Act and the Export Industries Act of 1963. Within three years of these legislations some 44 industrial plants were established, providing more than 2,000 jobs.

Early successes in significantly increasing the annual rate of growth of the gross domestic product distinguished the government's economic performance from that of its predecessor (Table 22). There had also been marked expansion in non-sugar agriculture, especially livestock, poultry and vegetables. Sugar, none the less, still dominated the economy, earning $37 million in 1963 compared with $26 million in 1960. These upward economic indicators gave the government much confidence in its programme. No serious efforts were made to restructure the distribution of economic resources, though occasionally mention was made of the need to nationalise the sugar industry. In general, the planter-merchant elite remained firmly in economic control, the result of the expansion of corporations such as Plantations Company Limited and the Barbados Shipping and Trading Company Limited. While the Democratic Labour Party prepared itself for a term of peaceful coexistence with the planter-

Table 22. *Barbados: composition of gross domestic product (at current factor cost),*
1955–80

Sectors	1955	1960	1970
Sugar	23.4	21.3	9.9
Other agriculture	11.8	6.7	4.8
Manufacturing	19.2	8.3	10.1
Construction	7.3	9.8	10.0
Wholesale retail trade	10.6	23.0	26.0
Tourism	n.a.	n.a.	n.a.
Government	8.7	9.8	15.6
Other			
Total	100.0	100.0	100.0
Sugar industry exports as a percentage of total domestic exports	93	93	60

merchants' corporate sector, its image grew in the popular consciousness as the long-awaited instrument of modernisation.

There were also significant changes, more difficult to quantify, but which illustrated the Democratic Labour Party's departure from the political vision of the previous regime. The black community certainly appeared more confident in its expression of its hitherto stultified nationalist sentiments. The rapidly expanding professional black middle classes, in particular, became the advocates of a revived radical political ideology that demanded the imposition of government pressure upon the white corporate elite in order to liberalise employment policies. In addition, black power activists urged government to use its fiscal and legislative power in order to democratise the ownership of economic resources.

In general, there was a distinct feeling within the country that society was being pushed away from its colonial foundations, and that the Democratic Labour Party regime represented the beginning of something new and progressive. For this reason alone, sections of the traditional merchant-planter community feared that the social and political basis of their elitism was under attack, and began to express their opposition to what seemed inevitable – the move towards political independence. For them, the constitutional break with Britain would be an act of near revolution given the 300-year-old mercantile legacy from which their political and economic vision could not be disengaged.

In all these developments, Barrow was hailed among nationalists, whites and blacks alike, as the leader most capable of harnessing the country's energies and directing them for socio-economic modernisation. By 1965, the British government was impressed by the Democratic Labour Party's economic record, and in a roundabout way accepted that Barbados was moving on a developmental path that should be encouraged. It was this imperial recognition, stated Professor G. K. Lewis, which, in the final instance, 'callously helped to destroy' the political reformist 'handiwork' of Grantley Adams. Barrow had certainly transformed Adams' colonial reformism into anti-colonialism and nationalism. On 30th November 1966, after long and testing negotiations, Barbados – following Jamaica, Trinidad and British Guiana – gained its full sovereignty, thereby becoming an independent State. Errol Barrow became the country's first Prime Minister and the then Governor, Sir John Stow, was re-appointed as the country's first Governor-General. The new State was given its blessing by the Queen of England and her government, and the colonial status which began in 1627 was now at an end.

CHAPTER NINE

Some post-independence trends

The entrenchment of Westminster-style government in the post-independence period was perhaps inevitable given the absence of political activity within the ruling Democratic Labour Party, or the opposition Barbados Labour Party, which sought to distance the island from the institutional and constitutional structures inherited during the colonial era. Independence within the confines of the imperial Commonwealth system was what the Democratic Labour Party government had proposed and attained in 1966, and the rejection of republicanism, in itself a popular measure, was perhaps the most obvious indicator of the limits which would be placed upon nationalism thereafter. The appointment of the last imperial governor as the first Governor-General of the free state was also symbolic of the gradualist and moderate nature of the transition implied by constitutional independence.

The demise of the Barbados National Party in the years after the 1966 general election, which was again won by the Democratic Labour Party, resulted in the development of a two-party political culture in which two labour parties, the Democratic Labour Party and the Barbados Labour Party, contested for the peoples' mandate. With the planter-merchant's political party discredited and removed from the political arena it was obvious that its members would seek protection for their vested economic interests within one or both of the dominant labour parties. Both parties had cultivated traditions of criticism of the oligarchical political attitudes and practices of the planter-merchant elite, but both had also sought to court its economic power and managerial expertise within their developmental strategies. These positions were not considered contradictory; a conciliatory arrangement between white corporate power and black political administrations emerged as the dominant political thrust of the post-independence period.

The Barbados Workers Union continued to maintain its firm support for the Democratic Labour Party, in spite of the fact that Frank Walcott, its increasingly powerful leader, had lost a seat for the first time while being a

Democratic Labour Party candidate in the 1966 election. This party-union alliance cannot be separated from the emergence in the early 1970s of the Barbados Labour Party as the umbrella for the protection and enhancement of the powerful corporate elements of the former Barbados National Party. While this new alliance was taking shape, the Barbados Labour Party sought to retain its image as a worker party by becoming a member of the Socialist International. The results were that the Barbados Labour Party drifted to the right of centre of the island's political spectrum, while the union-supported Democratic Labour Party, also with its share of mercantile support, confirmed its traditional image of being marginally left of centre. At the same time both parties continued to advocate policies based upon the assumption of the fundamental compatibility of worker and employer interests within the economy and society.

The leadership of the Barbados Labour Party had been hostile to the popularly elected socialist governments of Dr Jagan in British Guiana during the 1950s, and in the process revealed itself as a regional beacon of cold-war-style anti-communism; in the post-independence decades this ideological feature of the party was maintained. The Democratic Labour Party, which had grown out of the anti-colonial nationalist surge of the post-war years, while being supportive of liberation causes in Africa and Asia, for example, remained cautious on the question of white economic and racial domination in Barbados. Indeed, the all-black Assembly in 1970 found it necessary to prevent Trinidad-born, American black-power activist, Stokeley Carmichael, from addressing public audiences in Barbados during his short and well-policed visit, on the pretence of government commitment to non-racialist politics and the defence of white minority rights. The 1970 Public Order Act not only sought to suppress the black-power movement, but also to escalate police surveillance of known black-consciousness radicals. None the less, the Party won the 1971 general election with a handsome majority, including strong support from the grateful white community. Prime Minister Barrow had won fifteen years of unbroken rule. It was also in 1971 that the single-member constituencies were introduced.

The growing ideological polarisation of the region's politics during the 1970s did not succeed in exaggerating the political differences between Barbados' two labour parties. The pervasive black power movement of this decade had its advocates within both, though the leadership of the Barbados Labour Party, with its political image becoming increasingly associated with the interest of the corporate sector, remained sceptical if not critical of black radicalism. The economic crisis of the mid-1970s, which followed the escalation of oil prices, resulted in a premium being placed upon financial and managerial acumen within regional politics, rather than radical socio-cultural dynamism; this context was effectively exploited by the Barbados Labour Party in the 1976 general election. Now led by Tom Adams, son of Sir Grantley Adams, the Barbados Labour Party, with an undoubtedly private-sector image, was able to defeat the Democratic Labour Party and restore the sagging confidences of the corporate elite within the country's polity.

The Barbados Labour Party governed confidently under Tom Adams until 1985, in spite of increasingly popular accusations that it was concerned principally with white elite interest and defence of American imperialist strategies within the region. Tom Adams' leadership role in gaining the regional isolation of Grenada's socialist revolution in 1979, and in the implementation of the American invasion of the country in 1983, reconfirmed the party's image as opposed to socialist decolonisation. The sudden death of Tom Adams on 11th March 1985 left the party with an ideological and leadership crisis not dissimilar to that which followed Grantley Adams' departure for Trinidad in 1958. However, the massive electoral defeat of the Barbados Labour Party by the Democratic Labour Party in the 1986 general election – 24 seats to 3 – has been hailed as evidence of continuing opposition by the working class to the political dominance of big business, though it is also true that sections of the black middle class, and elements of the white community, attracted to the DLP's fiscal policies, contributed significantly to the electoral swing away from the government.

The development of radical political ideologies since independence, some of which tended to revolve around the socialist element within the Democratic Labour Party, did not succeed in mobilising forces for meaningful democratisation of economic resource ownership. In spite of the alienation of the planter-merchant elite from political office, its economic strength has grown considerably since 1966. During the 1986 general election, for example, a major argument levelled against the Barbados Labour Party government by Dr Don Blackman, a former cabinet minister who crossed the floor and joined the Democratic Labour Party, was that its policies were manipulated by the merchant class to the extent that it had become a puppet administration. Certainly, merchant corporations such as Barbados Shipping and Trading Company Limited (B.S. & T.) and Plantations Company Limited, both formed in the immediate post-First World War years, grew in size and strength during the post-independence period. By the 1970s, these companies had grown into conglomerates which exercised considerable economic power and political influence.

If labour governments of the 1940s and 1950s seemed unprepared to confront planter interests, then since 1966 they seem to have been equally unprepared to tackle the manipulative might of the commercial elite. By 1970, the B.S. & T. had expanded its operations into almost every sector of the economy to become the largest locally owned corporation in the island (Table 23).

The growth of the local corporate sector was directly related to the development of the economic integration of the Commonwealth Caribbean following the collapse of the Federation. Barbados played an important leadership role in this process, and took advantage of economic opportunities made available to it. The idea of a regional economic association was revived in the mid-1960s. At the initiative of Guyana

Table 23. *Barbados Shipping and Trading Company Limited (B.S. & T.) since 1970*

Subsidiaries of B.S. & T.
DaCosta & Musson Ltd
Manco Investments Ltd
S. P. Musson Son & Co. Ltd
Manning, Wilkinson & Challenor Ltd
Gardiner Austin & Co. Ltd
Bulkeley Estates Ltd
Tractors and Equipment Ltd
Bulkeley Factories Ltd
Musson (Jamaica) Ltd
Super Centre Ltd (supermarket chain)

Companies wholly owned by subsidiaries
DaCosta & Co. Stevedores Ltd
Ince & Co. Ltd
Fort Royal Garage Ltd
Perkins and Co. Ltd
Seawell Air Services Ltd

Companies controlled by subsidiaries
Applewhaites Ltd
West Indies Records (Barbados) Ltd

Other links made by B.S. & T. since 1970
Orange Hill plantation
Banks Beer
Areas in the tourist industry

(which had remained outside the West Indies Federation), articles of a Caribbean Free Trade Association (CARIFTA) were drawn up in 1965, and were accepted by Barbados and Antigua. The provisions of the Agreement were largely modelled on those of the European Free Trade Association. All twelve Commonwealth Caribbean countries were able to agree on the formation of a free trade area, based largely on the text of the 1965 Agreement, and CARIFTA came into existence in May 1968. At the same time, the Eastern Caribbean islands were developing closer forms of cooperation which culminated in the formation of the Eastern Caribbean Common Market in June 1968.

In October 1972, some of the CARIFTA member countries decided to form a Caribbean Community and Common Market (CARICOM). The Community, which came into being on 1st August 1973, represented a deepening of regional integration and has achieved such objectives as the establishment of a common external tariff, a harmonised system of fiscal incentives for industry, double taxation agreements, and the formation of a Caribbean Investment Corporation designed to channel equity funds to the less developed member countries. It initially comprised Jamaica, Trinidad and Tobago, Guyana and Barbados but by the end of July 1974, all the other CARIFTA members had acceded to the Community Agreement. Following independence, then, Barbados became increasingly immersed within the region's economy and polity, and in fact began to perceive its interests in regional terms.

The expansion of the white controlled and owned local corporate sector, in addition to the steady growth in the number of foreign multinational companies in tourism, manufacturing, banking and finance, stimulated the development of a black professional middle class which constitutes perhaps the most noticeable social feature of the post-independence era. The middle managers and clerical staff of these corporations were the material out of which the present cult of 'professional elitism' was created. These upwardly mobile groups filled part of the vast socio-economic gulf which hitherto separated the white elite from the black labouring masses.

To a large extent, the emergence of the middle classes had to do with social processes released by the Democratic Labour Party government free education policy in the early 1960s. For the first time in the island's history, society seemed fluid, and working-class families were able to produce individuals who could be found within all social groups. These social changes have been hailed by some as evidence of the basic egalitarian nature of the post-independence social order, though the argument has also been made that the rise of the black professional elite was more the result of

Daphne Hackett, a leading founder of the
Barbados theatre movement.

Frank Collymore, considered the father of the
Barbadian literary movement.

George Lamming, an internationally famous
Barbadian novelist and scholar.

Edward Kamau Brathwaite, world-famous
Barbados poet and scholar.

significant white emigration to places like Australia, South Africa, Canada and New Zealand, after the attainment of independence.

These developments in social structure had a significant impact upon the process of cultural institutionalisation that had been stimulated by constitutional independence. Certainly, radical elements within the black middle classes, under the influence of the Pan-American black consciousness movement of the 1960s and 1970s, appeared to be socially rejecting some formal aspects of their European cultural heritage and began the movement for the redemption and validation of their Afro-Barbadian traditions. In this regard, they were merely doing what the working classes had long been expressing – that there is a dynamic, legitimate Afro-Barbadian culture. The rural villages and urban slums gave form to a vibrant social culture whose song, dance, art, theatre, drama and language derived from a root long driven underground by the repressive plantation world, but awaiting an intellectual environment for its revival.

It was Elombe Mottley, son of Ernest Mottley, the conservative black spokesman for the discredited planter-merchant political party, the Barbados National Party, who appeared in the vanguard of the Afro-Barbadian cultural renaissance which is undoubtedly a most dynamic feature of the country's social life. The formation and development of 'Yoruba House', an organisation dedicated to cultural understanding and revival, under Mottley's directorship, provided a forum for cultural activity which was symbolic of the Afro-Barbados which world-famous Barbadian artists, novelist George Lamming, poet Edward Kamau Brathwaite, and the brilliant multi-talented Frank Collymore, had long been writing about.

In 1978 Edward Brathwaite was invited by the Adams government to conduct a survey of indigenous cultural activities and to draw up proposals for a national development plan for the cultural sector of the country. In his report, Brathwaite stated that despite individual efforts in various sections of the arts, it could not be said that Barbados had developed any significant institutional cultural infrastructure in the period prior to political independence. Elombe Mottley had been instrumental, along with Daphne Joseph-Hackett, in the establishment of the Barbados National Theatre Workshop, and Anthony Hinckson, poet-playwright, had pioneered the formation in 1969 of the Barbados Writers Workshop. Black Night, a grass-roots forum of writers, poets and dramatists, also under Mottley's guidance, led the way in the early 1970s, in the development of community/street art which drew upon the folk tradition. In June 1978, Mottley, along with the Ministry of Education and Culture, mounted an islandwide community and theatrical event, the traditional 'Crop-Over Festival'. It was a major achievement for the government of the Barbados Labour Party. There can be no doubt that this event, now an annual one, was the most remarkable folk-festival ever held in Barbados, and together with the National Independence Festival of Creative Arts which began in 1973, remains the beacon of the national cultural upsurge.

The institutionalisation of culture since the mid-1970s, in the form of a proliferation of theatre workshops, dance and musical groups, professional artists, writers and folklorists, all working within the Afro-dimension of social experience, attests to the extent to which the social culture of the country has been undergoing a transformation. Indeed, this socio-cultural independence had been emphasised by Prime Minister Barrow since 1961. He had never articulated national independence in exclusively political or economic terms. For him, it had to be first and foremost an intellectual process, whereby citizens should always, in his words, critically look at their 'mirror image of themselves'. His death on 1st June 1987 at the age of 67, was mourned by the nation with an unprecedented display of sorrow which expressed more than just the passing of a founding father of the State, but the tragic loss of its most popular nationalist leader of the modern era.

Since independence, then, there have been profound social changes and cultural developments, though the dominant economic and political trends were clearly to be anticipated. The island's economy did perform satisfactorily during the crisis years of the 1970s, and unlike many of its neighbours experienced no significant internal political turmoil. During these years, its role as a commercial centre for the Caribbean Economic Community increased in significance, and by 1980 it was undoubtedly the major centre for international finance in the Eastern Caribbean – a status it had held before during the formative years of plantation slavery. The country has certainly lived up to the challenges of nationhood, and citizens pride themselves for being among those American nations with the highest material living standards and greatest democratic freedoms.

Notes

Chapter One

1 G. T. Barton, *The Prehistory of Barbados*, pp. 6–13
  A. K. Bullen and R. P. Bullen, 'Barbados, a Carib centre', *The Bajan and South Caribbean*, 155 (1966), 20–2
  R. P. Bullen, 'Barbados and the archaeology of the Caribbean', *J.B.M.H.S.* 32 (1966), 16–19
  C. Cooksey, 'The first Barbadians', *Timehri*, 3:2 (1912), 142–4.
2 A. Boomert, 'Notes on Barbados prehistory', *J.B.M.H.S.* 38:1 (1987), 8–43
  P. L. Drewett, 'Barbados: the prehistory of the island'. University of London mimeograph, n.d.
  P. L. Drewett *et al.*, 'Archaeological survey of Barbados', *J.B.M.H.S.* 38:1 (1987), 44–80 and 38:2 (1988), 196–204

Chapter Two

1 G. A. Puckrein, *Little England: Plantation Society and Anglo-Barbadian Politics, 1627–1700*, pp. 42–50
2 R. Dunn, *Sugar and Slaves: The Rise of the Planter Class in the English West Indies, 1624–1713*, pp. 58–9
3 R. Ligon, *A True and Exact History of the Island of Barbados*, pp. 57–8
4 Ibid
5 Dunn, op. cit. p. 225
6 Ligon, op. cit. p. 54
7 Ibid, p. 43

Chapter Three

1 Ligon, p. 96
2 Dunn, p. 81
3 Ibid, p. 85
4 Ibid, p. 81
5 V. T. Harlow, *A History of Barbados, 1625–1685*, pp. 292–3
6 E. Williams, *Capitalism and Slavery*, 1975 edn, pp. 19–25
7 P. Curtin, *The Atlantic Slave Trade: A Census*, pp. 52–64, 89, 119
8 Ligon, p. 46
9 J. Handler and F. Lange, *Plantation Slavery in Barbados*, p. 25

10 H. Beckles, *Black Rebellion in Barbados: the Struggle Against Slavery, 1627–1838*, pp. 17–20
11 G. Hughes, *The Natural History of Barbados*, pp. 13–16
12 Dunn, p. 246

Chapter Four

1 R. Hughes, 'Barbadian sugar plantations, 1640–1846'
2 S. Carrington, 'West Indian opposition to British policy: Barbadian politics, 1774–1782', *Journal of Caribbean History*, 17 (1982), 26–50
3 G. Pinckard, *Notes on the West Indies*, vol. 2, 1808 edn, p. 132
4 W. Dickson, *Letters on Slavery*, p. 58
5 G. Pinckard, pp. 264–5
6 F. Bayley, *Four Years' Residence in the West Indies*, pp. 77, 436–7
7 J. Belgrave *et al.*, Letter of the Barbados Free-Coloured People to the Hon. John Beckles, 4th March 1817, CO 28/86, ff. 6–7

Chapter Five

1 Instructions for the Management of a Plantation in Barbados, London, 1786
2 Governor Leith to Bathurst, April 30th and September 21st, CO 28/85, f. 8 and CO 28/85, f. 36 respectively
3 A Report from the Select Committee of the House of Assembly appointed to inquire into the Origins, Cause, and Progress of the late Insurrection – April 1816
4 H. Beckles, *Black Rebellion in Barbados: the Struggle Against Slavery 1627–1838*, p. 114

Chapter Six

1 C. Levy, *Emancipation, Sugar and Federalism*, pp. 71–124
2 R. Carter, 'Public amenities after emancipation', in W. K. Marshall (ed.) *Emancipation II*, pp. 46–59
3 B. Gibbs, 'The establishment of the tenantry system in Barbados', in W. K. Marshall (ed.) *Emancipation II*, pp. 23–31
4 T. Marshall, 'Post-emancipation adjustments in Barbados, 1838–1876' in A. Thompson (ed.) *Emancipation I*, pp. 81–101
5 W. K. Marshall, 'Rock Hall, St Thomas: the search for the first free village in Barbados'. Paper presented at the 9th Annual Conference of Caribbean Historians, Barbados, 1977
6 W. K. Marshall *et al.*, 'The establishment of a peasantry in Barbados', in Blanca Silvestrini (ed.) *Social Groups and Institutions in the History of the Caribbean*, pp. 88–104
7 G. Belle, 'The abortive revolution of 1876 in Barbados', *Journal of Caribbean History* 18 (1984), pp. 1–35
8 W. K. Marshall, 'Nineteenth century crisis in the Barbadian sugar industry' in W. K. Marshall (ed.) *Emancipation II*, pp. 85–102
9 M. Sleeman, 'The agri-business bourgeoisie of Barbados and Martinique', in P. I. Gomes (ed.) *Rural Development in the Caribbean*, pp. 15–33

Chapter Seven

1　Report and Evidence of the West India Royal Commission, 1897
2　Report on the Census of Barbados, 1881–1891
3　V. Newton, *The Silver Men: West Indian Labour Migration to Panama, 1850–1914*
4　B. Richardson, *Panama Money in Barbados, 1900–1920*
5　B. Stoddart, 'Cricket and colonisation in the English-speaking Caribbean to 1914: steps towards a cultural analysis'
6　C. Karch, 'The growth of the corporate economy in Barbados: class, or race factors, 1890–1977', in S. Craig (ed.) *The Contemporary Caribbean: A Sociological Reader*, vol. I, pp. 230–4

Bibliography

Books

Alleyne, Warren *Historic Bridgetown*, Barbados, 1978

Anon. *Memoirs of the First Settlement of the Island of Barbados . . .*, Bridgetown, 1741

Augier, Fitzroy *et al. The Making of the West Indies*, London, 1960

Augier, Fitzroy & Gordon, S. *Sources of West Indian History*, London, 1962

Barton, G. T. *The Prehistory of Barbados*, Barbados, 1953

Bayley, Frederick *Four Years' Residence in the West Indies*, London, 1830

Beachy, R. W. *The British West Indian Sugar Industry in the Late Nineteenth Century*, Westport, 1978 edn

Beckles, Hilary *Black Rebellion in Barbados: the Struggle Against Slavery, 1627–1838*, Bridgetown, 1984

—*Afro-Caribbean Women and Resistance to Slavery in Barbados*, London, 1989

—*Natural Rebels: A Social History of Enslaved Black Women in Barbados, 1627–1838*, London, 1989

—*White Servitude and Black Slavery in Barbados, 1627–1713*, Knoxville, 1989

Beckles, W. A. *The Barbados Disturbances: 1937*, Bridgetown, 1973

Bennett, J. Harry *Bondsmen and Bishops: Slavery and Apprenticeship on the Codrington Plantations of Barbados, 1710–1838*, Berkeley, 1958

Bridenbaugh, Carl & Roberta *No Peace Beyond the Line: the English in the Caribbean, 1624–1690*, Oxford, 1972

Campbell, Peter *The Church in Barbados in the Seventeenth Century*, Bridgetown, 1982

Clarke, Charles, *The Constitutional Crisis of 1876 in Barbados*, Bridgetown, 1896

Craton, Michael *Testing the Chains: Resistance to Slavery in the British West Indies*, Ithaca, 1982

Curtin, Philip *The Atlantic Slave Trade: A Census*, Madison, 1969

Davis, Darnell *Cavaliers and Roundheads of Barbados, 1650–1652*, Georgetown, 1887

Davis, Kortright *Cross and Crown in Barbados*, Frankfurt, 1983

Deerr, Noel *The History of Sugar* 2 vols, London, 1949–50

Dickson, William *Letters on Slavery*, London, 1789

—*Mitigation of Slavery*, London, 1814

Dunn, Richard *Sugar and Slaves: The Rise of the Planter Class in the English West Indies, 1624–1713*, Chapel Hill, 1972

Edghill, J. Y. *About Barbados*, London, 1890

Frere, George *A Short History of Barbados*, London, 1768

Galenson, David *Traders, Planters, and Slaves*, Cambridge, 1986

Goodridge, Sehon *Facing the Challenge of Emancipation: A Study of the Ministry of William Hart Coleridge, First Bishop of Barbados, 1824–1842*, Bridgetown, 1981

Goveia, Elsa *The West Indian Slave Laws of the Eighteenth Century*, Barbados, 1970

Greenfield, Sidney *English Rustics in Black Slain*, New Haven, 1966

Hamilton, Bruce *Barbados and the Confederation Question, 1871–1885*, London, 1956

Handler, Jerome *The Unappropriated People: Freedmen in the Slave Society of Barbados*, Baltimore, 1974

Handler, Jerome & Lange, Frederick *Plantation Slavery in Barbados: An Archaeological and Historical Investigation*, London, 1978

Harlow, Vincent T. *A History of Barbados, 1625–1685*, Oxford, 1926

Hewitt, J. M. *Ten Years of Constitutional Development in Barbados*, Bridgetown, 1954

Higman, Barry *Slave Populations of the British Caribbean, 1807–1834*, Baltimore, 1984

Hoyos, F. A. *Grantley Adams and the Social Revolution*, London, 1974

—*Barbados: A History from the Amerindians to Independence*, London, 1978

Hughes, Griffith *The Natural History of Barbados*, London, 1750

Knight, Franklin *The Caribbean: The Genesis of a Fragmented Nationalism*, New York, 1978

Lamming, George *In the Castle of my Skin*, London, 1953

Levy, Claude *Emancipation, Sugar and Federalism: Barbados and the West Indies, 1833–1876*, Gainesville, 1980

Lewis, Arthur *Labour in the West Indies*, London, 1938

Lewis, Gordon *The Growth of the Modern West Indies*, New York, 1968

Ligon, Richard *A True and Exact History of the Island of Barbados*, London, 1657

Lowenthal, David *West Indian Societies*, New York, 1972

McCusker, John & Menard, Russell *The Economy of British America, 1607–1789*, Chapel Hill, 1985

Mack, Raymond *Race, Class and Power in Barbados*, Cambridge, Mass., 1967

Mark, Francis *The History of the Barbados Workers' Union*, Barbados, 1965

Marshall, Woodville K. (ed.) *The Colthurst Journal*, New York, 1977

—(ed.) *Emancipation II*, Bridgetown, 1987

Newton, Velma *The Silver Men: West Indian Labour Migration to Panama, 1850–1914*, Kingston, 1984

Orderson, J. W. *Directions to Young Planters for their Care and Management of a Sugar Plantation in Barbados*, London, 1800

—*Creoleana: Or Social and Domestic Scenes and Incidents in Barbados in Days of Yore*, London, 1842

Parry, J. & Sherlock, P. *A Short History of the West Indies*, London, 1956

Pinckard, George *Notes on the West Indies*, 3 vols, London, 1806 and 1808

Pitman, Frank *The Development of the British West Indies, 1700–1763*, Newhaven, 1917

Poyer, John *The History of Barbados*, London, 1808

Puckrein, Gary A. *Little England: Plantation Society and Anglo-Barbadian Politics, 1627–1700*, New York, 1984

Richardson, Bonham *Panama Money in Barbados, 1900–1920*, Knoxville, 1985

Schomburgk, Robert *The History of Barbados*, London, 1848

Sheppard, Jill *The "Redlegs" of Barbados: Their Origins and History*, New York, 1977

Sheridan, Richard *The Development of the Plantation to 1750*, Kingston, 1970

—*Sugar and Slavery: An Economic History of the British West Indies, 1623–1775*, Barbados, 1974

Skeete, C. C. *The Condition of Peasant Agriculture in Barbados*, Bridgetown, 1930

Spurdle, Frederick *Early West Indian Government*, Christ Church, n.d.

Starkey, Otis P. *The Economic Geography of Barbados*, New York, 1939, Westport, 1971

Sturge, Joseph & Harvey, Thomas *The West Indies in 1837*, London, 1968 edn

Thompson, A. (ed.) *Emancipation I*, Bridgetown, 1986

Watson, Karl *The Civilised Island, Barbados: A Social History, 1750–1816*, Barbados, 1979

Watts, David *The West Indies: Patterns of Development, Culture and Environment Change Since 1492*, Cambridge, 1987

Williams, Eric *Capitalism and Slavery*, Chapel Hill, 1944 and London, 1964, 1975

—*Documents of West Indian History*, Port-of-Spain, 1963

—*From Columbus to Castro: The History of the Caribbean, 1492–1969*, London, 1970

Worrell, Delisle (ed.) *The Economy of Barbados, 1946–1980*, Bridgetown, 1982

Wrong, Hume *Government of the West Indies*, Oxford, 1923

Articles

J.B.M.H.S. = Journal of the Barbados Museum and Historical Society

J.C.H. = Journal of Caribbean History

Barrow, Christine 'Ownership and control of resources in Barbados: 1834 to the present', *Social and Economic Studies* 32:3 (1983), 83–120

Beckles, Hilary, 'On the backs of blacks: the Barbados free-coloureds' pursuit of civil rights and the 1816 slave rebellion', *Immigrants and Minorities* 3:2 (1984), 167–188

—'From land to sea: runaway slaves and servants in Barbados, 1630–1720', *Slavery and Abolition* 6:3 (1985), 79–95

—'Plantation production and "white proto-slavery": indentured servants and the colonisation of the English West Indies, 1624–1645', *The Americas* 41:2 (1985), 21–45

—'The Slave Drivers' War: Bussa and the 1816 Barbados slave rebellion', *Boletin de Estudios Latinoamericanos y de Caribe* 39 (Dec. 1985), 85–109

—'"Black men in white skins": the white working class in West Indian slave society'. *Journal of Imperial and Commonwealth History* 15:1 (1986) 1–21

—'Black over white: the "poor-white" problem in Barbados slave society', *Immigrants and Minorities* 7:1 (1988), 1–16

Belle, George 'The initial political implications of emancipation: Barbados'. Paper presented at the 14th Annual Conference of Caribbean Historians Puerto Rico, April 16–21, 1982

'The abortive revolution of 1876 in Barbados', *J.C.H.* 18 (1984), 1–35

'The struggle for political democracy: 1937 riots'. Public Lecture, Bridgetown, 17th March 1987

Bennett, J. H. 'The problem of slave labour supply at the Codrington plantations', *Journal of Negro History* 36 (1951), 406–39

Boomert, Arie 'Notes on Barbados prehistory', *J.B.M.H.S.* 38:1 (1987), 8–43

Bullen, A. K. & Bullen, R. P. 'Barbados, a Carib centre', *The Bajan and South Caribbean* 155 (1966), 20–2

Bullen, R. P. 'Barbados and the archaeology of the Caribbean', *J.B.M.H.S.* 32 (1966), 16–19

Carrington, Selwyn, 'West Indian opposition to British policy: Barbadian politics, 1774–1782', *J.C.H.* 17 (1982), 26–50

Carter, Richard 'Public amenities after emancipation', in W. K. Marshall (ed.), *Emancipation II*, Bridgetown, 1987, pp. 46–70

Cooksey, C. 'The first Barbadians', *Timehri* 3:2 (1912), 142–4

Drewett, Peter L. *et al.* 'Archaeological survey of Barbados', *J.B.M.H.S.* 38:1 (1987), 44–81 and 38:2 (1988), 196–204

Dunn, Richard 'The Barbados census of 1680: profile of the richest colony in English America', *William and Mary Quarterly* 26 (1969), 3–30

Gibbs, Bentley 'Government and the problem of social reconstruction, 1838–1849'. History Department Seminar Paper, UWI, Cave Hill, 1976

—'The establishment of the tenantry system in Barbados', in W. K. Marshall (ed.), *Emancipation II*, Bridgetown, 1987, pp. 23–46

Gilmore, John 'Church and society in Barbados, 1824–1881', in W. K. Marshall (ed.), *Emancipation II*, Bridgetown, 1987, pp. 1–23

Hall, Neville, 'Law and society in Barbados at the turn of the nineteenth century', *J.C.H.* 5 (1972), 20–45

Handler, Jerome 'The Amerindian slave population of Barbados in the seventeenth and early eighteenth centuries', *Caribbean Studies* 8:4 (1969), 38–64

—'Aspects of Amerindian ethnography in seventeenth century Barbados', *Caribbean Studies* 9:4 (1970), 50–72

—'An archaeological investigation of the domestic life of plantation slaves in Barbados', *J.B.M.H.S.* 34:2 (1972), 64–72

Heuman, Gad 'Runaway slaves in nineteenth century Barbados', in Gad Heuman (ed.) *Out of the House of Bondage: Runaways, Resistance, and Marronage in Africa and the New World*, London, 1986, pp. 95–112

Hughes, Ronnie 'Barbadian sugar plantations, 1640–1846'. History Department Seminar Paper, UWI, Cave Hill, 1977

—'The origins of Barbados sugar plantations and the role of the white population in sugar plantation society', in A. Thompson (ed.) *Emancipation I*, Bridgetown, 1984, pp. 26–33

Hunte, Keith 'Church and society in Barbados in the eighteenth century', in Blanca Silvestrini (ed.) *Social Groups and Institutions in the History of the Caribbean*, San Juan, 1975, pp. 13–26

—'The Democratic League and Charles Duncan O'Neale'. Public Lecture, Bridgetown, 3rd March 1987

Innis, F. C. 'The pre-sugar era of European settlement in Barbados', *J.C.H.* 1 (1970), 1–22

Johnson, Howard 'Barbadian immigrants in Trinidad, 1870–1897', *Caribbean Studies* 13 (1973), 5–30

Karch, Cecilia 'The role of the Barbados Mutual Life Assurance Society during the international sugar crisis of the late nineteenth century'. Paper presented at the 12th Annual Conference of Caribbean Historians, Trinidad, 1980

—'The growth of the corporate economy in Barbados: class, or race factors, 1890–1977', in S. Craig (ed.) *The Contemporary Caribbean: A Sociological Reader*, vol. 1, Port-of-Spain, 1982, pp. 230–43

Lewis, Gordon 'The struggle for freedom', *New World Quarterly* III:1–2 (1966) [Barbados Independence Issue], 14–29

Lowenthal, David 'The population of Barbados', *Social and Economic Studies* 6 (1957), 445–501

Marshall, Trevor 'Post-emancipation adjustments in Barbados, 1838–1876', in A. Thompson (ed.) *Emancipation I*, Bridgetown, 1986, pp. 8–108

Marshall, Woodville K. 'The termination of apprenticeship in Barbados and the Windward Islands: an essay in colonial administration and politics', *J.C.H.* 2 (1971), 1–45

—'Rock Hall, St Thomas: the search for the first free village in Barbados'. Paper presented at the 9th Annual Conference of Caribbean Historians, Barbados, 1977

—'Amelioration and emancipation (with special reference to Barbados)', in A. Thompson (ed.) *Emancipation I*, Bridgetown, 1986, pp. 72–88

—'Nineteenth century crisis in the Barbadian sugar industry', in W. K. Marshall (ed.) *Emancipation II*, Bridgetown, 1987, pp. 85–102

Marshall, Woodville K. *et al.* 'The establishment of a peasantry in Barbados', in Blanca Silvestrini (ed.) *Social Groups and Institutions in the History of the Caribbean*, San Juan, 1975, pp. 88–104

Mathews, Christine 'Crisis in Barbados . . . with special reference to the Central Factories Proposal, 1897–1902'. History Department Seminar Paper, UWI, Cave Hill, 1975

Molen, Patricia 'Population and social patterns in Barbados in the early eighteenth century', *William and Mary Quarterly* 28 (1971), 287–300

Morris, Robert 'Slave society in Barbados', in A. Thompson (ed.) *Emancipation I*, Bridgetown, 1986, pp. 33–45

Phillips, Anthony 'The racial factor in politics in Barbados, 1880–1914'. History Department Seminar Paper, UWI, Cave Hill, 1973

—'The political elite in Barbados, 1880–1914: aristocracy, plantocracy, or bureaucracy'. History Department Seminar Paper, UWI, Cave Hill, 1976

—'The origins of the Bushe Experiment: a governor's eye view'. History Department Seminar Paper, UWI, Cave Hill, 1983

—'An assessment of the ideological position of Grantley Adams in 1937–38, 1948–49'. Paper presented at the 16th Annual Conference of Caribbean Historians, Barbados, 1984

—'The confederation question', in W. K. Marshall (ed.) *Emancipation II*, Bridgetown, 1987, pp. 70–85

Ramsaram, Ramesh 'The post-war decline of the sugar economy in the commonwealth Caribbean'. University of Hull, Conference Paper, Wilberforce Anniversary, July 1983

Roberts, G. W., 'Emigration from the island of Barbados', *Social and Economic Studies* (1955), 245–87

Rodney, Walter 'Barbadian immigration into British Guiana, 1863–1924'. Paper presented at the 9th Annual Conference of Caribbean Historians, Barbados, 1977

Sheridan, Richard 'The crisis of slave subsistence in the British West Indies during and after the American Revolution', *William and Mary Quarterly* 33:4 (1976), 615–41

Sleeman, Michael 'The agri-business bourgeoisie of Barbados and Martinique', in P. I. Gomes (ed.) *Rural Development in the Caribbean*, Kingston, 1985, pp. 15–33

Stoddart, Brian 'Cricket and colonisation in the English-speaking Caribbean to 1914: steps towards a cultural analysis'. History Department Seminar Paper, UWI, Cave Hill, 1985

Vaughan, H. A. 'The shaping of the new order: Barbados, 1834–46'. History Department Seminar Paper No. 9, UWI, Cave Hill, 1981–82

Ward, J. R. 'The profitability of sugar planting in the British West Indies, 1650–1834', *Economic History Review* 31:2 (1978), 197–212

Official documents and reports

Instructions for the Management of a Plantation in Barbados (London, 1786)

Jacob Belgrave *et al.* Letter of the Barbados Free-coloured people to the Hon. John Beckles, 4th March 1817, CO 28/86

A Report from the Select Committee of the House of Assembly appointed to inquire into the Origins, Cause, and Progress of the late Insurrection – April 1816 (Barbados, 1818)

A Report of a Committee of the Council of Barbadoes, appointed to inquire into the Actual Condition of the Slaves in this Island (Barbados, 1822)

Parliamentary Papers, Colonial Dispatches 1830–38

Report of Select Committee of the House of Commons on West India Colonies, 1842

Barbados Blue Books, 1845–1920

Report on the Census of Barbados, 1881–1891 (Bridgetown, 1891)

Report and Evidence of the West India Royal Commission, 1897

Report on the Elementary Education for the year 1899 (Bridgetown, 1899)

Henry Lofty, Report on the Census of Barbados, 1921

Proceedings of West Indian Sugar Commission (Bridgetown, 1929)

Report of the Acting Chief Medical Officer, 1929 (Dept of Archives, Barbados)

Report of the West India Royal Commission (Moyne Report), 1945

Official Colonial Correspondence CO 28, 30, 31, 33 series, Public Records Office, London

Governor Leith to Bathurst, April 30th and September 21st, CO 28/85

Unpublished theses

Belle, George 'The politics of development: a study in the political economy of Barbados', PhD diss., Manchester University, 1977

Davis, Karen 'The position of poor-whites in a colour-class hierarchy: a diachronic study of the ethnic boundaries in Barbados', PhD diss., Wayne State University, Detroit, Michigan, 1978

Drewett, Peter L. 'Barbados: the prehistory of the island', mimeograph, University of London, n.d.

Innes, Frank 'Plantations and peasant forms – Barbados, 1627–1960', PhD diss., McGill University, Montreal, 1967

Karch, Cecilia 'The transformation and consolidation of the corporate plantation economy in Barbados, 1860–1877', PhD diss., Rutgers University, New Brunswick, 1979

Manyoni, Joseph 'Social stratification in Barbados: a study in social change', PhD diss., University of Oxford, 1973

Will, Wilber 'Political development in the mini-state Caribbean: a focus on Barbados', PhD diss., University of Missouri, 1973

Index